MY
Times

MY
Times

Adventures
in the News Trade

JOHN CORRY

A GROSSET / PUTNAM BOOK
Published by G. P. Putnam's Sons / New York

A Grosset/Putnam Book
Published by G. P. Putnam's Sons
Publishers Since 1838
200 Madison Avenue
New York, NY 10016

Library of Congress Cataloging-in-Publication Data

Corry, John.
My *Times:* adventures in the news trade / John Corry.
p.   cm.
"A Grosset/Putnam book."
ISBN 0-399-13886-2 (acid-free paper)
1. Corry, John.   2. Journalists—United States—Biography.
I. Title.
PN4874.C688A3   1994   93-5871 CIP
070′.92—dc20
[B]

Printed in the United States of America
1 2 3 4 5 6 7 8 9 10

This book is printed on acid-free paper.

ACKNOWLEDGMENTS

I owe too many people for too many things to be able to thank them all. Nonetheless, at least some debts must be acknowledged. The Freedom Foundation and its executive director, Everette E. Dennis, sheltered me when I left the *Times*; the Bradley Foundation eased my way; the Media Institute and Patrick Maines always offered encouragement. There is also my agent, Kathy Robbins, who is simply better at what she does than anyone else.

For Abe and Arthur—who else

For Sue and Arthur, who et c.

CONTENTS

THE WAY WE WERE

any people long since retired or otherwise separated from *The New York Times* still refer to it
as "we"—as in, "We overplayed this story,"
or "We missed that story," or "What the hell do we think
we're doing with the front page?" The old reporters and editors who do this may never visit the *Times* newsroom, or
even know who's running it now, but they still read the
paper with great care and grumpy dissatisfaction; and while
most are convinced it is no longer what it was in their day,
they retain a professional interest in its well-being. That is
why they still say "we." The old reporters and editors
joined the *Times* when young, grew cranky in its service,
and seldom thought of working anywhere else. They signed
on for lifelong tenure. Young men and women who work in
the newsroom now, however, are more mobile. They are not
wedded to the *Times,* and most see it as a way to punch their
tickets before moving on to other things. There is nothing
wrong with this, but it does show how the newsroom has
changed. Journalism is more respectable, and so is the newsroom, and although respectability is nice, it neither inspires

nor engages, and it seldom gives way to mirth. You can take it or leave it alone, and while appearances are served, the soul is not nurtured. Respectability, unrelieved, is boring. Not long ago, though, mild raffishness, moderate dissoluteness, and minor deviancy were tolerated and tacitly encouraged at the *Times,* and this fact helped breed allegiance to the newsroom and to the style of journalism that was practiced there, too. The assumption was that certain social or psychological irregularities fit in with the newspaperman's trade and, in the appropriate circumstances, even contributed to his education.

I benefited from that assumption myself. When I was promoted from copyboy to clerk in the *Times* sports department in the late 1950s, I inherited from the previous clerk a sinecure that went with the job. Two bookmakers paid me twenty-five dollars a week to give them by phone the scores of late ball games. The two bookmakers—Jack and Manny—owned, or at least were the front men for, a nightclub near Times Square. When I got off work on Fridays, I would go there to get the twenty-five dollars, along with a chicken sandwich on toast, weak Scotch and water, and permission to sit with the bookies and watch the club's girlie show. Jack and Manny never talked about bookmaking, although on occasion they would fall into an expansive mood and elucidate the fine points of running the nightclub. I learned, for example, that when the girls came offstage and male customers asked to buy them a drink, the girls always ordered "wine." This would be a split of ersatz champagne—a mixture of cheap sauterne and ginger ale, brewed by the bartender in the club's kitchen and sold at exorbitant prices. The particular bartender who did this also saw to it that the bar had large ashtrays with hollow bottoms. When he put an ashtray back on the bar after emptying it, he would place it on top of any loose bills or change a customer had not retrieved. As often as not, the customer then forgot all about the money. Jack and Manny said the bartender made quite a bit of money this way, although they seemed to disapprove of his raw cupidity and called him a "dirtbag."

I always considered my time with Jack and Manny well spent, and I know now they were part of my education. I know also it was just as well I did not do postgraduate work. One Friday night, several men in dark suits filed into the club, nodded toward Jack and Manny, and walked past the stage into a back room I had not known existed. "Button men," Manny murmured. Minutes later, several more men entered. This time, however, one of them walked toward us. He appeared to be looking at me. Jack and Manny immediately jumped to their feet, and pulled me up with them. "This is Johnny Corry," Jack told the stranger. "He's been helping us out." The man stared a moment and mumbled something I could not hear. Then he went into the room I had not known existed. "Who was that?" I asked. "His name is Mr. Bender," Jack answered, but in a manner so discomfited I thought it best to leave. The next week, and for a while after, I received the twenty-five dollars by messenger. Then, one afternoon at the *Times,* I picked up the *Post* and saw a story about Tony Strollo, son-in-law of Vito Genovese, the Mafia boss of New York. He was missing, and the police thought he might be dead. The story mentioned that Strollo sometimes used the name Bender. The face of the man in the accompanying picture, of course, was that of the man I had met at the nightclub.

I never saw Jack or Manny again. In fact, Jack disappeared at about the same time as Mr. Bender. Naturally, I wondered whether he had been bumped off, too, possibly in the back room of the nightclub, where, just perhaps, the button men had also gotten Mr. Bender. A perfervid imagination is not supposed to be proper equipment for a young journalist, but I am glad I had mine. It enhanced the romance of the city and the newsroom, and made the two entwined. I could not divorce the one from the other, nor did I ever wish to: they were complementary halves, accessible in conjunction and mutually reinforcing.

When I was a copyboy in sports, I also worked part-time at the racetrack. For twenty-five dollars a week (all my outside work seemed to pay that) I wrote press releases and did other jobs for the press agent who promoted the steeplechase races at New York State racetracks. In steeplechase races, horses jumped over obstacles, and while this was exciting to watch, it did not inspire bettors to bet as freely as they did on the flat races. Bettors did not trust jumping races; they thought them exotic and perhaps unnatural. Bettors also noticed that steeplechase jockeys sometimes fell off their horses. This made wagering a more complicated exercise than God presumably intended it to be, so bettors stayed away from the steeplechase in droves. The total amount bet on a jumping race—there would be one on the race card every day—was always less than that bet on any flat race. Consequently, there would be smaller purses and less money around for the steeplechase people. They thought they should do better, and hired a press agent to promote favorable publicity about steeplechasing and change the bettors' habits. The press agent, in turn, hired me. This meant I could hang out in press boxes with big-time race writers. It also meant I could go anywhere I wanted to go and talk to anyone I wanted to talk to at the racetracks. I got to know trainers, jockeys, and grooms; I schmoozed with gamblers, deadbeats, and men who sold tipsheets. One August I spent my vacation at Saratoga, where I arose every morning at five to watch the early workouts and drink coffee around the old oil drums in which the grooms built smoky fires to ward off the dawn's dewy chill. In the afternoons I worked in the press box, and in the evenings I went to the horse sales, and late at night I joined the busted gamblers who waited at a newsstand on Saratoga's Broadway for the *Morning Telegraph* and the early line on the next day's races. I was in love with existence, and naturally I bet the horses, too.

One day I hit a thirty-five-dollar daily double. Jubilantly I collected the money, the most I had ever won on a single bet in all the time I had played the horses; it was also almost as much as my weekly copyboy's salary. Then, by chance, I saw an editor from the *Times* foreign desk. His name was Bob Simpson, and apparently he was on vacation. "Mr. Simpson," I said, and started to introduce myself. "Bet the Oil Capitol horse," he told me, and turned and walked away. When I looked in my program, I saw that Oil Capitol was the sire of a horse in the next race. As I recall, the race was for two-year-old maidens.

In a fit of daring, then, I bet the entire thirty-five dollars, and when the Oil Capitol horse came home rolling, I collected some $300. In the paddock area two races later, I overheard a young woman in a linen dress tell a young man in a madras jacket that "Daddy" had a horse in the next race, and that his trainer had kept the horse under wraps so no one would know what a speedball the nag really was. I no longer remember the name of the horse, but I do remember sprinting up to a betting window just before it closed and emptying my pockets. I won $1,200.

A digression now, but one bearing both on what happened next and on my formative period in journalism: One of my jobs at the track was to ghostwrite stories about steeplechasing for sports columnists who, when inspiration failed or, more likely, when they just wanted a day off, would put their names on my stories, and even publish them word for word. The old-time press agent for whom I worked, however, would always tell the columnists he had written the stories himself. This was because no columnist would want it known that someone else wrote his column for him, and while an old-time press agent would never spill the beans, a young unknown like me could not be trusted. Thus the old-time press agent always made it appear the ghostwriting was known only to the columnist and him. When the column was published, the press agent would send the columnist some booze. He observed a sliding scale when he did so. The columnist at the New York *Daily News,* for instance, would get one bottle, while the columnist at the *Journal-American,* a more discriminating man, would get two. On rare occasions, when the press agent had fobbed off a particularly dicey story, say, he might throw in lunch or dinner. It never occurred to me to feel moral outrage over any of this, and I enjoyed seeing my words in a newspaper, especially when they were printed as written. (The one-bottle man at the *Daily News* was a delight; he never changed a thing, not even a misspelling.) I had a problem only once: when the press agent told me to ghostwrite a piece for a columnist I greatly admired. This made me very sad; I had thought the columnist was above that sort of thing.

Fortunately, my distress did not last. When the column was published, it was no longer mine; it was the columnist's, transmogrified by his editing. My version, for example, had described a jockey as looking like "a weather-beaten Ivy Leaguer." The columnist turned this into "a Harvard man who had been left out too long in the rain." Wonderful, I thought, and was pleased to know the columnist had betrayed neither himself nor his talent. I did not know it then, but I was beginning to understand journalism. As a profession, it was not to be taken seriously, and whether one-bottle or two-bottle men wrote their own stuff or had others do it for them was a matter of no importance. The sole function of journalism is to inform and entertain, and while this is honorable, it is not elevated, and abstruse moral discussions about the trade are for the birds. On the other hand, journalism could be, and indeed should be, worthy of a journalist's very best effort. The columnist I admired must have been stricken by conscience when he thought of turning in an in-

ferior piece, especially one he had not even written. He had
worked almost as hard editing my story as he would have if
he had sat down and written it himself. Journalism is sanctified not by any misplaced sense of itself or puffed-up idea of
its own importance. It is sanctified only when someone
works very hard to produce it.

But back now to me, a dazed, dazzled copyboy wandering
through Saratoga's sylvan paddock with $1,200 in his
pocket. The story the columnist had edited had appeared in
the papers that very same week. It was about a jockey, and it
had praised him as a prince among men and a wonderful
rider as well. The jockey had never had such nice things said
about him before. Meanwhile, he knew I had something to
do with their having been said, and he wanted to do me a
favor. That day in the paddock, he gave me, as they say, a
horse. It was his mount in the next race, Hurst Park. The
horse had a very respectable trainer and was a first-time
starter in a jumping race. The morning line had him at
twelve to one. The jockey, who had a reputation for never
passing on useful information, or in fact ever saying much at
all, was adamant about Hurst Park and, by his usual standards, damn near loquacious. I remember his words precisely. "Bet the farm," he said, on Hurst Park.

So I did, putting the $1,200 down to win, with $400 at one
window, $400 at another, and the final $400 at a third. I
feared that if I put it all down in one place and at one time I
would depress the odds. Besides, I did not want to attract
attention. I saw myself as a serious gambler, and I thought
self-effacement more seemly than ostentatious display. At
post time I sauntered up to the press box, clamped one hand
over the twelve $100 win tickets in my breast pocket, and sat
on a folding chair. The race was to begin in the corner on the
far side of the track, and then pass by the clubhouse, make a
full circuit of the track, and end at the clubhouse. Coolly I
waited for the announcer to say "They're off!" When he

did, Hurst Park jumped out in front. He held the lead around the turn and down the stretch, and widened it as he went past the clubhouse. Then it was around the track, with Hurst Park still in front, and moving even farther in front at the far turn, backstretch, near turn, and coming into the homestretch. I could wait no longer, and rose from the folding chair. The press box had its own betting window, and it was there I would collect my money. As I mounted the short flight of steps to the betting window, though, I heard the crowd roar, and I turned and looked back at the track. Hurst Park had crossed the finish line first, but just before he did, my friend the jockey had fallen off his back.

This spoiled my career as a gambler. I never bet more than two dollars again. Nonetheless, in my grief that day I was not entirely inconsolable. In adversity I found sour pleasure. It seemed to me I had had an appropriate experience for a journalist. Journalists were rakish, intemperate, blithesome. They lived on the edge, and never worried about what followed. Today's story was what sustained them. What the hell; so I had dropped ten or twelve thousand dollars. Tomorrow I would do something else. I am not insisting this was a healthy, sound attitude, but it did have its merits, and it came naturally to me as a young man in the *Times* newsroom. News was what happened today, and a story was dead after that ("as dead as Kelsey's nuts," the old national news editor used to say), and playfulness kept things in perspective.

There was visible proof of this every day. Throughout the fifties and into the sixties, a serious card game got under way in back of the rewrite bank as soon as the deadline for the first edition had passed. The same cardplayers showed up for every game. The most devoted was an assistant city editor, a courtly man who wore a fawn Stetson hat in the office. When an officious columnist for the New York *Post* wrote that the *Times* sanctioned gambling, the *Times* publisher decreed that the card game be shut down. People in the newsroom were sad to see it go. The assistant city editor in the fawn Stetson even retired. The card game had been an agreeable tradition, proof that a newspaper office was a newspaper office, not a place of mere commerce. It confirmed that reporters were different from bankers and brokers and people who kept regular hours. Reporters moved easily between high life and low life, and were irreverent about both. When their stories were done they played cards. Never mind now that any number of reporters was intimidated by high life and uncomfortable with low life, and did not know pinochle from poker. What they thought about themselves was what counted. A card game was down-to-earth and unpretentious, and so was the newsroom, and so, in its way, was the news.

Things are different in the 1990s. When I visit the newsroom now, I am struck by its quiet. Reporters do not raise their voices or hang around after hours, and the atmosphere reflects a new sense of the news. Man bites dog would once have been a story, but it might not be now, unless it touched on racism, sexism, gay rights, or the rain forest. There is less emphasis on hard news or breaking news, and much of the old urgency of daily journalism has fled, along with the eccentric humor wedded to it.

I am thinking now of the night some twenty-five years ago when I thought Sylvan Fox had dropped dead. He was the best rewrite man in the newsroom, and Arthur Gelb, the metropolitan editor, worked him without pity or mercy. Arthur was not being cruel; he simply could not help it. A good rewrite man can work the phones, read the wires, talk to colleagues, and then organize a story and write it faster than anyone else. He is indispensable to the coverage of breaking news, and since Arthur saw the coverage as bounden duty, he would call on Sylvan Fox almost every night. Syl, a stocky man who wore glasses, and was on the side a fine classical pianist, did not complain. He also saw the coverage as bounden duty. Nonetheless, he did not smile very often, and on heavy news nights he smiled not at all. Arthur would want a new lead or an insert on deadline, and perhaps, just perhaps, if Syl thought he could do it, a brand-new story, too. Syl would always oblige, just as Arthur expected. Reporters and copy editors who sat nearby watched with interest. On routine stories Arthur would pass orders to Syl through intermediaries, but on big stories he would give the orders himself. One night, however, Arthur went too far. Syl turned white, let out a gasp, and slumped to the floor unconscious. "Jesus!" a young clerk on the metropolitan desk cried out. "Arthur, I think you killed him."

A stricken Arthur thought he had, too. When the paramedics from Roosevelt Hospital arrived with a stretcher to take the still insensible Sylvan away, Arthur knew he had to call Sylvan's wife. How could he tell her he had just killed her husband? As it turned out, though, Mrs. Fox, who was a nurse, reassured Arthur. She had seen Syl turn white and pass out before, and she said all he needed was rest. She was correct, and her husband returned to rewrite the next week. Most people in the newsroom thought it had been a close call, although when they talked about it, they could not stop themselves from grinning. No one wanted Syl dead, of course, but somehow the incident was cheering—the wound-up Arthur, stricken Syl, and "Jesus! Arthur, I think you killed him." It was all appropriate to the surroundings. Wasn't the newsroom supposed to be this way? Who ever said reporters were like other people? Arthur was unpredictable, and so was Abe Rosenthal, the executive editor, yet there was no question about whether they were real. They stalked the newsroom and made you crazy. They butted in and intruded. Young male reporters adopted them as father figures and then had to slay them, symbolically. One reporter I knew wanted to leave the *Times* to accept a fat book contract, but had to go into analysis before he could do it. The atmosphere was heated, immediate, and often anguished, and while reporters could turn sullen or angry, few of the good ones ever grew bored. They were alive and they knew it, people caught up in the news trade.

CHAPTER TWO

A PERFECT 1960s REPORTER

ow could you?'' the famous journalist David Halberstam asked. He had won a Pulitzer Prize and now wrote very long books, and once had been satirized in *Doonesbury*. I was about to enter the lobby of *The New York Times,* just as he was leaving. ''Hello,'' I had said carefully, but Halberstam's lips were tight and his eyes narrow, and for an instant I thought he might hit me. He did not. Instead, he seethed and glared and let me have it with, ''How could you?'' and then, words failing, let me have it with, ''How could you?'' again. David and I had worked together in the *Times* newsroom in the 1960s, a decade he enjoyed more than I, and then we both had left to write for *Harper's.* Three years after we got there, Willie Morris, the editor of the magazine, had fought with the owner and resigned in a high-minded and well-publicized huff, and when that happened Halberstam and I and most of our *Harper's* colleagues resigned with our friend Willie. There are rules about these things, and the rules are written in fire. When Willie walked, we walked. We had to. That was in 1971, and I had gone back to the *Times,* while Halberstam had gone off on his own and become a famous author. Now it was 1982, and he and I stood on West 43d Street outside the *Times* lobby, he enraged and I defensive, and both of us in the November cold a little breathless. It was the rules again; this time I had broken them. That was why he was so angry. Cultural and journalistic politics is no game for the fainthearted.

Still, the game can be exhilarating—which is why so many play it. Sex, money, and fame are attractive, but power or virtue is better, and power *and* virtue is best. I know because I have been there. I was, and am, a moderately successful, moderately endowed, and moderately passionate New York journalist, blessed professionally often by chance. My first task on my first day at the *Times* was to fill a paste pot—"Boy," a copy editor on the sports desk said tonelessly, and held out the sticky jar—and my last task on my last day, thirty-one years after the paste pot, was to write a television review for the Sunday paper in which I could deplore talk-show host Morton Downey, Jr., in particular and tastelessness in general, and warn that we were entering a new age of dumbness. In thirty-one years, therefore, I had gone from the paste pot to becoming a certified member of what the economist Joseph Schumpeter and others have called the "new class." My status was defined not by what I owned but by what I did, and my strength was in where and how I used words. I was, along with thousands of others of my kind, an opinion maker.

Halberstam was also an opinion maker, and what annoyed him so was a long story I had written about the novelist Jerzy Kosinski. Halberstam was not alone. *The Nation* termed the story "sinister," while *Newsweek* called it "embarrassing," and said that in publishing it the *Times* had "shocked its own newsroom." Actually, the newsroom was more titillated than shocked, because it loved gossip better than anything else, and this was so rich and fruity. Reputations were being shredded. Abe Rosenthal was under attack. He would call me at night and ask me how I was, and then I would ask him how he was, and when we finished talking I would wonder if we were both going down together. Cultural and journalistic politics gave no quarter. I will explain the Kosinski case later.

First, though, you should know about journalism. The principal thing to know is that the idea of journalism has changed, transformed by a conflation called media. New York is the media capital of the world, and everyone important who works in media knows everyone else, or at least seems to know all about everyone else. Gossip is rife, though deportment is civilized, and people at the top try not to argue. Most live between East 59th and East 86th streets, or in the better buildings on the Upper West Side, or in a few selected suburbs. Most believe the same things about life and art and politics. All of them read the *Times*. Consensus is formed not by conspiracy but by osmosis, and is enforced through moral persuasion. Usually this is not reprehensible, although you may have thoughts about how so few people in so small a place can have so much to say about what so many other people see on television or read in their newspapers and magazines.

You also should know about me. In most ways I am marked by my ordinariness. Most of what I have known I have known instinctively, and most of what I have felt I have felt not because I reasoned it out, but because I have breathed a certain air, moved through a particular place, and been touched by the people around me. Birthplace, birthright, and circumstance have formed me as much as anything else. This means I am less independent in my thinking than I would like to be. All opinion makers are this way, although they would lose their authority if they were to admit it.

I come from an Irish Protestant family in Brooklyn that arrived here in steerage and quickly forgot Ireland, but always remembered its Protestantism. My father once confessed to me that our name had been Curry, but my grandfather thought it sounded Irish Catholic, and so he changed it to Corry. "If someone asks what you are," I was told at an early age, "you don't say Irish, you say American." I heard little of Ireland. I heard we had been poor there, and that in County Armagh on New Year's Day, the minor nobleman who owned the property we lived on would ride a white horse past the tenants and tip his hat while they bowed or curtsied. The only other thing I heard was that Wolfe Tone, the greatest of Irish generals, had been a Protestant, and that Irish Catholic soldiers led by Irish Protestant officers could lick anyone else in the world. Protestantism confirmed my family's identity, separating us from benighted Catholics who confessed to priests, took orders from the pope, and worshipped painted idols. The Episcopalian Church connected us to a larger America. We believed in God, country, and respectable behavior. We had the faith of people who knew where duty lay. We had the faith of immigrants. My father wanted to reenlist in the Navy after Pearl Harbor, but he was forty-five and to my mother's relief the Navy said it could do without him. Even at age eight I understood his feelings. Patriotism has always seemed to me a desirable quality, and I know those who feel it are richer than those who do not.

Nonetheless, I did not like my childhood very much and longed for it to be over. (For that matter, I know few adults who thought much of their childhood, either.) God, country, and respectable behavior had limitations. I made the traditional escape of an intelligent child and found my freedom in books. As a boy I thrilled when I read the first sentence of *Scaramouche*—"He was born with the gift of laughter and a sense that the world was mad"—and it was one of the few lines in literature I was ever able to quote, although as a boy I would have been embarrassed to quote it. I read history books and novels like *Northwest Passage* and *Drums Along the Mohawk*. I romanticized the American past and thought that one day I might write a history book about the Hudson River. In college I applied myself to Kierkegaard and Niebuhr and tried to find God, but when I look back I suspect the search was more romantic than serious. In a fit of melancholy in my junior year, I pondered suicide. The improbable idea made me so nervous I never thought about it again. At twenty-three, after two boring years in the Army, I discovered George Orwell. I bought a paperback copy of *Homage to Catalonia* on an Indian-summer day and read it while I ate a hero sandwich in Greenwich Village. The paperback had the famous introduction in which Lionel Trilling said Orwell was a virtuous man. Lightning did not strike as I read it, although clouds seemed to roll back slightly. I finished the book and went on to Orwell's essays, diaries, and letters. He told me not what to think but how to think, and became a friend for life.

I was not heavily laden with intellectual baggage in 1968, when I left the *Times* for *Harper's*. In common with most of my kind, I did not think I had to be. I considered myself a reporter, a diligent collector of facts, who did not allow personal opinion to get in the way when he presented what he had collected. A reporter held himself above the fray and impartially evaluated all sides. A reporter prized objectivity. No one, of course, seems to believe that about reporters anymore, not even reporters themselves, although when everyone stopped believing it, something important went out of American journalism. Henceforth journalism would be practiced and regarded other than before. Its boundaries would widen but its soul would shrink, and polls would show that people no longer trusted it as they once had. Journalism was another casualty of the sixties.

Few reporters in those days quit the *Times*. The *Times* was the *Times,* as much myth as institution, and if you

worked there, it was home, church, and family. The *Times*
identified you to the world and to yourself. It was a place
that could inspire fierce loyalty and at the same time break
your heart. It was a place that allowed a young newspaperman to smell glory. "Not to have been involved in the actions and passions of one's time is to be judged not to have
lived," Justice Oliver Wendell Holmes wrote, and though I
now think Holmes was an elitist, as a young newspaperman I
found his words inspiring.

In the years after I filled the paste pot, I had moved from
the sports department to the national desk, and then had
become a Nieman Fellow in journalism at Harvard. I had
covered civil rights stories in Alabama and Mississippi. One
afternoon, on a lonely road in Lowndes County, Alabama, I
thought a Klansman would shoot me. I had been part of a
team investigating the assassination of President Kennedy.
A Dallas cop had thrown me out of Parkland Memorial Hospital when I tried to interview Jack Ruby before he died. I
had crossed the country and reported on the growing use of
drugs. One evening, outside a bookstore in Boulder, Colorado, two dealers tried to assault me. I had written the first
stories about William Masters and Virginia Johnson and
their research on the physiology of sex. It was a landmark
not necessarily in science but surely in taste and morals. I
had brushed up against national politics, the New Left, and
almost the entire Kennedy family, and I was briefly a media
celebrity. I was interviewed on the *Today* show and by Merv
Griffin. That was because I had written stories about Jacqueline Kennedy's suing the author William Manchester to stop
publication of *The Death of a President.* Then I wrote my
own book about Manchester and the Kennedys, while Gay
Talese wrote a story in *Esquire* about me, and Russell Baker
wrote a column in the *Times* about Talese's writing about
my writing about Manchester, who had been writing about
the Kennedys. It was incestuous, but so is much of journal-

ism; and when I went to *Harper's,* I was, in so many ways, a perfect 1960s reporter.

I loved everything about the magazine at once—its 118-year-old past and its promise for the future. Most of all, I loved its freedom. Willie Morris's idea of an editorial conference was two martinis in the Chinese restaurant around the corner. The alternative was a late dinner at Elaine's, the literary bar on Second Avenue, where Willie and I would muddle through the rest of the evening. Willie, who grew up in Yazoo City, Mississippi, and was educated at the University of Texas and Oxford, wrote his autobiography, *North Toward Home,* after becoming, at age thirty-two, editor of *Harper's.* On my first visit to Elaine's, he gave me a copy of his book. Across the top of the flyleaf he wrote: "July 27, 1968, the night Corry decided to work for Harper's magazine"; and under that: "To John, who is going to make my North Toward Home, through his own work, a confirmation of my own work, but at the same time a more complicated and richer understanding. Affectionately, Willie." Willie was in love with words and writers and the soul of the South and purple passages, and like me, he drank too much.

Willie was sentimental, sly, and mischievous. He was cherubic in face and florid in thought, and he adored being editor of *Harper's.* In *North Toward Home* he called New York the "Big Cave," and he dreamed brave dreams of conquest. They did not work out, and the cave would collapse, but his days were fine while they lasted. Willie thought *Harper's* was the center of the literary world, and in the strength of his conviction everyone around him thought it was, too. "Co-ree," he once said to me dreamily, "do you know this country has the one-two punch—Hemingway and Faulkner?" Willie was not just being whimsical; he wanted to be in communion with saints, and he looked to the big picture. One day I told him I wanted to try to get into Cuba for the tenth anniversary of the revolution. Fine, he said, and we went to the Chinese restaurant around the corner and drank martinis. Havana shuffled and danced for weeks and months before it eventually said it would accept me. Fine, Willie said, and we went once more to the restaurant. On the day I returned from Cuba, he asked me to meet him there again. I did, and while we sat at the bar I told him I wanted to write 5,000 words or so for the next issue of *Harper's*. Fine, he said, and did not ask about Fidel and the revolution, or the spirit of Che, or whether the *campesinos* were happy. It was enough that I wanted to write about them. Willie wanted you to write; he made you believe you could write. You wrote.

It was all so different from the *Times*. The newsroom had been layered with quirky editors who operated under a quirky committee system. A reporter felt he carried their weight on his back. *Harper's* was intimate: reception room, hallway hung with old magazine covers, a dozen modest offices. Willie had the corner office at the end of the hallway. He may have communed with saints, but you communed with him, and no one got in the way. Surely it was parochial, but I had a sense of having moved into a larger place than before, and in a very real way I had. I had stepped away from journalism and into the world of letters. I was no longer a reporter but a writer, and even if the distinction was not clear in my mind, it was certain I was meeting new people. *Harper's* was the hot magazine in New York in the late 1960s. There is always a hot magazine in New York, the magazine everyone talks about, incandescent in its orbit. Actually, everyone is not talking about the magazine, and the orbit one day will fade, but to be part of a hot magazine in New York is like winning at king of the hill. You gain entrance to social circles you did not know existed. It is still so in New York, though there is a difference between the late-sixties *Harper's* and the hot magazines now, and in the difference is the slow fading of the culture. Willie's magazine was *about* something; Willie cared, and late at night, when his cherubic look turned owlish, he would say that the magazine had to matter. He pronounced it "mattuh," but the meaning was clear, and to matter meant something important—life and death and American literature and the soul of the Great Republic. To matter meant width and breadth and vision. To matter meant you cared.

In time, these thoughts would mean a lot less. *Spy* could become a hot magazine in New York while inspired by no more than a compulsion to embarrass anyone mentioned in its pages. The literary-political matings of the sixties would ripen not as art or journalism but as dumb, empty media, and swallow up all distinctions. Everyone would be fascinated by the media, and everyone would be afraid of them, yet no one would be able to measure their dimensions, or know who or what would next swell their ranks. In the sixties, the historian Arthur Schlesinger, Jr., reviewed movies for *Vogue*; in the eighties, Phil Donahue moderated a debate among presidential candidates; in the nineties, Arsenio Hall went one-on-one with Bill Clinton. A historian and a fashion magazine lend each other cachet one day, and television entertainers and the political process do so the next. Differences are blurred, while status is served, and before you know it, you have *Spy*. On the whole, things were more sensible in the old *Times* newsroom and at *Harper's*.

Besides Willie, the editors at *Harper's* were Midge Decter and Robert Kotlowitz; besides me, the staff writers were David Halberstam and Larry L. King. David, who had won the Pulitzer for his distinguished reporting from Vietnam for the *Times,* was full of ambition, determination, and a large sense of self. "All that a writer has is his name," he would say, and talk about the need to protect his reputation. Larry, a witty, profane, and disrespectful Texan, introduced him to Nelson Rockefeller as "Frank Halpenstorm" one evening at Rockefeller's apartment, and watched David glower the rest of the night. The best, Larry recalled, came when they were leaving. "It's been good meeting you, Mr. Halpenstorm," Rockefeller said genially, unaware he had met the Pulitzer Prize winner. David was beside himself, and later spoke sternly to Larry, who apologized contritely and then, of course, told us about it the next day. "Mr. Halpenstorm, I believe," Willie said when David showed up at the office. David was so angry he stormed out.

It was a comfortable atmosphere, rent only by the usual personal crises, and I was pleased by my new circle. A *Times* reporter might walk with captains and kings, but he knew he walked with them only because he worked for a powerful institution. *Harper's* was an institution, although it was not nearly so grand, and you thought you could walk on your own. I went about and met lions. James Jones, the best war novelist of his time, was a gentle man. He drank orange juice to prove he could give up liquor. The playwright Arthur Miller was a rabbinical presence. You expected him to offer a blessing. Truman Capote was a mess. He was in love with an air-conditioning repairman, but the repairman had gone back to his wife, and Capote was sodden with grief and booze.

The poet James Dickey looked mad when he drank, and the novelist William Styron looked sad when he drank, but with Styron there was compensation. He would recite from *The Great Gatsby*. The passage in which Gatsby looks across the water at the green light blinking on Daisy's dock would move him to tears. Thinking about that gave Willie an elaborate idea. He would visit Styron at his house on Martha's Vineyard, and at a precisely chosen time of night suggest they step outside. Then he would mention the passage, prompting Styron to recite it and move himself to tears. Across the bay from the house, meanwhile, I would blink a big flashlight with a green filter. Styron would see it and gasp or worse, and Willie would ask thoughtfully whether something was wrong. Willie would deny, of course, that he saw the blinking light, too. I no longer remember why we did not carry out the joke, but it was just as well we did not: I think it would have finished Bill Styron.

For Styron already was wounded. Black intellectuals had criticized as racist *The Confessions of Nat Turner,* his novel about an 1831 slave rebellion in Virginia. Styron grieved over this as only a liberal southerner could grieve when his racial feelings were questioned and his sensibilities put in doubt. Nonetheless, he was reluctant to defend himself. Probably he did not know how. In the world of letters there was a right side and a wrong side, and no middle ground save dead silence. If you were on the wrong side you paid penance, hoping that eventually you would be redeemed. Styron paid penance, and indeed he would be redeemed, but for a while he was trapped by the counterculture. In the fearfully loony spirit of the time, you did not argue with black intellectuals on literary matters. If you did, it was proof you were racist, and possibly supported the war in Vietnam, oppressed women, and declined to save whales and dolphins as well. The climate was made up of Marxism, pacifism, and bad manners, and while one could live with the first two, the last was a great nuisance.

THE WORLD OF LETTERS, AND ALSO GREECE AND CUBA

Whatever its failings, the world of letters was rich with opportunity. Newspaper reporters were restricted to beats, but the world of letters allowed its members to go anywhere at will. At lunch one day in 1969, Arthur Miller, author of *Death of a Salesman,* arguably our greatest play, told Willie Morris that the fascist colonels running Greece had imprisoned that country's writers. Miller was president of the American chapter of P.E.N., the world organization of poets, essayists, and novelists, and P.E.N. was lending its prestige to an international campaign to free the imprisoned writers. Willie asked me whether I would like to go to Greece for a story; the United States had not paid much attention to the colonels since they had overthrown King Constantine two years before. This was my chance to expose the colonels and free the Greek writers, too. Of course I wanted to go. First, however, I checked back with Arthur Miller. We met and had a drink. I asked him for the names of the writers and anything he knew about them. What were they charged with? Where were they held? When had they been arrested? Miller said he did not have any of that information, but that P.E.N.'s international headquarters in London did. He was not embarrassed at not knowing the answers to my questions. I suppose he thought they were irrelevant.

That was the literary mind, as I would find: certain of the moral terrain but uncaring about the particulars. In the years to come I would see Arthur Miller again, and while we hardly were pals, he was part of my education. In the seventies, when I was back at the *Times,* he discovered a young man in Connecticut who had been convicted of killing his mother. Miller thought the state had made a shaky case, and he conducted his own investigation. He brought his evidence to the *Times;* the *Times* gave it to me. My cup overflowed, just as it had at *Harper's,* but whimsically this time I wondered how Miller's case would stand up before professionals.

I invited him to a squad room in East Harlem and asked him to present his evidence to some homicide detectives I knew. We sat at a long table—Miller at one end, a shrewd lieutenant named Herman Kluge at the other, homicide cops between. Miller made his case, most of it based on the notion that Connecticut state troopers had tricked the young man, Peter Reilly, into making a confession. Besides, Miller argued, Reilly just wasn't the kind of kid who would kill his mother. There was silence while the homicide detectives stared at the squad room walls. East Harlem that year had more murders than any other part of the city. Finally Kluge asked, "How far were the victim's panties pulled down her legs?" Miller said he did not know. The homicide sergeant next to me whispered, "This guy's read too much fucking Dostoyevsky." Miller was not pretentious and he wanted to be one of the boys, but he was mired in moral certainties. Peter Reilly was innocent because the state troopers insisted he was guilty. It was a way of looking at life and politics and all the great issues of mid-century.

Nonetheless, I also wanted to believe the young man was innocent. If he really had murdered his mother, I had no story. Prove him innocent, though, and I would earn the adulation of my peers and temporal glory. I went to Connecticut and talked to Reilly, who was out on bail, and anyone else I could find in Canaan, where the murder had been committed. Some townspeople thought the young man innocent; they had held a bake sale to help pay his lawyer. The Catholic pastor and local establishment backed the district attorney and state police. Most folks were indifferent and just wanted me to leave, but sustained by personal ambition and the grandeur of the *Times,* I persisted. The principal evidence in Reilly's favor, in my mind at least, centered on the time of night he and some friends had watched a Clint Eastwood movie on television. Amateur investigators in criminal cases always pick a small point they think everyone has overlooked and use it to convince themselves their man is innocent. My small point had to do with when, in the movie, Clint Eastwood shot some Nazis on a train. Someone who was with Reilly that night recalled that Eastwood shot the Nazis just before Reilly left the house where he watched the movie. According to the district attorney, Reilly then drove to where his mother lived and stabbed and beat her to death.

I checked with the New Haven station that had broadcast the movie. I was told the movie had not been shown at the time listed in the newspaper that day; it had been delayed by a ball game. I checked again to learn at what point in the movie Eastwood shoots the Nazis and at what time the scene would have been shown in Canaan. I found that the district attorney's chronology for the night of the murder was incorrect. This convinced me Peter Reilly did not have enough time that night to watch Clint Eastwood shoot the Nazis and then to kill his mother.

It was a small point, perhaps, but it was all my own; and because it was, I seized on it. Not only did I want to write a

good story, I wanted to have Peter Reilly's conviction overturned. I wrote a long article for the *Times,* laying out the
evidence as I saw it. Then, without telling anyone, I gave a
copy of the article to Mike Wallace of *60 Minutes.* Mike, I
said, here is a terrific investigative piece; the work is done,
and all it needs for television are pictures. However, I told
him, *60 Minutes* must not air its version until after the *Times*
has published mine. Wallace agreed. Subsequently, the
Times published my story as a two-part page-one series. A
week or so later, *60 Minutes* presented its version, without,
of course, mentioning me, even though it was only showing
my story with pictures. Connecticut was embarrassed by all
the media attention. It might have withstood the *Times,* but
throw in television's most popular news program and the
pressure was too much to bear. The state gave Peter Reilly a
new trial and eventually set him free.

This is a splendid example in miniature of how much of
my world operated. Arthur Miller manipulated the *Times.* I
took over and manipulated *60 Minutes.* We all manipulated
the State of Connecticut, even if it is impossible to tell who
did what precisely. Everyone involved had a proprietary interest. Everyone knew everyone else. Journalism, politics,
and ego mingled. Ego is the motive power behind so much
in the media. A year after my story appeared, one of the television networks presented a two-hour docudrama, based on
a book about Peter Reilly by a free-lance writer. For the
most part it showed how state troopers persuaded Reilly to
confess after they picked him up. As I watched I grew sulky.
The movie said nothing about the terrific job I had done to
get him a new trial. Then, in the last line of the movie, a
character mentioned that Arthur Miller was interested in the
case and would speak to *The New York Times.* I brightened
up when I heard that. Why yes, I thought; they've finally
mentioned me.

I do not mean to be picking on Arthur Miller, but he was

an exemplar of the literary intellectual with a penchant for speaking out on public affairs. In that first encounter, at *Harper's,* I thought it strange he was so poorly informed about Greece even though he led the P.E.N. campaign, but I did not think about it very long because I was happy to go to International P.E.N. headquarters in London. I more or less assumed what the story would be, anyway. Army colonels were army colonels and I knew what to think of them. Of course they imprisoned writers; that was what colonels did. I flew to London and went to the townhouse headquarters of P.E.N. Arthur Miller had sent me, I said. A pleasant woman there told me she had heard about the imprisoned writers, but she did not know about names, dates, or charges, either. I asked her to please check around. She said she would, though she sounded distressed and suggested I come back the next day. I did go back, and met another woman, less pleasant than the first, who told me that P.E.N. wanted to free the writers but that it did not keep track of each one. Please give me the name of an imprisoned writer, I said; any name will do. The woman looked cross and said she had no names, and it was clear we had nowhere to go. The next day I flew to Athens.

In Athens, I told myself I was a reporter and not a writer. I presented myself at the United States embassy and in a very loud voice asked an American diplomat how Greece was doing under the military junta. I spoke loudly because I wanted the Greek employees in the embassy to hear me, and I practically shouted when I mentioned I was staying at the King George Hotel. The Greek Foreign Ministry had booked the room for me, and it was distinguished by its view of the Parthenon and the listening device in the air vent. (Finding the listening device required no imagination on my part; a previous occupant of the room had written, "This room is bugged," on a matchbook and left it where I would find it.) The day after I visited the embassy I had a call at the hotel: a

Greek employee at the embassy inviting me to tea. He was a small man in a seersucker suit, and over pastries he said he would help me. The day after that, another Greek man called and told me to go to a telephone kiosk outside the hotel and dial a certain number. I did, and was told to walk several blocks and then take a taxi for several more blocks, and then to call a different number from a new telephone. I did that, too, and received new instructions: Walk two blocks in one direction and two blocks in another, and enter the apartment building on the corner; hurry past the concierge, without speaking, and take the elevator to an upper floor; get out and walk one flight down. Knock on the apartment door at the end of the hall. Needless to say, I enjoyed all of this immensely.

It was the world of the Greek underground, wrought from high tragedy and farce, and another step in my education. In that particular apartment on that particular day, I met Amalia Fleming, the Greek widow of Sir Alexander Fleming, the discoverer of penicillin. Lady Fleming was cheerful and rumpled and full of contempt for the colonels. "Do not worry about them," she said as she shook my hand. "They are very stupid men." She explained that midafternoon was the best time for clandestine meetings because the police took naps after lunch. That morning, she said, she had taken taxis around Athens while she distributed clothes and small sums of money to the families of political prisoners. The police had followed her everywhere, but now she was sure they were dozing. I liked Lady Fleming at once, and it is a solemn fact that when I entered the apartment building I had noticed two men in a car sound asleep.

Military dictatorship in Greece had an antic quality; so did its opposition. At my second meeting with Lady Fleming, the young communist student who answered the door said she and her colleagues would smuggle me into Averoff prison in Athens so that I could interview inmates who had been tortured. That made me nervous; a diplomat had told me the colonels' cops broke the heads of reporters they caught snooping. On the other hand, I did not know how to refuse the offer gracefully. What if I looked like a coward? I asked the student how I would enter the prison. She said I would climb down from a rooftop and get in the back of a truck; then I would be driven into Averoff, where a sympathizer would help me out of the truck and lead me surreptitiously to the prisoners. I pondered this awhile and eventually asked how I would leave. Of that she and her colleagues were not sure; I might have to hide where the guards could not find me until that had been worked out. I turned down the offer to be smuggled into prison.

I suppose I am making Greece sound comic. Some of it was comic: amateur revolutionaries and Keystone cops and, most comic of all, a reporter who thought he could make much sense of it. When Thucydides wrote his history of the Peloponnesian War, he complained that "the task was laborious because eyewitnesses of the same occurrence gave different accounts of them as they remembered, or were interested in the actions of one side or another." Nothing had changed 2,400 years later. Communists, fascists, monarchists, and opportunists chewed up the truth like old bones. The CIA was mentioned by all sides. "Have you heard the latest?" Greeks said when they passed on fat clots of rumors. Someone had disappeared. There would be a counter-coup. The colonels were fighting with one another. It might have been only a game, except the police did take people away, and to join in the game was to try not to drown in paranoia. In Salonika one night I was followed, and I was frightened because the man following me was so obvious about it. One way a police state works is simply by letting you know it is there.

The atmosphere had the appropriate effect on me. I became wan in spirit and apprehensive of mind and cursed myself as both fool and coward. I left the King George and the listening device I had once found so amusing, and moved from place to place; the last room I stayed in had a concrete floor with a hole in the middle for the toilet. I talked to sad Greeks and mad Greeks, and Greeks who laughed and Greeks who lied and Greeks who were far braver than I. A former tank commander, still loyal to the king, was hiding out in the back of a men's haberdashery. Army officers he once served with were imprisoned in an old hotel near Athens. The hotel windows were nailed shut, and twice a day two guards took each officer downstairs for a walk around the lobby. If he were caught, the former tank commander told me, he would be shut up in the old hotel or perhaps even killed. Why did he not flee Greece? He was in love with an American woman who lived in Athens, and he could not bear to leave. Months later in New York, I heard he had disappeared and most probably had been killed. That monarchist was purer in spirit and less confused about his politics than any writer I knew.

In the end I triumphed over the colonels. Just before I left Greece, the prime minister called a press conference to denounce as slander the rumors that political prisoners were being tortured. By then, however, I had statements from dozens of Greeks who had been tortured and were willing to be identified and to identify their torturers, too. I did not get the statements because of my skill as a reporter, though; I got them because Lady Fleming handed them to me. I had skulked around Greece for a month, looking over my shoulder, drinking ouzo, and feeling the romance of far places, but not finding out much about prisoners. Then I was called back to the apartment. With whispers and murmurs while young communists guarded the door, Lady Fleming gave me the prisoners' statements, all neatly typed on onionskin paper. Each was more piteous than the last—terrible stories of beatings, brutality, and rape. How could I tell whether they were true? I could not, but I acted on faith and accepted them.

I packed the statements in my suitcase and gave copies to an American diplomat. I was worried I might be searched at the airport before I left Athens, and the diplomat had offered to send the copies to me through the sacrosanct diplomatic pouch. As it happened, I was searched; the police had my name on a list. A uniformed man pulled me off the line of passengers at the Pan Am gate and put my suitcase on a table. Then another uniformed man pawed through my belongings. Eventually he arrived at the sheaf of onionskin paper. He picked it up and stared at it, and panic rose in my throat. The inflammatory words he stared at indicted the government and proved the prime minister a liar. I wondered whether the American embassy could obtain my release before the Greek cops beat me up. Then, however, the man stuffed the paper back into the suitcase and motioned me to board the plane. I was halfway across the Atlantic before I realized it had all been in keeping. The man could not read English.

So ended my Greek adventure. I think of it now as a learning experience. I learned that when I looked at the world, my view was directed by other people. They told me where to look and what moral judgments to make about what I saw. The same burden Thucydides had had of not knowing whom to believe could disappear when everything was laid out in advance. This was a great convenience, but it did not help you get at the truth. A reporter who is told where to look and how to look is a reporter on his way to tunnel vision. He may get details right but the mosaic wrong, and on matters of real importance he may get everything twisted. Arthur Miller and P.E.N. and the world literati were wrong. The colonels were hard men, but they did not seem to be imprisoning artists and writers. The composer Mikis Theodorakis was under house arrest in a mountain village, although few

Greeks seemed to care about that, and most didn't like Theodorakis. It was true that eighteen Greek writers had signed a declaration saying freedom had died and that two or three were called to police headquarters and questioned, but then they were released. Arthur Miller and his literary colleagues looked at the world ass-backward. They made a moral judgment first and then filled in the particulars, when they ought to have done it the other way around. The world was more complex than they thought.

The world was more complex than I thought. Communists helped me in Greece and so did United States diplomats, and bilious rumors to the contrary, the CIA had not installed the colonels. I wrote a story Willie put on the *Harper's* cover. Sheila Berger, the art director, who later married the writer Tom Wolfe, illustrated it with an engraving depicting the death of Socrates and words from a prisoner's statement: "I was arrested on April 13, 1968. Security Director Koletis and Deputy Director Pechnikas had me beaten on the soles of my feet, my hands were wrung and I was kicked on the back while hung from the feet. . . . On April 16 Christakis and Kalyvas crushed my genitals." Some prominent members of the Greek-American community protested and said I had been duped, but they produced no evidence and, I was told, they had business connections with the colonels. Meanwhile, I received a letter with a Paris postmark from Lady Fleming. "Well done," she wrote. "You and I will beat the colonels." That pleased me, although I was reasonably sure the colonels would beat themselves, and I had said so in *Harper's*. The colonels had no philosophy, religion, or politics to sustain them; they had nothing except their ambition, and it was obvious other Greeks would soon throw them out.

I WAS BEGINNING to learn a historic truth: Governments like the colonels' come and go because their support is thin and their purpose narrow and their police take naps after lunch. Other governments, however, can stay on forever. The same year I was in Greece I was in Cuba, where I found a Marxist-Leninist revolution was more beguiling than a military coup. Cuba was all flags, bright posters, and stirring music. The revolution met you at the airport and put you on a bus to the hotel. The revolution liked you and was sure you liked it as well. How could it not? The revolution had much of my times behind it. I remember being on a subway in 1957 when I read the first story Herbert Matthews wrote about the then obscure Fidel Castro and his brave rebels in the Sierra Maestra. I wanted to get off at the next stop and make my way to Cuba and join them. Matthews was the legendary *Times* correspondent who had made his reputation covering the Loyalist side in the Spanish Civil War. Ernest Hemingway called him "the straightest, the ablest and the bravest correspondent, a gaunt lighthouse of honesty." Well, perhaps, but years after I had thrilled to Matthews's story on the subway, I went back and reread it and realized it was terrible. The gaunt lighthouse was a rotten reporter. He saw through a romantic haze, and what he could not see he guessed. Castro, Matthews wrote, was "the rebel leader of Cuba's youth" and "a flaming symbol." The Cuban government did not and could not know that "thousands of men and women are heart and soul with Fidel Castro." Clearly, Matthews found, "General Batista cannot possibly hope to suppress the Castro revolt."

In fact, Castro had only eighteen men with him in the Sierra Maestra on the night Matthews interviewed him, and he was hardly a military threat. Matthews was seeing what he wanted to see. Other Cuban rebels fought Batista in the late 1950s, and many did it more effectively than Castro, who never saw much combat. But none had Castro's feel for publicity or his skill at manipulating the media. Castro's people in Havana obtained thousands of reprints of Matthews's articles and mailed them all over Cuba. Perfectly ordinary Cubans who had not thought about Castro before read that he was now their new leader. Recruits began trekking to the Sierra Maestra. Back in New York, meanwhile, where he had returned to his regular job writing editorials, Matthews was visited by the Cuban academic who had ordered the reprints. Ruby Hart Phillips, the resident *Times* correspondent in Havana, had put the academic in touch with NBC; he had been interviewed on Dave Garroway's *Today* show. Matthews put the man in touch with CBS. Three months later, the network televised a special, *The Rebels of Sierra Maestra—Cuba's Jungle Fighters.* ("Jungle" was a fanciful touch; Fidel was still in the mountains.) That same month, *Life* ran a big picture spread. Batista was baffled. Why was so much attention being paid to a man who had done no more than raid a few police stations? Batista, an old-style caudillo, never did understand. The new era was beyond him. Castro entered Havana on January 1, 1959, at the head of a column of troops. Matthews and Phillips were there to greet him. Coincidentally, I was on a subway when I read about that, too. I remember once again being thrilled.

I do not think Castro was able to take over Cuba because of Herb Matthews or Ruby Hart Phillips; the cartoon in William F. Buckley's *National Review*—Castro sitting atop a map of Cuba, the caption reading, "I got my job through *The New York Times*"—was going too far. Still, I do think the *Times* helped. When it spoke, the White House and State Department listened. "In the eyes of nearly all his compatriots," Matthews wrote, "Dr. Fidel Castro is the greatest hero that their history has known." Batista lost his Washington support. American statesmen and politicians read the news stories and dumped the old caudillo. Castro brought Phillips an orchid from the mountains on the day he swept triumphantly into Havana. I never met Mrs. Phillips, who retired soon after that, but occasionally I saw Matthews, an immaculately dressed, ascetic-looking man who seemed uncomfortable when he visited the newsroom. He still wrote editorials, but when he asked to write more news stories about Cuba in the 1960s, *Times* editors said no. Castro had turned the country into a police state while he executed or imprisoned both old comrades and opponents. Matthews's byline would be an embarrassment, a reminder of stories the paper wanted now to forget. (His editorials, of course, were anonymous.) Matthews retired in 1967, after forty-five years at the *Times,* and while he never recanted publicly—indeed, he seemed to apologize for Castro until the end—he must have been quite sad. He had fallen in love with the revolution, but somehow he had been betrayed. Matthews died in 1977 in Australia. I don't think he ever went back to the *Times.*

In 1968, I decided to see Cuba myself. If I had been at the *Times,* I would have had no chance of getting in. Havana was now barring reporters. At *Harper's,* however, I was supposed to be a writer. Havana liked writers. Writers were blessed by creative imagination and not constrained by facts the way reporters were. Writers understood. When Castro first visited New York, Norman Mailer announced that "it was as if the ghost of Cortez had appeared in our century riding Zapata's white horse." Castro, he wrote, was "the first and greatest hero to appear in the world since the Second War." The sixties were full of encomiums like that— rich, ripe, and essentially goofy. They colored their time and shaped people's views and left a residue that persisted years later.

I resolved to approach Cuba with an open mind. Willie Morris, of course, thought that was fine. My problem was getting a visa. I went to the United Nations to solicit Cuban delegates for help. They shrugged and said help was unlikely; only Havana could issue visas. I went back a second time and pleaded. By then at least they knew my name. A few weeks later, while leafing through old issues of

Harper's, I saw a cover story by C. Wright Mills, the Columbia sociologist who applauded Castro in his book *Listen, Yankee.* I returned to the UN, taking the old copy of *Harper's* with me. I remember waving it at a stern Cuban diplomat in a black suit. Surely, I argued, a magazine that put C. Wright Mills on the cover was a magazine that understood the tide of world history. A few days before Christmas, I heard Havana had granted me a visa. I heard it from a friend, who had heard it from the Cuban delegation. The Cuban delegation, however, had forgotten to tell me. I called the UN. Oh yes, a delegate said lazily; present yourself at the Mexico City airport one week from today, in the morning, and you will get a seat on the flight that afternoon to Havana. The casualness was disarming, although now I had only seven days to have the State Department validate my passport for travel to Cuba and the Mexican Foreign Ministry to grant me a permit to return to Mexico. There were no flights between the United States and Cuba; Mexico City was the way in and out. The late-adolescent in me was thrilled. That week exists like a series of snapshots: Christmas Eve, and I am alone at the bar in a hotel in Mexico City, drinking margaritas and feeling exquisitely sad. Christmas Day, and I am in Chapultepec Park with thousands of poor Mexicans who picnic in silence while I wander among them in my Brooks Brothers suit. The day after Christmas, and I am at the Foreign Ministry trying to find the clerk I am supposed to bribe so I can obtain the permit to return to Mexico from Cuba. I could not find him; when I left Cuba, I came home by way of Spain.

My own little group of Americans who flew into José Martí Airport in Havana on December 27, 1968, was made up mostly of young radicals who cheered when the plane touched the ground. They were there to help harvest sugar cane. Some were members of Students for a Democratic Society, and a few were young Trotskyists or militant chicanos.

There was a contingent from the counterculture press. There were also dour-looking unaffiliated individuals who declined all conversation. My traveling companions were not representative of the Americans Cuba usually attracted. They included no Protestant clergymen, assistant professors, Quaker activists, or old relics of progressive causes. They included no one older than thirty-five. Cuba was having a mild problem. The year, 1968, had started out quite nicely. The Cultural Congress in Havana was a great hit. Jean-Paul Sartre and Simone de Beauvoir had attended, along with the usual crowd of world artists and intellectuals. Everyone had gone home pleased. Some months later, however, Castro declined to criticize the Mexican government when its police killed student demonstrators. After that he defended the Soviet invasion of Czechoslovakia. Meanwhile, there were reports that Cuba was rounding up homosexuals and putting them in camps. The bloom was off Castro's rose in advanced circles, and although the bloom would never entirely fade, Cuba had grown more cautious about visitors. The revolution wanted no ingrates. To help celebrate the tenth anniversary of the day on which Castro had brought Mrs. Phillips that orchid from the mountains, Cuba summoned mostly the young. There was a Spanish term for them: *los invitados,* the invited ones.

I remember best a skinny girl with an uncombed mass of dark hair and her pale, skinny male companion. She was fierce and he was sullen, and they spoke to me only once: at a dockside ceremony in Havana where the revolution was honoring heroic sailors. We were part of a crowd that stood under flapping flags and heard speeches and canned music, and when the ceremony was over they approached. They said they did not understand why Cuba had admitted me; I was part of the "imperialist" press and a member of the "bourgeoisie." I argued about the imperialist part, but surrendered on bourgeoisie. I had a crew cut and wore shirts with button-down collars, and was trying to look like a product of my middle-class time and place. If I advertised my background, I had decided, Cubans would tell me what they thought about the United States.

Would Cubans insult me? In fact, two did, but one did not count because she was a young communist functionary showing off for her peers and the other was Armando Hart, a high party official, who seemed so equally composed of pathology and ideology that he could be discounted, too. On the other hand, the skinny girl with the dark hair and her pale, skinny male companion were abusive. They hated what I represented: from crew cut down I looked like a congeries of middle-class, middle-American, white Protestant virtues. The skinny girl said I was a "jackal." In retrospect, I rather like that, but at the time I was mildly depressed. Until then I had been enjoying myself in Cuba. Foreign visitors were shepherded about and taken only to places the government wanted them taken to, although imaginative souls could manage short sorties on their own. That was because the anniversary of the revolution had brought people from all over the world and the hospitality apparatus was strained. Efficient dictatorships use hospitality as a method of control. Visitors who are wined, dined, and courted do not get around on their own; they always have someone with them.

A plump man named Oscar was supposed to look after me, but with so many visitors in Cuba, Oscar was quite busy. I slipped away and took walks and rode buses around Havana. The city was running down like a tired clock and there was an air of decay, but the Cubans I met were friendly. "Yo estoy journalista para un periódico in Nueva York," I would say in my minimal Spanish, laboriously explaining that I had paid my own way and was not an *invitado*. I suspected most Havanans did not like the freeloading foreigners who seemed so enthusiastic about the revolution, and I suspected most would prefer being in

Miami. Castro had allowed some bars to reopen temporarily for the anniversary, and one night I wandered into a bar for a drink. The handful of men there fell silent. I made my little speech about being a "journalista" and not an *invitado.* I was ignored. The men began talking again among themselves. I finished my drink and got up to leave. When I did, one of the men walked over to me, gripped my shoulder, and stared hard in my eyes. He said, very quietly, "Fuck Fidel."

I learned that you see what you want to see in a revolution. I learned also that attraction to Cuba was in proportion to distaste for the United States. The *invitados* were inspired not so much by the enthusiasm they felt for one side as by the contempt they felt for the other. They were people without a country and so they had to invent one. Their Cuba was an imaginary place, just like their North Vietnam. If reality intruded they would invent a new country—China, say, or Nicaragua. Most radicals behave this way. The little band of Americans under Oscar's care was put up at the Hotel Nacional, an imposing old pile with a great portico and long driveway that once had been filled with tourists. It was supposedly the second-best place to stay in Havana. The revolution's most distinguished guests had rooms in the Havana Libre, once called the Havana Hilton. The Nacional was dowdy but had a faded period charm and a cigar shop where foreigners could buy Havanas, while the Havana Libre was plastic-tacky. Neither hotel had Cuban guests; both catered only to foreigners. Indeed, the government saw to it that you were more likely to meet other foreigners than to encounter ordinary Cubans—a manipulation far beyond the coercive powers of the fascist Greek colonels. Ordinary Cubans did not hang around the hotels, and if they had tried, the security people would have chased them away.

As a privileged person, though, I could sit in the lobby of the Nacional or the Havana Libre late at night and watch world travelers come and go. South American leftists were furtive. Americans were reverential. The occasional African or Asian looked lost. Brotherhood and international solidarity aside, you knew instinctively in communist Cuba which person you could speak to and which person you could not speak to. You sensed who was "with the revolution," as the Cubans said, and who was open to doubt. One night in the lobby of the Havana Libre, the writer Susan Sontag and I stared at and through each other; we both understood there would be no mix. The next night in the lobby, I met Renata Adler of *The New Yorker*; we talked until almost dawn. It may seem frivolous to say you simply smell someone else's politics and then react accordingly, but that is what seems to happen. One day I unhesitatingly introduced myself to a stranger on a Havana street. He turned out to be the British historian Hugh Thomas, whose book on the Spanish Civil War I had admired, and who was then writing a history of Cuba. When two strangers meet in a closed society it is unlikely one will tell the other what he thinks. Thomas and I talked only in generalities and I never saw him again, but I knew when I left him he would be scornful when he wrote about Castro.

Feelings were charged among foreign visitors to Cuba. You picked up their vibrations. My own vibrations must have been palpable. I was torn between the wish to believe Castro was benign and skepticism that he was. The wish came naturally to journalists of my generation. We were heirs to the tradition that had shaped Herb Matthews. You did not wish to believe in Greek colonels, but you wished to believe in Fidel. You wished to find some redeeming quality, some sense of purpose, some hint his revolution had merit. The wish might have been hidden, even from you, but it was lodged in your brain and sat in your mind and tempered your critical judgment. Certainly it tempered mine. The revolution, for example, was fond of statistics; it served them up in great heaps. It told you the literacy rate in Cuba had climbed to 96 percent, cattle herds stood at 15 million head, and that for each 537 citizens there were, say, 1.3 physicians. There was no way to prove or disprove the statistics, and it was likely most were fake, but I accepted them with few reservations. In a sense, it was a relief. If you credit a leftist revolution or political movement with some positive accomplishments you feel freer to explore its disasters; you already have shown you are fair-minded. Most journalists, I think, operate in this way.

Cuba itself was a hoax, a charade, a mime show mounted for partisans. I was escorted to model farms, schools, and cooperatives. I met heroes of the revolution who said they had carried bombs, messages, or supplies to Fidel in the mountains. Mime show aside, the proper response was mixed feelings. You thought the revolution had not been a complete bust. The poorest of the poor, especially in rural areas, apparently had amenities they did not have before, and it seemed likely they supported Castro. Still, how could you really tell? It was impossible to go anywhere without government assistance. You could not hire a car or buy a train ticket. In Havana you could not even flag a taxi.

I beseeched Oscar to help me get a bus or train reservation so I could go somewhere unescorted. He said he'd see, but it was obvious he wouldn't, so I decided to act on my own. I had met an Italian woman who was staying at the Nacional in a room much nicer than mine. She was a longtime guest, a devoted communist, and more important, one of the best-looking women in Havana. It seemed reasonable to think she knew a commissar, possibly well, maybe even Fidel. I went to her room and had a calculated tantrum. I said the revolution was being shortsighted by not encouraging me to move around; God forbid, but it was almost as if no one wanted me to see the real Cuba. The Italian woman said it saddened her to hear me say such things, but what could she possibly do? After all, she was not a government official. Two days later, however, the desk clerk at the Nacional handed me a pass that would get me on a bus to Oriente province at the other end of the island. Aha, I thought; how smart I was to figure that out; now I can do some real reporting. The bus took me to Oriente and dropped me off at a white concrete hotel miles from any town. It had a swimming pool with no water, an open-air bar under a canopy, and long-haired Germans as guests. When I got to my room I saw a small balcony. I stepped outside and heard a voice. It was Oscar, a beer in his hand, two balconies away. He had just checked in, he said, that morning. I did not get to do much real reporting.

Nonetheless, I could find out some things. Cuban prisons were filled, and freedom of thought was nonexistent. The man in the bar who said "Fuck Fidel" was either brave or stupid. On the other hand, some citizens clearly were enamored. "You don't understand," a Cuban writer told me, "the question of individual liberty is irrelevant in a revolution." He argued that freedom did not matter so long as peasants went hungry in Colombia or workers were shot in Peru. The writer was a nice man and obviously sincere, but we were on opposite sides of a chasm. To love the revolution, you had to love Fidel.

On New Year's Day, I heard him speak to hundreds of thousands in the Plaza of the Revolution in Havana. It was as Berlin must have been in 1933. A restless energy swept through the crowd like a sirocco. Castro was a thug, but his oratory gripped Cubans by the throat. Although my Spanish was terrible, his words got to me. Still, I was no different from anyone else. How I evaluated what I saw depended on what I wanted to see. A pleasant communist from Pakistan told me she had been shocked when she saw the great number of police in New York. A society that needed so many armed men, she insisted, must be near collapse. I politely pointed out that soldiers with Czech assault rifles stood on almost every Havana street. That, she replied, was different;

the soldiers protected the people. To believe was to believe fully, and to believe less than fully was to begin to feel a great doubt. One had to buy the whole package, or else throw the package away.

It is reassuring to identify with historical forces and think you stand on the side that will win. But to stand with the revolution in Cuba, you had to doubt your own senses. Cuba looked, felt, and smelled like a place run by a despotic Groucho Marx. It was high comedy and low camp. It was a country where nothing worked and everything was closed or out of order. Toilets did not flush and buses broke down and a lot of the people looked droopy. Churches were closed and stores were empty and movie theaters were open only on Sundays. *Posadas,* the Havana hotels where couples went to make love, had declined in number from twenty-five to twelve in a year and now were open only on Fridays and Saturdays. The price was $3.50 for the first three hours and fifty cents for each additional hour, and the desk clerk was supposed to give guests paper slippers. Did Sartre and de Beauvoir ever go to a *posada*? Did they even know *posadas* existed? I got away from Oscar one night and went to a *posada* with a pleasant companion. We joined a long queue, but when the desk clerk heard there was an American on line he became so flustered I thought it best to leave. The revolution tolerated sex but did not really like it, which was why the *posadas* were fading. Totalitarianism has a moralistic strain that makes for its joylessness, a condition its supporters ignore.

One day Oscar gathered us up at the Nacional and took us to the ceremonial opening of a farm. Castro was supposed to show up, too. We waited in the hot sun but he did not come, and while officials made dull speeches about Cuba's "new man" I slipped away and fell asleep under some coffee bushes. I was awakened by voices. Susan Sontag, Cuban officials, and campesinos with machetes were bearing down on me while they earnestly examined the bushes. I sprang up in their midst. They looked surprised. I did my best to look casual. It was a perfectly ridiculous scene. Months later, I read a magazine article Sontag wrote about her visit to Cuba. "It seems sometimes," she said, "as if the whole country is high on some beneficent kind of speed, and has been for years." It was as though we had visited two different places.

HARPER'S COMES UNDONE

ew York in those years was delicious for me. As I
said, it is a fine thing to be part of a hot magazine.
The world comes to you (or so you think) and
holds itself up for inspection. I pronounced judgment on
things I never even could have speculated about at the
Times. Willie Morris encouraged writers to follow their interests. I wrote a story about sex and politics in Washington,
D.C., and fell in love with a woman I interviewed for the
story. My love affair grew more intense as my marriage
grew worse, and I made many trips to Washington on the
Eastern air shuttle. This was part of my education, too. Sex
scandals or purported sex scandals proliferated in Washington in the seventies and eighties like a new strain of virus,
but I knew nothing very different had gone on for years.
Washington was not, and still is not, a good town for
women. When prominent men there look for someone other
than their wives to take to bed, they look to women whose
social status is below their own. They screw down, so to
speak, and not up. Prominent men in Washington fear being
rebuffed more than most men elsewhere do, and they seek

out women they think are least likely to rebuff them. A rule of thumb is that middle-aged conservatives are randier than their liberal counterparts, but the liberals are more likely to act. It is a mistake, though, to think there is a lot of sex in Washington. Cabinet secretaries and their deputies begin work at eight A.M. and stay in their offices until late at night; presidents and their men live in a fishbowl. When Morris Udall was Democratic whip in the House, he told me perhaps a third of the congressmen were unfaithful when they had the time, but that this was only a guess and in any case it was not important. Mo Udall was right about the relative importance, although as journalism has given way to media you are not likely to know it.

Willie titled my story "Washington, Sex and Power." It ended with an imaginative peroration: "It could be a spectacular thing for the country if the President, his Cabinet and any number of other important men in Washington . . . were from time to time locked up in a whorehouse, not a fine whorehouse on the Upper East Side of New York, but something sweatier and more imaginative, where someone like Jean Genet was the idea man." This, I said, would make the important men feel guilty and, therefore, more sympathetic to all the rest of us. Southern conservatives would bleed for the black man, liberals would lay off the labor unions, and everyone would want to get out of Vietnam. Did I know what I was talking about? Perhaps not, but no matter. Opinion makers are not required to stand by their opinions. The same issue of *Harper's* that featured "Washington, Sex and Power" had articles by Arthur Miller, David Halberstam, and John Kenneth Galbraith. Our names were all on the cover. Miller wrote about Thailand, and Halberstam wrote about Nixon, while Galbraith, in the longest, most graceful, and most authoritative of the articles in the issue, wrote about the economy and the future of the Democratic Party. "The Democratic party must henceforth use the world socialism,'' Professor Galbraith declared forthrightly. ''It describes what is needed.'' Years later, in a television interview, I heard him deny he had ever said any such thing.

Meanwhile, my education continued. When the nation swept up the debris left by Watergate, I accidentally learned that the Nixon White House mistakenly had tapped my Washington love's phone and taped our conversations. Political operatives had confused one bedroom with another; the Watergate spooks simply dialed a wrong number. They listened for days and then, overcome by embarrassment or decency, decided to destroy the recordings. It was a lesson of sorts for me. The approved moral conscience worries about government intrusion and the threat to civil liberties, but I do not think Washington is ever well organized enough to threaten our liberties very much. It is constrained by bureaucracy, law, and timidity, and as a practical matter I would rather be wiretapped by the FBI, say, than by a hungry young member of the media. The old newsroom legend was that whiskey was the bane of the *New York Herald Tribune* and sex the curse of the *Times,* but while I was at *Harper's* and for some time after, I was afflicted by both. I do not regret very much, but I am embarrassed by some things I said and did. My embarrassment is entirely appropriate, and I often have thought the media would be a healthier force in American life if the people who worked in them felt embarrassment over their old improprieties, too. If they did, they would not invade private lives in the way they do, and beat up so many innocent people.

I did not know it in those years, but I was present at the birth of neoconservatism. Midge Decter was handmaiden to my introduction. Midge, a *Harper's* editor, was married to Norman Podhoretz, the editor in chief of *Commentary,* and I liked her very much. She was tough-minded and wise and usually on the verge of wry laughter. Podhoretz was earnest and pugnacious, and appeared midway between savant and elf. When I met him he had just published *Making It,* his book about growing up in Brooklyn and then becoming a big-time literary intellectual. The other New York literary intellectuals were mad at him because he revealed their "dirty little secret": They wanted to be rich and famous. No one, however, called Podhoretz a neoconservative then. The term was not applied until the late 1970s, when it was meant to be derisive, but Midge and Norman and their allies liked it and started to call themselves neoconservatives, too. Whatever neoconservatism is, or is supposed to be, it is inseparably bound up in my mind with West End Avenue in Manhattan and a couple of Chinese restaurants nearby on Broadway. The people who would later be identified as neoconservatives all seemed to live around 100th Street and West End Avenue (as it happened, I lived at 89th and West End), and if they did not live there in reality, they did so in spirit. The neighborhood was home to the old left and its multiple derivatives and political-literary battles that went back years. The first big battle was between the Stalinists and everyone else; it left a fault line that endured in the world of letters. Out of its dust and smoke came Midge and Norman and a few friends, fiercely determined, loudly outspoken, and in my memory, all dining on wonton soup.

The radicalism of the sixties dismayed these veterans of the old left; the presidential candidacy of George McGovern in 1972 made them sever their ties to the Democratic Party. Adrift in politics, they picked out the parts of the conservative political agenda that pleased them, particularly in foreign affairs. Traditional conservatives were full of passions, impulses, and high feelings, but never knew how to express them. The neoconservatives sat at typewriters in their apartments and wrote articles and essays that put the high feelings into words. Temporarily, the men around Ronald Reagan embraced them, and for a moment it appeared these neoconservatives might overturn the political culture. In fact, they

were never numerous enough or influential enough to overturn very much. They were, and are, a handful of people who
all seem to know one another by first name, although you
can't always be sure of that. In the 1980s, *The Village Voice*
identified me as one of five members of a neoconservative
conspiracy plotting to take over the *Times*. I was warmed by
the recognition, but I had never met two members of the al-
leged conspiracy, and the other two I only had passed in the
halls. The *Voice* also published a story—"The Corry
Cabal"—that said I used my secret power as a *Times* critic
to twist public television for my own nefarious political purpose. It was exhilarating to think that I led a cabal, and once
again I was warmed, although I had never laid eyes on two
of the three people I was supposedly leading. If you were
going to be a neoconservative, it was more *gemütlich* in the
late 1960s, before the tiny movement had a name, and at
least then you were clear about the other players. They
could, and occasionally did, fit into a booth in one of the
Chinese restaurants. Whatever eminence or notoriety they
would later achieve, in the beginning they were just the
bunch around Norman and Midge.

Propinquity to West End Avenue, though, was no guaran-
tee of friendship. Norman and Midge no longer spoke to
Norman Mailer, or perhaps he was not speaking to them, but
anyway there had been a great fight. Senator Henry Jackson
was the favored politician, although Daniel Patrick Moynihan was coming up fast. Relationships were always being
ruptured and new alliances formed. One night over a buffet
table at a party, I talked to the writers Irving Howe and Murray Kempton, who were not talking to each other. Later that
night either Kempton or Howe—I am no longer certain
which—asked me, "How could you speak to that son of a
bitch?" There was real anger in the apartments on West End
Avenue, along with a certain amount of self-satisfaction in
feeling how angry you could get. I was not angry at anyone

in particular, although it was inevitable I would end up
choosing sides. There was no precise moment when I did
this—there never is in these matters; life's accretions just
grow up around you—but inasmuch as I made a conscious
choice, I did so early one evening at the bar of the Chinese
restaurant around the corner from *Harper's*.

Midge was there—a rare occurrence, since ordinarily at
that time she was hurrying home to look after Norman and
the four children. Midge and I were waiting for Willie and
Larry L. King. Larry lived in Washington, but swooped into
New York now and then to argue and drink and in a rusty
voice tell stories about Texas. He had worked as an advance
man for Lyndon Johnson when Johnson was in Congress,
but the job had been a flop. The end came when Johnson
stopped at a Texas town where he thought he was supposed
to shake a few hands and then go somewhere else. When he
got there, however, he found he had to give a speech. Johnson gave the speech and afterward was very angry. "God
damn it, King," he said, "I thought it was supposed to be
just coffee, bullshit, and doughnuts." I was never sure when
Larry told the truth and when he made things up, but it never
really mattered. He was fun to be around, and he could use
obscenities more inventively than anyone else I knew. Once
I heard him describe a poorly lighted street as being "as dark
as six feet up a bull's ass."

Midge and I sat at the bar and talked about movies. I had
just seen *Diary of a Mad Housewife* and thought it annoying;
she had seen *Easy Rider* and thought it worse. The critics
loved both movies, which were supposed to be about aliena-
tion. I remember that night thinking the popular culture was
slipping out of my grasp. Never before were so many people
supposed to feel so much self-pity. Never before were so
many people supposed to think they were victims. Everywhere, it seemed, you heard keening. The woman in Washington had told me that she attended a memorial service for

Robert Kennedy at his old home in McLean, Virginia, and that at the end of the service everyone had held up lighted candles and sung "We Shall Overcome." She said Shirley MacLaine had stood next to her sobbing and singing louder than anyone else. But what, my love asked impatiently, did Shirley MacLaine have to overcome? She was rich and famous, with a husband who lived in Tokyo and a daughter who boarded at school. I did not know what she had to overcome, either, but her sobbing exemplified the compulsion to bear witness to real or imagined injustice and express a general grief. In galleries on 57th Street in Manhattan, artists draped their canvases to show they were against the war in Vietnam or Spiro Agnew, and in apartments off Central Park, fashionable people fought racism by holding fund-raisers for the Black Panthers. High style and political causes joined in a way unbecoming to both. It was fun for the participants but deleterious for everyone else. You did not have to be prescient to figure out where the country was being driven, or the mess this would get us into. What would happen now to the old immigrant faith?

Midge said I should write about it. I said I didn't know. Larry and Willie swept in with a lot of hoo-hawing and ordered the usual martinis. Willie had gone to a black-tie dinner party the night before, uncomfortable because he wasn't wearing the right shoes or shirt. But then, he said, Arthur Schlesinger, Jr., arrived by taxi and stepped in a pile of dog shit. "All over his itty-bitty patent-leather shoes—dog shit," Willie said happily. "Boy, did it stink." Willie did not dislike New York intellectuals, but he preferred them at their least rarefied, and certainly so did I.

I had a feeling the times were leaving me stranded. The country was awash with new therapies, ideologies and religions; gurus were swarming in flocks. The new politics supported the skinny girl on the dock in Havana. Just as she had said, the oppressor was supposed to be me—white, middle-

class, and a family man, a tool made to beat up the victims.
Midge argued that night that the politics of moral purpose
was replacing the politics of compromise. Moralists, she declared, despised democratic coalitions. They wanted it all
their own way. I agreed. Moralists blighted the twentieth
century; Orwell had taught me that. *Harper's* kept getting
manuscripts from writers who said America was mean, self-
ish, or crazy. We were having two conversations by then at
the bar. Larry was talking about how he got a Dallas Cow-
boy drunk one night and how the guy went out with a hangover the next day and helped beat the Philadelphia Eagles.
Willie was hooting and hollering and egging Larry on.
Midge said good night to us all and sensibly went home to
Norman. By then, however, I had made my decision: I was
going to take sides; I was going to write my opinion.

I wrote a piece titled "The Politics of Style." I said our
troubles began when Robert Frost read a poem at the inauguration of John Kennedy. Hardly anyone remembered the
poem, but everyone remembered how attractive Frost
looked when he read it. And that, I declared, was "the first
sign that from then on it would not matter so much what you
said but how you said it." Henceforth the appearance of
commitment would be what counted in politics. We had entered the age of style over substance. The path was clear for
John Wayne and Jane Fonda. I mentioned the Black Panthers, the women's movement, the Nixon Justice Department, and *Vogue* and *Harper's Bazaar*; I assailed Eugene
McCarthy, former attorney general Ramsey Clark, and Dr.
David Reuben, who had written *Everything You Wanted to
Know About Sex, but Were Afraid to Ask.* Mostly, though, I
criticized radical-left politics, which I found dogmatic, self-
righteous, and boring. The week the commentary appeared,
Willie and I went to a fund-raising party at Harry Belafonte's. I no longer remember what the fund-raiser was for,
but I remember the two writers who angrily braced Willie,

asking him how he could publish such trash. Willie looked sheepish. He said he had made a mistake. "That John Coree," he said gravely, "is an unprincipled son of a bitch." The two writers became even angrier, and one began shaking his fist. He said I was worse than unprincipled; I was, well, despicable. "You should tell him," Willie finally said, and pointed to me. "That's Co-ree." I had been standing there all the time, of course, but until then Willie had not introduced me. I balled my fists and tried to look fierce. Willie choked with glee. The two writers turned and fled Belafonte's apartment.

I was learning that opinion makers played for blood. Nietzsche was right when he said God was dead, and warned that redemptive politics would replace redemptive religion. It was what made the cultural-political wars so nasty. Those two writers at the party had invested all passion in their political faith; they had invested their identities, too. Attack that faith and they became terribly upset because you were attacking them. Yet there is a difference between playing for blood and splattering real blood, and while the first may make you apoplectic, only the second can hurt you. That was useful to know, and a way to keep things in perspective. In the meantime, it was nice to be noticed. Offer an opinion and everyone knew who you were. That may be a sorry reason for writing an article or otherwise performing in public, but it is probably universal among members of the media. Many come from backgrounds like mine, distinguished by neither wealth nor family position. Many are out of the middle and lower-middle classes. If they rise high in the media, though, they become part of an aristocracy, with specified rights and privileges and a wide range of perks, from free theater tickets and preferred tables in restaurants to the power of advice and consent. This last is the greatest and most attractive of the perks, and the one that causes the most contention. Media stars are not elected by popular vote, although they influence people who are, and to be a media star is to rise above mundane restrictions. Some media stars are comfortable with fame, and some find it a burden, and the ones who find it a burden are more responsible about their role in society than the ones who do not. They feel guilty about their power and influence, especially when they come from the lower-middle classes.

Harper's had no true media star except David Halberstam, who achieved stardom when President Kennedy spoke critically to Arthur Hays Sulzberger, the publisher of *The New York Times,* about Halberstam's reporting from Vietnam. His public success was then assured, with or without the aid of his considerable talent as a reporter. There is no firmer way for a reporter or correspondent to become a star than by being questioned or reprimanded by a government figure. Next best is to be questioned or reprimanded by a publisher, editor, or network executive—the person for whom he works. The general rule is that the reporter will come out on top if it appears he has antagonized someone important. It is even better for him if there seems to be an attempt to silence him because he has expressed an unpopular view. Other reporters and correspondents will rally 'round him, and he will be praised for his tenacity and courage. Look closely, however, and you often will find that the unpopular view he is expressing is shared by most of his colleagues.

There was an element of this when *Harper's* came undone. Willie, Midge, David, Larry, and I had been having a fine time, but the magazine was not making money. Faint rumblings came from Minneapolis, home of John Cowles, Jr., who was both chairman of the board of *Harper's* and president of the Minneapolis Star & Tribune Company, which owned *Harper's.* Emissaries from Minneapolis showed up occasionally in New York and spoke solemnly to Willie, who would jolly them through dinner or lunch. I did not know why the company had bought *Harper's,* although I assumed it was because the Cowleses, a famous publishing family—Gardner Cowles, Jr., John Jr.'s uncle, owned *Look*—found it prestigious. John Jr. appointed as publisher William Blair, an amiable advertising man who probably was better at his job than I thought. Willie was suspicious of Bill Blair, and so Willie's writers were suspicious, too. It was a reflex action. Blair, I think, was trying, but he was part of the countinghouse and I was a writer, and in my reckoning that put us on opposite sides. Consciously or not, all the editorial staff felt the same. Among ourselves we referred to the owner as "John Jr.," but Bill Blair, poor man, did not earn our affection; he was simply "Blair."

Harper's circulation was a mystery, and so were its business practices. It shared an advertising staff with *The Atlantic,* even though *The Atlantic* was *Harper's* chief rival in terms of audience and general appeal. The advertising salesmen were friendly men in pin-striped suits, who all seemed to belong to the Harvard Club. I liked them, but thought it a mistake to pay them straight salaries rather than have them work on commission. *Harper's* carried mostly institutional advertising—automobiles, airlines, book clubs—and toward the end of Willie's editorship, not nearly enough of that. He once told me offhandedly that our circulation was 400,000; later he told me it was higher. In fact, I don't think it was ever more than 350,000. Willie didn't know it, but the figures he used reflected the arcanum of magazine circulation. The 400,000 figure included a great many unsold copies. It is customary now for magazine and newspaper editors to involve themselves with the business side of their publications—there is a drab corporate mentality in big media—but not long ago editors and business people operated in separate cultures. Willie lived on one side of the great divide, while Bill Blair and John Jr. were on the other. When I look back, I am surprised we all lasted as long as we did.

"I tell you, Co-ree," Willie said to me one day. "Blair is going to do me in." Willie had said that before, but this time he sounded serious. Blair, he said, was a "money man," and money men did not understand literary men. Willie said Blair wanted to take his magazine away. The two had scarcely spoken for months. Blair had proposed they have dinner together and discuss their misunderstandings, but the meeting had been a flop. Willie arrived late and left early, and when I saw him later that night he said Blair had talked about changing the "direction" of *Harper's*. Willie refused to discuss it, and got up and left. I should have known then it was all over; changing the direction of *Harper's* was unthinkable. Any newspaper or magazine reflects the tastes and interests of the people who write and edit it. *Harper's* reflected our beings; *Harper's* was where we lived. But an owner must live, too, and John Jr. was losing money. Every so often in the publishing world an owner asserts himself in a dispute with the editorial staff. The owner is usually polite and the staff is always aggrieved, but there is never any doubt about who will win. Nonetheless, there is room for maneuver. Willie maneuvered, and although his defeat was preordained, in a media way he won.

Willie had devoted almost an entire issue of *Harper's* to "The Prisoner of Sex," a long meditation by Norman Mailer on the women's movement. There was precedent for giving up the whole issue to one article. Three years previously, just after he became editor, Willie had bumped into Mailer on Madison Avenue. Mailer told him he was going to join the March on Washington and protest the Vietnam war, and Willie asked him to write about it. Mailer marched, was arrested, and spent a night in jail, and then went to his house in Provincetown, Massachusetts, to write 10,000 words about the transcendental experience. He called Willie and said he wanted to write more. Willie told him he could, and risked his professional future. Monthly magazines run on deadlines and printers' schedules, and must be put together weeks before they appear, or they will not appear at all. Mailer pressed up against the deadline, without knowing when he would be finished. Willie and Midge Decter flew to Provincetown and sat in Mailer's kitchen while Mailer passed out pages from his study. Willie got excited reading and so Mailer got excited, too. *Harper's* was put on hold while Mailer kept writing. The result was the brilliant "The Steps of the Pentagon." It was published in hardcover under the less apt title *The Armies of the Night,* and it was the finest piece of literary journalism to come out of the sixties.

I was on an airplane when I read it, going somewhere for the *Times.* I no longer remember my destination, but I remember whole sentences that danced off *Harper's* pages: Bella Abzug had a voice that could boil the fat off a taxi driver's neck; Eugene McCarthy's eyes were cold as a monastery floor. The strength of the piece was in Mailer's imagination and in his willingness to risk looking foolish when he used it. He never had written so well before, and I do not think he has written that well since. "The Prisoner of Sex," the book-length piece he wrote for *Harper's* three years later, was a tedious lamentation about women. ("You know what Mailer is?" Midge said when she read it. "He's a nice Jewish boy.") It had flashes of brilliance, along with a great many dirty words, but for the most part it sank like a stone. On the other hand, Mailer was then the leading contender to be the country's great man of letters.

It was a coincidence, though, that the story appeared when it did—just before John Jr. summoned Willie and Blair to Minneapolis for a meeting. Willie resisted the trip; in fact, he behaved very badly. He declined at first even to return John Jr.'s phone calls. In any other business, I suppose, he would have been fired at once, but the Cowleses were old-fashioned. Amenities were observed. Willie and Blair eventually did go to Minneapolis and meet with

John Jr. and the *Harper's* board. As Willie recounted it later, Blair did most of the talking. I am sure that is true. I cannot imagine Willie in those circumstances chattering away. Already he could hear the death knell. A poll commissioned by John Jr. found that many *Harper's* readers did not like what they read, and John Jr. made clear he did not like much of it, either. He mentioned the piece by Mailer. He also said, lightly, I guess, that the dirty words Mailer used had upset his father. Blair said delicately that the magazine had received favorable notices among "Eastern communicators," but that circulation had dropped to 325,000 and advertising sales were off by eight percent. I was not there, so I can only imagine the scene, but in my mind I see Willie first charming and funny, then defensive and nervous, and finally humiliated and scared.

Willie did not say much when he returned to New York. He sat in his office and brooded. Occasionally, he would call in Midge, who would talk to him gently and then, when she left him, look as if she might burst into tears. Willie was in an untenable position. John Jr. had neither fired him nor asked for his resignation, but he had declared that in the interoffice struggle he supported Blair. Perhaps if I had owned *Harper's* and was losing money and its editor would not return my phone calls, I would have done that, too. I did not think this at the time, of course; all I knew was that Willie was wounded. Yes, he was never much of an administrator. He commissioned pieces late at night at Elaine's and then forgot he had commissioned them. Office procedures were a shambles. I do not think I bothered to turn in an expense account that final year. Unhinge a single part in the process, though, and everything would fall apart. Willie could not share power with Blair and edit *Harper's*.

So Willie did the only thing he could do. He quit. He did not do it meekly or in prolonged conversation; he was in the office one day and the next day he was not. As *Newsweek* reported, he caught "the entire communications industry by surprise.'' It was a wonderfully dramatic gesture, and it set off a tremor in the world of arts and letters. Norman Mailer said he would never write again for *Harper's*. Arthur Miller, William Styron, and other writers sent a telegram to John Jr. and asked that Willie be reinstated. The *Times, The Washington Post,* and other newspapers carried stories about Willie's departure, and so did the newsmagazines. Implicit in all the stories was the feeling that Willie had been forced to leave. As he told one reporter, ''It boiled down to the money men against the literary men, and, as always, the money men won.'' Strictly speaking, that was true, but no story attributed any fault to Willie, while most mentioned the book-length piece by Mailer. Willie, they said, been brave to print it; the pressure and criticism had forced him to resign. I think I believed it myself.

Halberstam, King, Bob Kotlowitz, Marshall Frady, another staff writer, and I howled out our pain to John Jr., who flew in from Minneapolis and met with us in a suite at the St. Regis Hotel. It was brave of him to do so. We were all inflamed by our cause. In our hearts, we knew the game was up and Willie would not be invited back, but nonetheless we enjoyed the drama. We filed into the suite and sat on hard-back chairs while John Jr. faced us on a yellow sofa. Nervously he read a statement. It noted *Harper's* treacherous financial situation and the poll that showed our readers did not particularly like us; subscription renewals were declining. The summing up was cogent. ''The magazine, as presently constituted,'' John Jr. said, ''cannot live only on favorable press notices and dinner-party conversation.'' We struck back, politely at first and then with increasing indignation. Didn't he understand what *Harper's* did in the world of letters. Didn't he understand what it did for democracy? We sounded terribly pompous, although what we said was true. American culture was richer and finer with Willie in place than it was going to be without him.

John Jr., however, persisted. Finally he said of *Harper's,*

"It's not a proper mix." What did he mean? He didn't know, but driven by our goading he blurted out that, like the people in the poll, he was "bored" by what he read. The truth was I was bored with some of it, too, although it was the last thing I would have admitted. We asked John Jr. if he would accept Bob Kotlowitz as the next editor—Midge had resigned the day after Willie—but he said only that Bob would be among the candidates; the final decision would be made by Bill Blair. That was the end of it. *Newsweek* reported the meeting thus:

" 'All right, John,' interjected Corry, 'are you telling us that the magazine will change but you won't say in what direction, and that Blair will remain in power?' Cowles replied: 'Yes, that's pretty much the case.' At that point, Larry King, a rusty-bearded Texan, stood up. 'Screw it,' he drawled. 'There's no reason to stay here,' and he stormed out of the room—followed rapidly by Corry, Halberstam and Frady. Kotlowitz stayed for a short while, but he too resigned the next morning."

That was the way it was, except that Larry had said "Fuck it" not "Screw it." Meanwhile, for all our devotion to Willie, not one of us knew where he was. He had gone to ground somewhere and did not reappear for days. When he turned up, he was proud and hurt but full of plans for the future. He would move to the Hamptons and write; he would never forgive John Jr., although what had happened was all for the best; New York had never been right for him, anyway. Willie was correct about New York. He had arrived too young and flowered too early and been scorched by his own incandescence. Willie did move to the Hamptons and live awhile in the afterglow of *Harper's,* but he did not write much; eventually he returned to Mississippi. He gave me three of the best years of my life, and I shall owe him as long as I live. I have seen him only a few times, though, since working at *Harper's.* He seldom returns to New York.

CHAPTER FIVE

HOME AGAIN

When I left *Harper's,* in 1971, I had a wife and two young daughters and, common to my kind, absolutely no money. In my soul I had known the *Harper's* period would not last, but my soul had never worried about how to support itself. Halberstam, as I said, went on to writing more books. Larry King returned to free-lance writing, and in a speculative mood wrote the book for the musical *The Best Little Whorehouse in Texas.* It turned out to be a great hit. Marshall Frady became a correspondent for ABC. Bob Kotlowitz became an executive in public television and also wrote novels. Midge Decter wrote books and articles and became doyenne of the neoconservatives. I had vague ideas about free-lancing, but remembered a conversation I had had with a free-lancer whose work I admired greatly. In the previous ten years, he said, his annual income had ranged from $3,500 to $10,000, with the higher figure coming from a book that almost killed him. At *Harper's* I was paid a princely $25,000 a year and had a generous expense account, and still was always broke. Most writers I know give the impression they are better off financially than they really are; it has to do with their self-esteem. Newspaper reporters, on the other hand, complain all the time.

I needed work, and Eugene Patterson, the managing editor of *The Washington Post,* called me. Would I fly down to Washington to see him? I did, and we talked. The *Post* wanted me to be its bureau chief in New York. I made a counterproposal: What about my moving to Washington and covering Congress, especially the House, which seemed to me then, and still does now, livelier and more interesting than the Senate? Patterson pretended he didn't hear, and again offered me New York. Then we had a drink with Katharine Graham, the *Post*'s owner. I think I knew by then I did not want to work for the paper. Patterson was admirable and Mrs. Graham was gracious, but the *Post* newsroom felt precious. It was like a salon full of clever people who were unhappy they had not been invited somewhere else. The *Times* had had unhappy people, too, but the unhappiness was different. People there had thrown tantrums. I did not accept Patterson's offer to join the *Post,* but said I wanted to think about it. That was agreeable to him, and as a matter of form he wanted me to talk to Ben Bradlee, the paper's executive editor, when he got back from vacation. He said it would be a "courtesy call." We set a date for the following week.

I remember the day clearly: it was cold and rainy in New York, and the taxicab drivers were on strike. I had difficulty that morning getting from West End Avenue to La Guardia Airport to take the shuttle. In Washington also it was raining, and when I arrived at the *Post* on 15th Street my feet were wet and my trousers felt like damp rags. I announced myself and was shown a seat outside Bradlee's office. He looked out and saw me, and busied himself at his desk. He fussed for a while, making sure I knew he was in no hurry to greet me and had other things on his mind. Finally he beckoned me in. The first thing he said was, "Tell me, what makes you think you can handle this job?"

It was a disastrous meeting, and lasted no more than five minutes. I pointed out that I had not sought the job at the *Post;* the *Post* had sought me. I added "God damn it" for emphasis. Bradlee said stiffly that I had been writing "long form," meaning the stories for *Harper's,* and that newspaper reporting was different. I reminded him I had been a reporter at the *Times,* which, of course, he already knew. I added, childishly, I suppose, another "God damn it" for emphasis. I did not like Bradlee and he did not like me, although it was impersonal on both sides. He was out of Georgetown; I was out of New York. I thought him fake patrician; he probably thought me rude. Perhaps we both were right. Georgetown was charming but not serious. Townhouse and boutique blended. The *Post's* coverage of government and politics has reflected this for years. The heart of the paper is in its life-style sections—brightly written, gossipy, and snippy—and the pulse beat resounds on page one. Liberal Democrats are treated far better than conservative Republicans, but a good scandal, real or imagined, can do in either. Everyone in Washington who is involved in government and politics reads the *Post,* and everyone is afraid of it, and not many people like it, but hardly anyone complains in a voice loud enough to be heard. People worry that if they complain their careers will be damaged, and they are right to worry as they do. The *Post* is custodian of manners and morals in a very small city.

Gene Patterson was waiting for me when I came out of Bradlee's office. "Oh, oh," he said, when he saw me gritting my teeth, "Ben did it again." Patterson, who soon would leave the *Post,* explained that Bradlee had expressed doubts about my having come from *Harper's*; he had reservations about the "New York literary crowd." I now know that meant nothing; I am wiser about men and institutions. Patterson should not have approached me while Bradlee was on vacation. Bradlee thought he was being upstaged. Most institutions work in this manner, and so do the people who run them. Personal vanity and small insecurities are as important as great principles in the way in which they handle their business. Still, Bradlee's instincts about me were correct. The *Post* and I would have made a sorry mix. A few years later, when I was back at the *Times,* it tried to hire Sally Quinn, who had been the *Post*'s most prominent life-style reporter and then briefly was cohost of *The CBS Morning News.* The *Times,* which was in its own paroxysm of change over life-style coverage, offered Sally a job. She seemed to accept it; then she seemed to turn it down. Abe Rosenthal and Arthur Gelb did not know what to think. They asked me to talk to her. She and I took a walk one afternoon on the East Side. She said she thought she would be unhappy at the *Times.* I did not feel the slightest bit disloyal when I agreed. Sally Quinn was pure *Washington Post,* a flower wholly grown in its hothouse. She went back to Washington and shortly after became Bradlee's third wife.

Meanwhile, I had become a small footnote in *Times* history: I had been rehired. Restless people had always left the *Times* and taken their ambitions elsewhere. Nowhere was it written the paper would not employ them again, but somehow it never did. Former reporters seldom visited the newsroom after they quit. They knew they had dissolved the familial connection by leaving. Occasionally, a retired reporter or editor might drop by to visit, but he would look lost after only minutes and realize he no longer fit in and quietly slip away. The newsroom was not sentimental. It lived in the present, measuring time by the daily editions. A reporter existed only as long as his story. A byline confirmed his identity, and when the byline disappeared he was gone, his years in the newsroom recalled only by old clippings no one wanted to read.

Nonetheless, a reporter, an old friend, had called and asked how I felt about working once more for the *Times.* This was no idle conversation. Abe Rosenthal and Arthur

Gelb had asked him to make the approach. I understood perfectly; it was a matter of institutional pride. Welcoming back
a prodigal son broke tradition. God forbid, but what if he
should spurn the welcome? The *Times* had to sound me out
first. The truth was I yearned to go back, but I did not want to
look overly eager. I had memories, too. I remembered the
first time I met Abe: in the mid-1960s, after he had returned
from a brilliant career overseas and was city editor and I was
deputy to Claude Sitton. Sitton had covered the civil rights
movement, defying mean southern sheriffs, bomb threats,
and Klansmen, and became one of the country's best-known
reporters. He deserved a Pulitzer Prize, and when he did not
win one, the *Times* in partial recompense promoted him to
national news editor in New York. Mean southern sheriffs,
bomb threats, and Klansmen were one thing, though, and
contests with other *Times* editors were another. In New
York, Sitton was no good in that most enduring contest: getting control of the most reporters or the most space in the
newspaper.

Unskilled in newsroom ways, he kept losing daily battles.
This had a progressive effect: the more he lost, the less
equipped he was to fight the next time out. He hesitated
when making decisions—a sure way to newsroom oblivion.
Abe, by contrast, never hesitated at all. He passed on to Sitton a posthumous psychiatric study of Lee Harvey Oswald.
He said it might be worth a story from the national desk. Sitton, sensing peril, gave the study to me. He knew Abe was
moving up through the *Times* hierarchy, perhaps going all
the way to the top. He would not want to dismiss any story
suggestion of Abe's. But what if he thought Abe had made a
dumb suggestion? How could he tell him that? Such small
matters might affect a newsroom career. Sitton did not want
to risk offending Abe and jeopardizing his own future. It was
prudent to allow me to decide what to do with the psychiatric
study.

I read it and dismissed it. Abe, however, followed up with

Claude Sitton, who referred him to me. I told Abe I had thrown the study away. He asked coldly why I had not sent him a memo. I said I had not thought it necessary. Abe's coldness turned to anger. He said I had not been "courteous," whereupon I got angry, too. I rose from my chair and said I did not need a lesson in manners from him. We glared at each another like two kids in a playground, scuffing the dirt by the swings. Abe turned red, looked as if he might choke, and then wheeled and walked away. We ignored each other for a long while after, averting our eyes whenever we passed in the newsroom. We did not speak again until the week I told *Times* editors I was thinking of joining *Harper's*.

My wife and I were having dinner on a Friday night at Sardi's. Abe was sitting on a banquette with Arthur Gelb. Abe said hello from a distance; Arthur came over and sat down at our table. Do not go to *Harper's,* he said. He and Abe would find a place for me on the city staff; the paper was on its way to great things. I listened but was not moved. I had had enough of *Times* editors. That afternoon James Reston—"Scotty" to a generation of journalists who admired him for his two Pulitzers and his acquaintanceship with numerous world leaders—had puffed on his pipe, looked very solemn, and asked me whether I would like to be national editor. Reston, up from Washington, where he had spent most of his career, was conducting a brief interregnum in the newly created position of executive editor. Clifton Daniel, the managing editor, a pleasant, decent man, was being hung out to dry. Reston was presiding over the change. Would I like to be national editor? A wonderful movie showed itself in my head. If I were national editor at age thirty-five, I would be managing editor at forty and inherit the executive editorship soon after that. I would run the whole world from West 43d Street.

Or so I believed, at least in that first rosy glow. Several hours later, or around the time I sat down at Sardi's, a colder truth set in: Reston had not offered me the job of national editor; he only had asked whether I might like it. That was a trap. I must be resolute, I told myself, or I will fall in unawares. Editors sang siren songs while you shattered yourself on the rocks. The newsroom ran with treacherous currents as ambitious men formed alliances and sought the big prize: control of the entire paper. My imagination grew perfervid at the thought of my narrow escape. Consequently, Arthur's entreaties that night left me unmoved. He leaned over the table and waved his arms, and in a hushed voice mentioned Lincoln Steffens, James Thurber, and Damon Runyon. He said they would all be working now for the city desk, if only they weren't dead. The *Times* was entering a new golden age; henceforth it would be run for reporters and not editors. New York would be a treasure chest, with each story a glittering prize. Everything would be mine if I stayed on and worked for him and Abe. The last thing Arthur said was that we should all sit down soon and talk. For a moment he almost had me. Then I recalled my conversation with Reston a few hours earlier. The last thing he had told me that Friday afternoon was not to make a hasty move; we would meet for a drink the next week. The siren song faded away then. I resigned from the *Times* early Monday morning.

BY 1971, WHEN I RETURNED, the paper was beginning a metamorphosis, although from the outside it didn't show. The newsroom looked the same: rows of gray steel desks on a gray linoleum floor; no pictures, plants, or carpets. Old rituals still abided. The best reporters were assigned desks in the first two rows of the newsroom. A reporter who covered the St. Patrick's Day parade wrote the story with a green ribbon in his typewriter. A reporter banished to rewrite worried that he had fallen from grace. When the senior editor on duty shut down the newsroom at three a.m. he always yelled

"Good night." The last spittoon had disappeared a few years back (the copyreader who used it had retired) and so had the last green eyeshade, but the general ethos still seemed to be 1940.

The picture was deceptive. Abe Rosenthal had become managing editor two years before and was rewriting the newsroom rules. A revolution was in progress. Lesser editors still fought to control the most reporters or the most space in the paper, but now they answered to him. Meanwhile, the city desk had been renamed the metropolitan desk and Arthur had become metropolitan editor, presiding over what may have been the most impressive collection of talent ever to staff a newsroom. Young hungry reporters and old seasoned reporters made up an eclectic mix, joined only by their disdain for *Times* editors. There was nothing personal about this; good reporters hated editors as a matter of course, and the better the reporter the more likely he was to show it. The legendary Homer Bigart sat at the first desk in the first row, and next to him sat Peter Kihss; and while Homer sat upright and sneered, Peter hunched over and muttered. Into this volatile mix came Abe and Arthur; Abe was the most powerful figure in American journalism at mid-century, and Arthur was his chosen instrument in remaking the *Times*. Abe's background was in foreign affairs, but Arthur knew the city. He had been a local reporter and then a theater critic, as well as the paper's chief cultural correspondent. Abe was analytical; Arthur was intuitive. Abe thought logically and sequentially, carefully weighing and sorting out facts. Arthur worked out of a creative imagination and saw possibilities where no one else did.

Abe and Arthur made a remarkable team. They were wildly in love with what they were doing. They had been copyboys together in the 1940s. They were best friends and closest colleagues. They both married young women who were newsroom clerks. Neither had ever worked anywhere else than the *Times* and neither had ever wanted to work anywhere else, either. In the *Times* table of organization, Arthur was always ranked one or two places beneath Abe, but in the newsroom they were thought of as a pair. When reporters talked among themselves, they referred not to "Abe" or to "Arthur" as separate entities but to a collective "Abe and Arthur." Abe's more prominent rank was signified by his always being mentioned first, but the assumption was that two souls somehow lived in one body.

Nonetheless, there were distinguishing features. Abe intimidated reporters by high intelligence and sheer force of presence. Arthur maneuvered them by enthusiasm for whatever occupied him at the moment. Abe seemed to be a contradiction: at once sentimental and sensitive, and cold and indifferent. Arthur was no contradiction at all. His cunning was as apparent as his lack of malice, and while one could imagine Abe squinting down a gun barrel and disinterestedly squeezing the trigger, it was hard to imagine Arthur even nursing a grudge. Institutions perpetuate themselves and have lives of their own, but they are inseparable from the people who run them, and to think of the *Times* was to think of Abe and Arthur.

I was assigned a desk in the second row, on the aisle, a few feet from the men's room. It was a lovely vantage point—in front of me the metropolitan desk and Arthur and all the other important desks that made up the *Times,* and in back the rows and rows of other reporters in the newsroom. The place has changed since then, and looks and feels now like an insurance company or impoverished savings and loan, but in those days it was the last of the great newsrooms. Everything was exposed, especially the psyches of the people who worked there. There was a new show every day. The temperature climbed after four P.M. as reporters banged away at typewriters to make the first edition and their body heat rose in the air. They scowled and sighed and murmured.

Everyone had his own style. You could talk to some reporters while they were on deadline; others snarled at any interruption.

I was one of the reporters you could talk to. I cultivated insouciance, killing time as gracefully as possible until there was no time left to kill. My game was to turn in the last page of a story at the last minute, in part because it was the only way I knew how to write and in part just to show I could do it. I raced against the clock whether I had two weeks, two days, or two hours to write, holding back until there was no time left and then hurling myself against the tape in a desperate lunge just before collapsing in a heap and pretending there was nothing to it. I was a trial to myself and my editors, although this in no way distinguished me in the newsroom. Many people there were talented and many were ambitious, and the most talented and most ambitious were the ones most drenched with angst. There was a morale problem at the *Times* when I went there as a copyboy, and there was a morale problem when I returned from *Harper's,* and there was a morale problem when I left years later. Feeling unhappy was a tradition, as much a part of the *Times* as Cheltenham bold or Bookman italic type. You had to keep all that in perspective, however. Feeling unhappy at the *Times* also put you outside yourself and in touch with large issues.

Times people were unhappy because their abilities were unrecognized or their stories butchered or their talents misdirected by the less able. They were unhappy because the paper was not what it should be. Exactly what it should be was seldom made clear, although it was the most public and personal of institutions. People inside and outside the newsroom wrestled for its soul every day. The *Times* blessed foreign policy initiatives and Broadway shows. It certified candidates and causes and political fancies. World figures had lunch in the publisher's dining room on the fourteenth floor and presented their solemn cases to editors who had to feign interest. Capturing the attention of the *Times* was important; everyone agreed on that, especially the people in the newsroom. How a story was played and who made the assignment and why and whether the reporter was in anyone's hip pocket were matters of interest. You speculated, you wondered, you allowed your imagination to roam. You looked for political intrigue. You could always find it, even if you had to invent it, and the invention usually centered on Abe and Arthur.

We speculated about them endlessly. It was part of our entertainment. They speculated about us, too, although less for entertainment than out of necessity. They were determined to remake the world's greatest newspaper, and to do it they needed us. Arthur and I got along well from the start, but in the beginning Abe and I made each other nervous. Women may think male relationships are uncomplicated, but two men can like each other and still paw the ground when they meet. As a first-grader I had a fight with my classmate Billy Boswell, whose father was a lieutenant in the fire department, and I pushed Billy so hard he plopped down in the pail of water used for soaking blackboard erasers. I was sent to the principal's office and confronted with the awfulness of my sin. My mother was called from home to come fetch me, while I was made to sit in an empty classroom and wait. I remember my humiliation. I remember my gratitude when the principal's secretary—a tiny woman named Miss MacAteer—told my mother I really wasn't a bad boy. When she summoned me from the empty classroom she noticed I had started to leave but then returned to the desk where I had been sitting and solemnly raised the seat. Only a nice boy would do that, Miss MacAteer declared. The rules said the seat had to be left up; obviously I respected the rules.

Well, I did, but I also had to sock poor, unoffending Billy. A fire department lieutenant was important, a man you looked up to and respected. Of course I had to sock his son: I couldn't very well sock the father, so the son was the next best thing.

At age six, my psychological-political-social structure was already showing: obedience to the rules, along with the need to challenge the man who seemed to run things. One could have predicted my life right there. A boy of six who must raise the seat of his desk because the rules say he is supposed to is unlikely to be anything but a conservative as an adult. Even at six he has begun to cherish order, regularity, and a feeling that the social contract demands responsible behavior. On the other hand, a boy of six who is compelled to push the son of a fire department lieutenant into a pail of water is likely to fight with authority figures when he grows up. It was inevitable Abe and I would be uneasy with each other early on. The man who ran the *Times* was the most powerful journalist in America, and part of me wanted to push him into a pail of water.

CHAPTER SIX

THE BEST
OF ALL POSSIBLE EDITORS

𝕴 have lived all my life in New York City and probably I will die there, although I have never been sure how much I actually liked the place. I am not alone in this. People no longer live in New York as much as try to survive it, and while the city has always been tough, it now sometimes seems almost barbarous. There was no precise moment when the precipitate slide began, but in my mind it was on a summer day in 1981 when I was crossing Columbus Avenue and nearly got hit by a van. The driver had jumped a traffic light. I realized that a growing number of drivers was jumping traffic lights and that the social contract was close to default. I suppose I had known this awhile, but to live in New York you either ignore impending disaster or accept it as part of the scene until it achieves the immediacy of a mugging, say, or a careening van. That day on Columbus Avenue I thought about leaving the city. Soon it would be inhabited only by the very rich and the very poor, and ruinous municipal policies were sure to overcome both. Who would know that better than a reporter for *The New York Times*? In the ten years since I had left *Harper's* and returned to the newsroom, I had roamed the city almost at will, exercising a newspaperman's sovereign right to poke his nose anywhere he chooses. I thought of stories I had covered only blocks from where the van almost hit me.

West 79th Street, for example, was where the dismembered body of a former policeman had been found stuffed into garbage cans. The cans were outside an Italian restaurant where my daughters and I sometimes ate dinner. West 74th Street was where an old man had been stabbed to death in a brownstone. It was a nasty crime, but I remembered it as easy to cover. You did not often get a murder in a good neighborhood early on a mild, sunshine-filled day. I was able to visit the scene, wait for the pomaded television reporters to leave, and then interview cops and neighbors, and still find time to eat before I wrote my story. West 77th Street was where Macy's blew up the big balloons the night before the Thanksgiving Day parade. I had written a piece about how parents and children showed up to see Snoopy. West 77th Street, however, was also where a multiple murderer had lived. According to one cop's estimate, he might have killed as many as nine people. I wrote about that case, too.

Why, yes, I thought that day on Columbus Avenue, it is time to leave the city, although the impulse to flee was not new. Severing a connection to New York was a lifelong doomed obsession. Even as a boy I had thought I would leave. I wanted to be a farmer and drew diagrams of what my farm would look like. I wondered whether I would be better off with Berkshire or Duroc hogs. For a while I was going to raise Plymouth Rock chickens, but then decided on Rhode Island Reds. I never discussed my farm with anyone, nor did it ever occur to me to do so, and the closest I ever came to an agricultural life was when I planted chives in a Kraft cheese box on the fire escape outside my bedroom window. Perhaps I knew even then that my life lay in the city. I will always be ambivalent about its allure, but by now I know I belong there. I have traveled far enough to know where I should live. At the *Times,* I was a very good New York reporter.

In part that was Arthur Gelb's doing. A good editor knows a reporter must play to his strength, and Arthur saw to it that I played to mine. I was comfortable with different people in different places, but I was most comfortable on the street. My talent was an ability to hang out and chat up the folks, probably because I had grown up with so many just like them. All neighborhoods in New York have a way of being alike, and a reporter who understands this can go any-where he chooses. It is banal to say people are all the same, and in these days of mandatory multiculturalism hardly any-one may believe it, but if nothing else the shared perils of urban living make us all brothers and sisters. Only the most thoughtful New York politicians, however, have understood this, and the failure to understand it is a principal reason for the city's decline. New York now has a larger budget than the nation of Greece and more municipal employees than Britain has soldiers and sailors. Yet no one in the city can fig-ure out how to empty overflowing trash baskets, allow an ambulance to pass unimpeded through traffic, or keep guns and drugs out of children's playgrounds. City government is out of touch with the people it is supposed to serve, and the rich who get richer and the poor who get poorer suffer indig-nities whenever they walk the street.

Even though I may have been ambivalent about New York, Arthur had no uncertainty at all. He was sure it was the richest, ripest, most fascinating place in the world. The arts thrived, while commerce flourished and the riffraff added color. Arthur was the best of all possible metropolitan editors. He was hardly naive, but he looked at New York like a lover. He had read Lincoln Steffens's *The Shame of the Cities* when he was a teenager, and said that famous book about municipal corruption had led him toward journalism;

he also should have acknowledged Damon Runyon. Runyon created a rowdy, sentimental, and engaging New York, possibly because he had been born in Kansas. For that matter, O. Henry was born in North Carolina, and spent much of his life in Texas. Arthur came out of a different immigrant tradition. He had been born in an apartment in back of a store in East Harlem, to Czech immigrant parents who prospered and then moved to the Bronx. His father, Daniel, had run away from his home in a Carpathian village and arrived in New York in 1901. His mother, Fannie, left the same village eleven years later, and by chance ran into Daniel, whom she had never known in the village, in a park on the Lower East Side of Manhattan. Daniel was a cigar-maker and Fannie designed children's dresses, and after they were married and the cigar-makers went on strike, Fannie persuaded Daniel to put his old trade behind him and open a dress shop. Arthur spent much of his childhood there, and in later years he would always recall this time with affection. Apparently, everyone in the neighborhood knew Fannie Gelb, and everyone sought her advice. Arthur would curl up under the cutting table in back of the store, and listen to his mother deal with crises and problems until he fell asleep. I think he was getting his first lessons in how to handle reporters.

When Arthur outgrew the dress shop, however, a different New York took hold. As an adolescent he fell in love with the theater and glamour and lights. He would walk all the way from the family's apartment near the Grand Concourse in the Bronx to the theater district in Manhattan to attend Saturday matinees; then walk all the way back to the Bronx. I am sure he saw the city itself as a theater production, with himself as an actor in a brilliant though yet unwritten role. As a grown man he still imagined the same production, although by then he was its director, calling characters onstage and making them appear in the *Times*.

Arthur had gone to the paper at age nineteen, dropping out

of City College because he yearned for a glimpse of a larger world before Selective Service called him into the army. The call never came; weak eyesight kept him from induction, but he did find his true vocation. He tried to get a job at *PM,* a now defunct daily. There were no openings, but the city editor at *PM* knew the woman who was secretary to Edwin L. James, the managing editor of the *Times,* and called her. Could she find a place, the city editor asked, for a bright young man? James's secretary said he could start as a copyboy the next day.

And so Arthur found his vocation, and he knew it right from the start. The *Times* newsroom was full of men who wore eyeshades and had elastic bands on their sleeves, and talked into upright telephones. When they stopped talking they banged away at black Remington typewriters, and after every page or so yelled ''Boy!'' The copyboys all sat on a long wooden bench. When a reporter yelled ''Boy!'' the copyboy at the end of the bench would hasten to the reporter, pick up the copy, and run it to the city desk. Then he would return to the wooden bench, sitting this time at its other end and joining the other copyboys as they slid in unison toward the takeoff point each time another reporter yelled ''Boy!'' The head copyboy was a one-armed man named Tim; his subordinate was a dwarf named Sammy. Arthur's salary was sixteen dollars a week, and he worked from six P.M. until dawn, although the hours passed quickly. Arthur had seen *The Front Page* by Ben Hecht and Charles MacArthur, but here it was for real. He was smitten the first time he saw the newsroom. Edwin James wore yellow spats and a cravat with a diamond stickpin. Every night when the first edition was put to bed, he would emerge from his office and get his bets down with Angelo or Phil, the *Times*'s two resident bookmakers. They were newsroom clerks, but as bookmakers they made more money than any of the reporters. Arthur pulled James's byline file from the *Times* morgue the first week he was in the newsroom. He found the stories from World War I and the stories from postwar Europe and, fluttering out of the manila folder, the story that began: "Paris, May 21—Lindbergh did it. Twenty minutes after ten o'clock tonight suddenly and softly there slipped out of the darkness a gray-white airplane as 25,000 pairs of eyes strained toward it."

Everything seemed so right. Arthur's heart was full of joy. The year was 1944, and when he left the newsroom as managing editor forty-six years later, the newsroom had changed, but in essential ways he had not. He was still smitten by what he was doing, just as he had been when he slid down the copyboys' bench. Whatever his prestige as managing editor, though, it was during his ten years as metropolitan editor that he had left his most indelible mark. He had directed reporters, critics, and editors with enormous affection, endless enthusiasm, and serpentine guile; he had thrown out ideas like seeds, and then moved on and thrown out more. He had operated on overdrive, and had grown bored when things became quiet. Meanwhile, it had been generally agreed in the newsroom that even though many of Arthur's ideas were brilliant, others did not stand up. For elucidation you had to make Arthur focus, which was not always easy to do. He was famous for his ability to be absorbed in whatever he was absorbed in, to the exclusion of everything else. I knew a senior editor who was offered a better job at another newspaper. He decided to take it, but as a courtesy thought to tell Arthur first. Each time he approached him, however, Arthur was either distracted or busy. The editor finally caught his attention with a memo: "Dear Arthur—I quit."

With persistence, of course, Arthur could be run down. Then a reporter or editor was faced with the difficulty of getting him to reconsider a past position, or to accede to whatever it was the reporter or editor wanted—a new beat or assignment or, likely as not, a raise. Arthur's adroitness in these encounters knew no bounds. Reporters skilled in hounding recalcitrant city officials for a straight yes or no would not have the slightest idea where Arthur had just come down on an issue. The reporters would prepare their arguments with care, often working up grand passions when they tried them out first on their colleagues. Then, confident they could speak clearly and logically, they faced Arthur. Lesser confrontations took place at his desk in the newsroom, and the more serious ones in his office, a small room with sofa, desk and chair, and walls hung with *Times* memorabilia. Watching the afternoon traffic in and out of Arthur's office was a favorite newsroom diversion. Determined reporters walked in, and baffled reporters walked out, struggling with bewilderment or vexation. "What did he say?" a friend might ask. "Damned if I know," would be the answer. Once, while campaigning for a raise, I decided to move obliquely. Reporters picked up their checks on Wednesdays, and so on three successive Wednesdays I stuck one of the long yellow checks in my shirt breast pocket, and let it stick out like a flag; then I borrowed ten dollars from Arthur. I thought it a nice sum, paltry in a way, but large enough to be noticed. I was reminding Arthur I needed more money. But each time I asked for the ten dollars, Arthur just handed the money over without comment or change of expression. I paid him back when we reached thirty, and when I did he grinned for an instant and then turned his head away. Nice try, he seemed to be saying, but you still are not getting a raise.

Arthur often assigned stories no other editor would assign. One of his techniques was to overwhelm a reporter with what seemed to be genuine enthusiasm. Arthur's enthusiasm, however, often would be in inverse proportion to the soundness of the story he was assigning. That is, a good story required almost no display of enthusiasm; an unsound, or marginal, story would be assigned with a great show of fervor. The more fervor Arthur displayed, the less likely the reporter would be to question the assignment. Why, of course, the reporter would say, and go off in full-throated cry. Late one afternoon Arthur swept down on me with great urgency and said that I had to get to West Point by dark. Benedict Arnold's ghost, he said, had been seen the night before at the military academy. I grabbed a photographer and told him we had to hurry, and we raced away in a car. Halfway to our destination, the photographer asked me what, exactly, he had to shoot. Benedict Arnold's ghost, I said weakly. The photographer looked at me strangely, and I realized Arthur had done it again. He had wound me up and sent me off on another goofy assignment. Still, Arthur's genius was such that, improbable as it all might have seemed, a reporter usually found a story. I did write a piece from West Point, and the photographer actually did take pictures. They were mostly of lights and shadows on stone parapets, but if you looked at them imaginatively, they could be of Benedict Arnold.

Arthur oversaw coverage of all New York City and the tristate area—New York, New Jersey, and Connecticut. The part of the city he loved best, though, was the part inhabited by theater producers, press agents, and homicide detectives, and politicians, writers, and actors. In other words, Runyon's city. Arthur was sure there was a broken heart for every light on Broadway, and on slow days in the newsroom he sometimes insisted I find one. Once I had to hang out in a taxi-dance palace, the last one left in Manhattan, looking for a hostess with a hard-luck story—two small kids in a cold-water flat, say, and a husband on the lam from the law. The holiday season was particularly perilous. Sentiment and cynicism ran a close race and usually ended up dead even. Knowledgeable reporters tried to avoid Arthur between Thanksgiving and New Year's Eve or, failing that, to appear preoccupied with real or imaginary stories that demanded all their time. One year I failed to do either, and spent the day before Christmas in an orphanage outside New York City writing a story about lonely children that would make readers cry on Christmas Day. One New Year's Eve, I sat until dawn at the bar in the Oak Room of the Plaza Hotel, looking for the bittersweet glow that so famously touches the city amidst the celebration. I did not find it, and went instead to the newsroom that morning and wrote a story about the dour bartender. Arthur was disappointed, but was man enough not to show it.

I liked those years in the newsroom very much. There was a vitality that seems absent now. It could give way to frenzy, and reporters, including me, could sulk like spoiled children, but boredom was fleeting and there was always the promise something interesting might happen tomorrow. A good reporter could be prince of the city if only he stayed on his toes. I had a sense of what it would be like on the night in 1971 when Arthur and I were in Sardi's discussing the possibility of my returning to the *Times.* Even before I said I would return, he gave me my first assignment. "New York in microcosm," he said earnestly. He said the paper was always looking at the "macrocosm," and that it was time it lowered its sights. " 'City Block,' that's what we'll call it," he continued. "A series—'City Block,' what it's really like to live in New York, New York in microcosm." He said I would choose a single street in the city and write about it as if I were covering a foreign country; no one had done anything like that before, and I was the only one who could do it now. "Everyone," he said, "will be talking about it." I think it was the first time I heard Arthur say that. Over the years I heard him say it many times again. Arthur smothered you with affection, and then yanked at your ego. "Everyone will be talking about it" meant everyone would be talking about you. Arthur's other routine blandishment, "There's a great deal of interest in this,'' was extended mostly to younger and less sophisticated reporters, usually when they were being assigned very dull stories. It meant that Abe Rosenthal or perhaps even Arthur Ochs ''Punch'' Sulzberger, the publisher, had a personal interest in the story, but that Arthur, constrained for reasons of delicacy and newsroom policy, was unable to say as much. Arthur would be so serious the reporters would believe him.

That night at Sardi's, Arthur and I talked about all the good things we would do together. When I got home I realized I had not actually said I was returning to the *Times*; it was something that had just happened. Meanwhile, I was not sure about microcosm and macrocosm, although the idea of writing about a single street was intriguing. But where would I find the street? I strolled about Manhattan a day or so to no particular avail. Characteristically, Arthur jumped in. Early one evening, we were walking on the Upper West Side. This is it, Arthur more or less said, when we got to West 85th Street. He was right; diversity made West 85th a very suitable choice. The better-off residents—loosely speaking—lived at the Central Park West end of the block, and the less well-off lived at the Columbus Avenue end, and in between were most of the social shadings that transfigured Manhattan. It was neither the best nor the worst street in the city, and for many of the people who lived there it was a way station, a place to stop indefinitely while they gathered new riches or exhausted old treasures, and then moved up or down life's ladder. It had sixty buildings, mostly brownstones and limestones and, I once reckoned, some 1,700 people. There was no one famous, although Jascha Heifetz's parents once lived there, as did, according to rumor, Enrico Caruso, even if no one knew where. Shere Hite lived in a basement apartment at 2 West 85th, but that was before she wrote *The Hite Report* and went on all the talk shows.

In the beginning, though, was my mission: New York in microcosm. I would write about how people lived as opposed to how press, politicians, and social scientists only said they did. Right, Arthur said, but insisted each story have a theme: landlords, say, or crime. We argued about that. In my mind, West 85th Street was a collection of short stories, all of which happened to be true. There was the old man at the end of the block who lived alone and never spoke to a soul. There was the prostitute who darted home between tricks to make sure her daughter was still sleeping. There was the man with no visible means of support who had lived thirty years with a parrot. There were young families starting out and widows and widowers for whom it was all over, Holocaust survivors and illegal aliens, fresh kids with big dreams and tired people with no dreams apparent, plus the usual assortment of eccentrics and crazies. "A theme," Arthur would say, "a core—you organize each story around an issue." Well, yes, I would say, I understand what you mean, but the important thing is the people. Once I hit him with Alexander Pope: "The proper study of mankind is man." Arthur blinked but stood his ground, and wanted to know what that man thought about the sanitation department. Garbage collection, he said, could be a theme. Arthur was thinking like an editor and I was thinking like a writer, and perhaps we both were right. The *Times* was not the appropriate place for articles that strained to sound like O. Henry. On the other hand, the proper study of mankind really is man, and press and politicians had forgotten that in the apocalyptic sixties.

It was easy to insinuate myself into West 85th. I walked over there one morning and sat on a stoop. The street was lined with stoops and stairs, which was another reason it was a good block for me. No one builds houses with stoops or stairs anymore, and this is too bad because they are fine places for neighborly exchanges. The second day I sat on a stoop I met the mailman. His name was Nick and he had been delivering mail to West 85th Street for nine years. He knew more about the people who lived there than anyone else. It was not that Nick pried. In fact, he was very discreet, but his job had made him expert on demographics. For one thing, he knew about checks—welfare checks on the first and sixteenth of the month, Social Security checks on the third, dividend checks almost anytime. Nick knew who was needy and who was not, who was unemployed and who was retired, and for that matter, who was living in sin. He delivered letters addressed "Miss" to young women who lived with young men and pretended to be married. Nick knew which buildings had high turnovers of tenants and which buildings were stable, and where people went when they moved. He knew the social ecology. When he had begun delivering mail to West 85th, people who were due welfare checks would wait for him on the corner so they could get the checks before their landlords did. If the landlords got the checks first, they would cash them and take out the rent, and then give the tenants the remainder. Many of the people on welfare had lived in rooming houses, but as the neighborhood grew more prosperous the rooming houses had been remodeled, and most of the welfare recipients had moved God knows where.

When people on West 85th Street said it was a "good block," they always meant the same thing: that it was free of violent crime, and that even though they kept their doors double-locked and bolted, they were reasonably sure they would not be mugged on the street or murdered while they slept in their beds. Fear of crime was, and is, the largest cloud overhanging New York. It darkens bright days and imprisons a populace, and no city booster can explain it away. When Nelson Rockefeller, as governor, sent state troopers into the Attica Correctional Facility in upstate New York to free hostages taken by rioting prisoners, trigger-happy

troopers killed nine hostages as well as twenty-eight convicts. Editorial writers and columnists immediately condemned Rockefeller for the bloodbath. I was asked to report
on what the people on West 85th Street thought. I found they
disagreed with the editorial writers and columnists. It was
not that they venerated Nelson Rockefeller—he was too remote to concern them at all—but the collective wisdom of
the people on the street was that the Attica convicts had to be
stopped, and that even a tragic use of force was better than
no force at all. But the story I wrote did not reflect this. Journalistic practice demanded that I plunge West 85th Street
into at least a partial state of mourning. I quoted the few people who deplored Rockefeller's use of force, and tried to
give them equal time with their neighbors. In truth, though,
the block was almost unanimous in its feeling. The deaths
were the lamentable by-product of the need to be firm with
criminals. "Good block" was code language everyone understood. West 85th Street was a good block in 1971 because no one had been murdered there in years. In the
sixties, a man had been killed in a knife fight at one corner,
and a young woman raped in a rooming house, and a man
strangled with a telephone cord in another rooming house.
But few people on West 85th Street could even remember
their names.

Meanwhile, I wrote stories with themes, occasionally pit-
ting my sense of propriety against that of *Times* editors.
How did you establish the truth about life in New York? For
example, in the microcosm where real people lived, as opposed to the macrocosm where one only thought they did,
dog shit was a huge item. People on West 85th Street
stepped in it all the time and loathed it when they did, and as
an unpleasant fact of urban life, it ranked second in their
consciousness only to violent crime. It seemed to me I
should write about this, if only for the challenge. Arthur,
however, said no. Damon Runyon, I suppose, would have

said no, too. I understood why, and in fact I was relieved, but clearly, as an urban chronicler I had shirked my duty. When Ed Koch came along as mayor several years later, he required dog owners to clean up after their pets, and then went on to win two more elections. He had a surer sense about neighborhoods than did the *Times*.

Arthur and I, however, did not disagree often. I kept sitting on stoops while I explicated themes and tried to plumb life in the city. What was it like, for instance, to fall in love on West 85th Street? Could you fall in love at all? I believed you could, but I decided big-city life militated against it. The unmarried young on West 85th talked about "relationships" and how hard it was to find them. They were not merely whining. The transience of their lives and the impermanence of their surroundings did not allow relationships to thrive. What was it like to grow old on West 85th Street? That was hard, too, and it was all the harder when the elderly were alone. They were more diverse in their tastes and temperaments than the young, but so many of them lived in isolation. What was it like to be a small landlord on West 85th Street? It was to be a member of a desperate gentry joined in the mysteries of plumbing, painting, and rent-collecting, while sharing the melancholy thought that their tenants all despised them. Still, the landlords did more than the most enlightened city planners to keep the street free of junkies, prostitutes, and random lowlifes. They would lie through their teeth about vacancies so as not to rent them apartments. A pity, I thought, that so many small landlords in other parts of New York had been forced to abandon their buildings. A city bureaucracy grown remote from urban realities had put them out of business. The ones who survived had to make their own arrangements. After I mentioned in a story that landlords paid sanitation workers to pick up extra loads, the most prominent landlord on West 85th Street begged me never to do it again. The system, she said, was working. She was right: New York has always been run on honest graft, and I never mentioned the payoffs again.

I hovered around West 85th Street for a year. Some residents declined to speak to me. Others, on reading my stories, said I was getting everything wrong. On the whole, though, I made a lot of new friends. I enjoyed exploring the microcosm. What was it like to own an automobile on West 85th Street? It was a mug's game, a constant skirmish with policemen, car thieves, and other automobile owners who wanted to park where you did. What was it like to see spring arrive? It was to be rejuvenated, really, and to be in a happier time than the Christmas holidays, which left so many unmarried, divorced, and otherwise single people depressed. What was it like to bring up children? It was trying, laborious, and complicated—which was why the street seemed nearly childless. It was not actually that, but for the most part children were tucked away, emerging hesitantly from the brownstones and limestones each morning, and then being virtually secreted back to them at night. There was something unnatural about their absence.

I do not mean to make West 85th Street seem unhappy. It had its pleasures and triumphs, as did even the meanest streets in other parts of the city. But what I remember most about the microcosm I explored was the isolation of some people who lived there. Every so often I saw an elderly woman come home after shopping. She had lived for twenty-five years in one of the last rooming houses at the Columbus Avenue end of the street, and she was always alone. I found out she had received no mail in years, and apparently only once had had a visitor, a woman her own age who never visited again. One day she collapsed in the hallway of the rooming house and was taken to a hospital. She refused to stay, and after sitting up in a wheelchair all night returned to West 85th Street. She collapsed on the stoop this time, but was adamant about not going back to the hospital, and was carried up four flights to her room. She went to bed but was unable to rise, and a trip down the hall to the bathroom was out of the question. Two volunteers from a charitable organization began visiting her; despite their ministrations the room became fetid and foul.

The two volunteers, both lovely people, did what they could. Once, while combing the old woman's hair, they even made her laugh, probably for the first time in years. Yet soon it became obvious the old woman was dying. "I hope you won't think I let you down," one of the volunteers said softly to her one afternoon, before calling 911 from a pay phone. Two policemen arrived at the room ten minutes later, and then backed quickly away. "God," the older cop said, while the younger one started to vomit. The ambulance attendant who came later refused to touch the old woman, and so the ambulance driver and one of the cops wrapped her in a blanket and carried her down the four flights of stairs. When they got to the street, a neighbor who lived only a few buildings away pursed her lips and said, "Who's she?"

The nurses and doctors at the hospital were efficient and even kindly, but there was only so much they could do. Red and purple bruises spread around the needles stuck in the old woman's thin arms, while her breathing became more labored. "She's a very tough lady," a doctor said dispassionately, "but you've got to look at her as a medical problem. It hurts when you stick needles in someone, and there comes a time when death is better than the pain of staying alive. Then you don't fight as hard for the patient anymore, and they just slip away."

The next morning the old woman died. That afternoon the two volunteers and I returned to her room. None of us knew much about her, and we thought we might find the name of some friend or relative to call. We found no name, although we did find four postcards—from Paris, Lake Placid, Pittsfield, Massachusetts, and Miami Beach. They were all impersonal, and the last one had been mailed in 1961. We also found a note the old woman had written to herself: "This little friend of mine is from abroad, Oslo, the cleanest and most beautiful city in the world. Her family noble and very wealthy. Told little girl, New York, see world, come back home. Lived the way she was accustomed to on Park Avenue. Her millions dwindled to almost nothing. She didn't go home, but took job with wealthy families as nurse, companion, secretary. Moved over to West Side. Took this little room. Kept it." There was also an address book, its pages blank. There were two pairs of white gloves wrapped in tissue paper, and four neatly folded lace handkerchiefs tucked in a plastic bag. There was not much to connect the dead woman with her past, but one small package helped. Inside were five photographs, all carefully preserved and mounted on thick cardboard. One was dated 1899. The largest showed a man, a woman, and a girl of perhaps ten. She had a ribbon in her hair and a sash around her waist, and she smiled serenely while she held the man's hand. The resemblance was clear. It was the same little girl who had grown up, and died in New York that morning.

THE RISE AND FALL OF JOHN LINDSAY

New York suffered a financial crisis in the seventies, and though it was a very big ongoing story, I paid it almost no attention at all. In the seventies I was suffering my own crises. They centered on a broken marriage and two children, and questions about whether the city was busted had a detached and abstract air. Besides, I did not write about the financial crisis, and nothing can be so remote to a reporter as a story some other reporter covers. I remember that famous headline in the New York *Daily News*—"Ford to City: Drop Dead"—when the White House said it would not take heroic measures to bail out a foundering New York, and I remember the wife of a bank chairman telling me she was worried her husband would be blamed for the city's problems. I also remember going out and drinking with a former cop who had risked his life in undercover narcotics and then been laid off so the city could save on his salary. Otherwise, I paid little attention to the financial predicament, although when I met someone who was trying to solve it or perhaps had helped start it—in New York, that could easily be the same person—I would pretend I was

knowledgeable about it indeed. As a reporter I was supposed
to know about these things, and while I was not likely to fool
many people in the newsroom, my reporter's credentials
gave me status among civilians. Part of the media game is to
appear to know more than you really do, and those who play
the game best get to pontificate at will.

There was a consensus among opinion makers and other
smart people that a principal cause of the financial crisis was
the failed reign of Mayor John Lindsay. It was conventional
wisdom and surely it was at least partly true. Nonetheless,
Lindsay was as much a product of his time as Bob Dylan,
and he had been abetted by co-conspirators. In the peculiar
climate of the sixties, the city was ripe for a quasi-Messiah.
On the day Lindsay was elected mayor in 1965, a Quaker
from Baltimore named Norman Morrison set himself afire
near the entrance to the Pentagon and burned to death. I went
to Baltimore the next day, talked to his friends, and then
wrote about him for the *Times*. Days later, a twenty-two-
year-old pacifist named Roger LaPorte set himself afire in
front of the United Nations. I wrote about that, too. Morrison
had left no note behind him, although LaPorte said he was
protesting "war, all war," and my stories suggested that im-
molation was a principled act and not an act of derangement.
Perhaps that was easier to believe then than now. On the
night LaPorte died, New York was struck by a power failure
that plunged the whole city into darkness. Nothing moved or
worked, and millions of people were stranded; there was,
however, little public disorder. When the next blackout
struck, a little more than a decade later, thousands were arrested for looting. New York had become a more fearful
place in a very short time, and it was Lindsay's misfortune to
have presided over the change.

New York had an eccentric changing of the guard in the
1970s: John Lindsay to Abe Beame to Ed Koch. The
princely Lindsay was mayor just before the fiscal bottom

dropped out, and he passed on to the bureaucratic Beame a
city in parlous condition. Obviously Lindsay had to be
blamed for something. On the other hand, he was being
blamed for everything that had gone wrong, or was about to
go wrong, or would certainly go wrong in the future. The
problem was that Lindsay had been a myth to begin with,
and when a myth dies, it leaves a huge void. Lindsay's critics were like disappointed lovers. They had offered him their
hearts, but now they pursed their lips and shook their heads
whenever they heard his name. It was not that they really
disliked him—he was always hard to dislike—but why, they
wondered, had they once been so smitten? Lindsay was
wryly aware of the fall in his reputation, and I think he felt
almost relieved. Perhaps it was because he no longer had to
keep acting like a child of fortune. I was at City Hall in the
waning days of his administration and mentioned to him that
I was late for my older daughter's birthday dinner. He wrote
a note: "Dear Colette—Please excuse your father for being
late on your tenth birthday. It's my fault—like everything
else! Warm regards and Happy Birthday! John Lindsay."

Lindsay could laugh at himself: a rare enough trait for any
politician, and a particularly admirable one for a man who,
the year before he left City Hall, foolishly sought and feck-
lessly lost the Democratic presidential nomination. Actually,
his career had been full of wrong turns. He should not have
run for mayor; he should not have changed his party affiliation from Republican to Democrat; and he should not have
been so close to the *Times*. If he had not run for mayor he
would have remained in Congress, a less demanding place
than City Hall, and one where his faults would not have
become apparent. If he had not changed parties he would
have been appointed to Robert Kennedy's Senate seat when
Kennedy was murdered, and been in a better position to run
for president. If he had not been so close to the *Times* he
would not have suffered such a steep decline when he fell.

Lindsay had charmed New York and raised its hopes when he was elected mayor. In a decade that prided itself on looking to the best and the brightest, no one appeared better or brighter than he. Arthur Gelb had met him when he was a congressman representing the toniest neighborhood in Manhattan, and when Lindsay first spoke of running for mayor, Arthur arranged lunch at Sardi's so Abe could get to know him, also. Abe, new as city editor, had just made Arthur his deputy, and both were determined to light up the *Times.* Lindsay was a man on fire, too. That day at lunch, Abe and Arthur sized him up, while he sized them up, and all three thought about how they might go on together. Lindsay needed the *Times* if he was to be elected and then run the city, and while the *Times* cannot be bought, it can be influenced, especially by men of high calling. The liaisons do not always last, though some become real marriages, but they all begin as hot flirtations. Abe and Arthur were enchanted by John Lindsay. The good-looking Episcopalian was strong and confident, but with a lovely sense of humor and just the right touch of deference. I heard Abe and Arthur hugged each other on election night and yelled, ''We've won.'' That was bad form for objective newsmen, but understandable at the time. Abe and Arthur were young, and so was John Lindsay, and they were arriving together as new princes of the city.

The excitement was not confined to the newsroom. On the tenth floor of the *Times,* editorial writers swooned away, while columnists and commentators everywhere compared the new mayor to John Kennedy. In fact, Lindsay was a much nicer person than Kennedy, but the comparison was apt and everyone agreed he was destiny's tot. His campaign ads had shown him in shirtsleeves, jacket slung over one shoulder, a serious look on his face. He was pristine but tough, and gazing eagle-eyed at a golden future. He was as handsome as young Gary Cooper, and just as winsome, too.

Showmanship had always been prized in New York politics, but his charisma was brand-new. True charisma is rare among politicians. John Kennedy had it, and I am sure FDR had it as well, but lesser men show us only its shadow. True charisma inspires, engages, and summons us to greater things. It hints at shared adventures in which we may be faced with some peril. True charisma is exciting. Ronald Reagan had a comfortable presence, not a charismatic one. Conservatives are never charismatic. They either embrace the status quo or look to the past, and charisma must suggest a direction toward the future. Those who want to go in that direction surrender to the charisma and its heady intoxication. Those who would prefer to go elsewhere are not much affected. The media and the upper classes wanted to march with Lindsay, but even from the start the lower middle class knew it wanted to stay home.

In the 1972 movie *The Candidate,* Robert Redford played a guileless young politician with a tough, smart media consultant who guides him through an election. When he wins, the Redford character turns to the consultant and in bewilderment asks, "Now what do I do?" The character of the media consultant was based on David Garth, who, in real life, had done the ads for John Lindsay. Media consultancy was in its infancy then, and electoral politics was on the verge of great change, not only in the United States but wherever there were elections. In California an amiable man named Stuart Spencer was preparing Ronald Reagan to run for governor with a campaign that used computers, sophisticated polling techniques, and television ads rather like those Garth was doing for Lindsay. Spencer was, and is, a southern Californian, and Garth is purely New York, and while neither knew the other, they used the same approach. The artfulness of their ads lay in the artlessness. Garth showed Lindsay in shirtsleeves, and Spencer showed Reagan as a talking head; and although Lindsay was seen as more glamorous, the messages were the same: The candidate is sincere, and able to deal with our problems. The conservative Reagan and the liberal Lindsay were our first great television candidates. Years later I asked Spencer how important television was in politics, and he smiled at the innocence of my question. "Politics," he said, "*is* television." He was overstating, but Reagan by then was in the White House, and so perhaps he was not overstating by much.

Lindsay, meanwhile, was Garth's first big client, and in the insular world of New York their union was immediately blessed. Garth cut his eyeteeth in politics as a volunteer in the quixotic 1960 presidential campaign of Adlai Stevenson, and he had shown his toughness by standing up to the Kennedys. At the Democratic National Convention he reportedly distributed forged gallery tickets to Stevenson supporters and helped stage a tumultuous demonstration; he also let it be known he had tapped the Kennedy phones. Garth was a macho liberal. In New York that was a style that played well, and while Garth did not court high-ranking editors, he spoke to reporters in a tough-guy way that enchanted them. Dealing with him made them think they were tough guys, too. The short, stocky Garth scowled, blustered, and said fuck this and fuck that. Moreover, he knew everyone and everything, and was devoted to liberal causes. Lindsay was a Republican, but Garth knew that the affiliation was shaky and that, once elected, he would do the right thing. Lindsay did; he embraced sixties orthodoxy and ran with it.

Charisma rests on the promise of action, and the politician who has it must appear to act boldly, or else the charisma will fade. Lindsay was bold from the start. After taking the oath as mayor on inaugural day, he dashed off to save the city. Subway and bus workers had crippled the metropolis with a transit strike. Mike Quill, the head of their union, could call it off, but he was hospitalized after suffering a heart attack. New York was entranced when the newly sworn-in mayor rushed from City Hall to Quill's bedside. The patrician mayor faced off against the stricken union leader—Irish, irascible, propped up against pillows, and for all anyone knew, maybe dying. It was a wonderful moment for Lindsay, and when he emerged from the hospital he was triumphant. The strike is over, he said; the transit workers will get a new contract. In fact, the new mayor had surrendered to Quill's demands, and from now on, municipal labor unions would impose onerous financial burdens on the city.

I do not know whether anyone noticed, though. Charisma makes you look at the man rather than at the consequences of what he is doing. A charismatic politician liberates the press's imagination and allows it room to maneuver. The press sees stories where there really are none, and embellishes them with a romantic glow. The *Times* assigned more reporters to City Hall than it had before, and more than it has since. Lindsay was fun to cover. It was even fun when City Hall began to suspect that Quill had faked the heart attack. "When you elect a matinee idol for mayor, you get a musical-comedy administration," said Robert Moses, the old master builder, but he was a man outliving his time and for years had been a curmudgeon. Meanwhile, Abe Rosenthal was winning an increasing number of battles with other editors over who would control space in the paper. Lindsay, his big running story, began to get more attention in the *Times* than anyone else in the country, and his national reputation grew. Television had not yet developed a mind of its own and still looked to the *Times* for guidance. If the *Times* thought Lindsay was important, the networks thought likewise. The country was starting to tear itself apart in social and political upheavals, yet Lindsay looked to the future. The possibility may have appeared slender at first, but soon it seemed quite real: The mayor of New York was on his way to the White House.

Lindsay thought he was, too. Reporters responded to this

and were beguiled. It was clear John Lindsay loved being John Lindsay. He told me once that if he had not gone into politics he might have become an actor, and I think he might have. Lindsay was magnificent when a riot erupted in Harlem and he walked the streets there to calm it. No other political figure could have done so with such panache and presence, but essentially his was an act of showmanship: John Lindsay playing John Lindsay. He played the role in all shadings. In his second term as mayor, it was rumored he was having an affair with Bess Myerson, a former Miss America and a political person herself. The rumors were inevitable—after all, they were two of the best-looking people in the city—and I asked him who had started them. "I did," he said happily. He had not, of course, but the roguishness appealed to him, and he was pleased to think other people might find him so dashing. In truth, he was one of those men who was old-fashioned and gallant with women, and then delighted in off-color jokes with the boys.

There was no one moment when his career fell apart. It was more an accretion of incidents. Lindsay may have been brilliant at playing himself, but he was not very good at playing mayor. Other politicians always had suspected he was not one of their own. Percy Sutton, the borough president of Manhattan during the Lindsay Administration, is a thoughtful man, and I once asked him what he thought of John Lindsay. "The problem with Lindsay," Sutton said slyly, "is that he won't stay bought." In other words, he did not play by the rules. Politics is about compromise and cutting deals, and then upholding your end of the bargain. That was how things had been done in Plutarch's day, and that was how things were done now in New York. Multiple interests were reconciled, not necessarily fairly, but with a sense that everyone's interests had been at least recognized. Everyone was supposed to get a piece of the pie, and while some would get far smaller pieces than others, it was understood they could always try to get more. This was the politics of inclusion—messy, inefficient, and often corrupt, but workable when government dealt with real people. Lindsay's politics were different. They were inspirational, not practical, and inseparable from his own person. John Lindsay was an elitist. He inspired the upper class and the media because the upper class and the media were full of people who wanted to be just like him. They bought his style and appropriated his aspirations, and found in them what they wanted to find in themselves.

It was fitting, therefore, that lower-middle-class cab drivers became the first and fiercest of Lindsay's critics. Early on as mayor he said cab-driving was not a suitable job for blacks, and that blacks should do something better. As it was, though, most cab drivers in New York were Irish, Italian, or Jewish. The new mayor had simply dismissed them. Many cab drivers refused to go to Harlem, Bedford-Stuyvesant in Brooklyn, or anywhere in the South Bronx, saying crime made these black neighborhoods too dangerous. Lindsay moved to enforce rules that would require the drivers to pick up anyone who hailed them, and go wherever they were told. He also legalized previously unregistered fleets of gypsy cabs, allowing them to service Harlem and other black neighborhoods. The intent was noble but the result was a flop. Gypsy cabs began cruising other areas of the city, taking business away from regular cab drivers. It became difficult to ride in a cab in New York without hearing a driver say something about that goddamn Mayor Lindsay.

He could have withstood the cab drivers; the white middle class was something else. Lindsay was perceived as a man who favored blacks at the expense of all others. Soon after he took office, he created a civilian board in the police department to investigate complaints about police brutality. It was not a bad idea, but it had an unintended result: it polarized the city along racial lines and gave demagogues on both sides an issue. Legitimate reservations about the board were dismissed. The argument degenerated into a question of whether New York would stand with blacks in the ghettos or whites in the outer boroughs. Lindsay was no help. He warned whites that abolition of the civilian review board could lead to race riots. In effect, he endorsed the idea that violence was a legitimate form of political protest. Middle-class whites became alarmed and then resentful, and when they had a chance to vote on whether to abolish the board, they did so in great numbers. The board lost by a two-to-one margin in a citywide referendum, and the schism between black and white grew.

It grew even further when Lindsay moved to integrate middle-class neighborhoods with housing developments that would bring in poor blacks. He also proposed the busing of white students to schools in black neighborhoods. *Times* editorial writers cheered him on, and so did people who wrote papers for foundations, but it is unlikely any of them lived in the neighborhoods that would be affected. Those neighborhoods were heavily Jewish—which probably was why they were chosen. Everyone knew Jews supported liberal causes, and Lindsay knew he had the Jewish vote. He even had campaigned at Jewish resorts in the Catskills the summer before he was elected. Then, when King Saud showed up in New York, Lindsay had boycotted a luncheon for the Saudi Arabian king because the Saudis did not recognize Israel. Lindsay never imagined he might have a problem with Jews. He was wrong.

Most New York Jews were poor to middle-class, and they clung to their homes and neighborhoods because they had nowhere else to go. The first wave of Jewish immigration had brought German Jews to the city more than a hundred years before. The second had brought the huddled masses of Eastern Europe and Russia early in the century. The German

Jews prospered. Some built commercial empires, endowed hospitals and museums, and attended Temple Emanu-El on Fifth Avenue. Lindsay had known them for years, and they were among his most devoted supporters. The other Jews, far larger in number, had settled on the Lower East Side, and then followed the city's subway lines as they spread through the Bronx and Queens. Their sons and daughters attended the city colleges, and went into one of the professions. Their less studious or less gifted children toiled in the commercial arteries of the city or drove taxis. These Jews were decent, warm, and generous. They were aggressive, outspoken, and rude. They were flesh-and-blood people who did not lend themselves to abstractions.

Lindsay's problems with these Jews came early, and the problems with the Jewish cab drivers were only the first. Lindsay championed community control—the political euphemism for the cry "Power to the people!"—and called for it in the city school system, with neighborhood boards elected to run things. It was not a terrible idea, but it had a serious flaw. The boards would function like old-fashioned political clubhouses, with nepotism and petty corruption, but without the discipline enforced by an old-fashioned clubhouse boss. Elected board members, amateurs in educational matters, would interfere with dedicated teachers and principals, a great number of whom were Jewish. Lindsay also promoted an open admissions policy in municipal colleges and universities. Admission had been competitive, based on merit alone, and Jews had attended the tuition-free colleges in large numbers. Open admission was meant to give blacks and Hispanics a chance, and compensate them for past injustices. This devalued the ethic that had allowed so many Jews to better their lives and move up the social ladder. Parents may have grown up in tenements and worked in sweatshops; their children were supposed to work hard in school and go on to win college scholarships. Jews had struck a bargain with society, but the bargain was being overturned by the mayor of New York.

It is no good saying the Jews or any other members of the white middle class were being racist in this case, or that ethnocentrism made them oblivious to the hardships of others. Racism existed, but much of the middle class was only a generation away from hard times itself, and it had gotten where it was by recognizing certain rules. Responsibilities went with rights, and society demanded certain standards of behavior. Lindsay did not disagree with any of this, although he never understood what it meant. The warrior prince accepted the political culture of the sixties, which insisted that behavior was an individual matter and that there was an inalienable right to behave however one chose. Lindsay meant well, but it is impossible to build a civilized society if everyone wants to do his own thing. Other people will have to get out of the way, and in New York they were the people who had the most to lose if they stayed. The middle-class flight from the city intensified, and has not been stanched since. The poor had to stay in New York, the rich could afford to immunize themselves, but those in between exercised their option and fled. Innate good sense and everyday experience told them the city was in trouble. Drug use, vagrancy, and the fathering of illegitimate children are all matters of behavior, but if behavior is an individual choice, then no one has the right to overrule it. One enduring legacy of Lindsay-era politics is the burden imposed on the city to clean up the messes its own citizens make.

The disparity between Lindsay's promise and his performance was appreciable. He had raised expectations so high there was no way he could meet them. Charisma is the most attractive but least substantive of political qualities, and it is useless as a guide to predicting what a candidate will do after he is elected. By the end of Lindsay's first term as mayor, New York was having second thoughts. Lindsay consulted again with David Garth, and they devised a strategy for reelection: The mayor would publicly acknowledge that he had made some mistakes. He would never be quite specific about where he had gone wrong, yet his contrition was appealing. The strategy worked. Lindsay lost Republican support, but he ran as an independent and was reelected in 1969. It may have been his finest hour. He had shown he could rise above party and win just by being John Lindsay. There was renewed interest in his possible presidential candidacy. In the wake of Hubert Humphrey's defeat in 1968, left-wing Democrats thought Lindsay might salvage their cause. He was certain to become a Democrat in time for the 1972 elections. The hope was that he could fill the void left by the death of Robert Kennedy, and also attract Eugene McCarthy's old supporters. The scenario was not entirely implausible, and surely Lindsay would have made a more formidable presidential candidate than George McGovern, the eventual nominee. What might have happened, however, will never be known. Lindsay's national reputation went into decline during his second term as mayor. The *Times* seemed to turn against him, and the romance that began with lunch at Sardi's went sour.

It was inevitable, really. No one announced that the mayor had had his day, but a love feast can go on only so long before there are dues to pay. There always had been some skepticism about Lindsay in the newsroom, skepticism being a natural condition among reporters; the suspicion is that only the glib, superficial, or phony can climb to the top, while those with integrity are hobbled. Not all reporters believe this, and some fall in love with politicians and under no circumstances renounce them. Still, misplaced or not, skepticism is more common than blind allegiance, and this is just as well because it helps keep journalism healthy.

Lindsay's charm was a two-edged sword. It may have left reporters beguiled, but it left them also restless. Too much charm eventually makes reporters want to stick their fingers in someone's eye. Lindsay's bright prospects intensified the urge. The mayor was climbing to the top, possibly all the way to the White House. Abe Rosenthal was climbing likewise, to the top of the *Times*, and their interests seemed intertwined. Abe had not yet learned that an editor is supposed to be above suspicion. He palled around with Robert Price, generally agreed to be the ablest of Lindsay's advisers. With the odd streak of innocence that would mark his reign at the *Times*, Abe saw nothing wrong with this. He liked Price, and Price appeared to like him, but Abe was breaking a cardinal rule: An editor is not supposed to hang out with a news source. Abe's relationship with Price did not affect the coverage of Lindsay in any important way; it may even be argued that it made it more knowledgeable. Nonetheless, it heightened the reporters' urge to stick their fingers in someone's eye. Price showed up in the newsroom one night while the reporter who covered City Hall was writing a story. Price looked over his shoulder and commented on what he saw. That was an egregious breach of *Times* etiquette. The newsroom was supposed to be off-limits to politicians. Price was presuming on his friendship with Abe. Actually, he had betrayed it.

That was the beginning of the end of John Lindsay; the process was irreversible. A congressman who did not like Lindsay quietly passed on to Arthur some documents about corruption in the city's Human Resources Administration. This could have been ignored or pursued only halfheartedly, but Arthur organized an investigative team of five reporters. They put together a series that began under the headline "Millions in City Poverty Funds Lost by Fraud and Inefficiency" and went on to detail "chronic corruption." Lindsay was embarrassed. This was his first real scandal, and it left him off balance. To hell with his erstwhile friends Abe and Arthur; he took his case to James Reston. Reston was uncomfortable with Abe and paid no attention to Arthur, and he adored upper-class reformers. He listened while Lindsay complained, and then told him to talk to Punch Sulzberger. Lindsay did, and the publisher listened, too. In the newsroom eleven floors below, Abe and Arthur were suspicious. Abe by now was deputy managing editor; Arthur had replaced him as metropolitan editor. Abe's next move up, to managing editor, presumably would pull Arthur onward and upward. Everything, though, depended on the publisher's blessing.

The *Times* had never been much for uncovering local corruption, and the stories about the Human Resources Administration, Arthur's first big project as metropolitan editor, were about people stealing money, a topic the *Times* ordinarily left to the *Daily News*. The *Times* was going off in an uncertain direction, and if Sulzberger did not approve, the course would be altered. But he held firm, and because he did, Lindsay would become a dead duck. It was as if the *Times* would now do penance for having lost its head in the first place. Besides, Arthur was now running the city staff, and bursting with impulses and energy. Imaginatively he appointed Martin Tolchin as his new bureau chief at City Hall. Not long before, Marty had worked on the "women's pages," covering news about children. He found that the Lindsay administration was using outside consultants to help it run the city. Arthur wanted to know all about them. Marty discovered that they were well paid, but their duties ambiguous, and he wrote a series. Lindsay again was embarrassed. Both the Human Resources Administration and the consultants were identified with the high-minded policies he favored, but high-minded or not, they were beginning to look precious and perhaps even flaky.

A consensus was being formed. It was true Lindsay had closed Central Park to traffic, making it safer for bikers and joggers, but bikers and joggers were in the minority to begin

with, and in the neighborhoods of New York the beneficence
bestowed on Central Park was seen as an upper-class privi-
lege. When a snowstorm crippled the city, it left the middle-
class borough of Queens in particularly bad shape. City
snowplows, it turned out, were all shoveling streets in Manhattan. Queens residents blamed Lindsay. The snowbanks
on their streets were proof that he cared not at all about them,
and they set up a monstrous cry. Naturally, Arthur sent reporters to Queens to record it. When Lindsay visited the
snow-bound borough, residents leaned out the windows of
their apartments and booed. It was not just the snow, of
course. It was Lindsay's whole stewardship of New York.
Yet he still was John Lindsay. A woman rushed up to him in
Queens that day and told him to pay no attention to the people booing. He was, she said, "a wonderful man." Lindsay
brightened, his spirits momentarily revived. "And you're a
wonderful woman, not like those fat Jewish broads up
there," he said, gesturing toward some women booing. The
quotation never appeared in the *Times*. Arthur could be
tough, but he was never malicious. You don't kick a man
when he's down.

Lindsay's greatest trial, however, came about because of
a cop, Frank Serpico, who a few years later would be played
in a movie by Al Pacino. Serpico had gathered evidence
about corruption among his fellow cops. He and another police officer, David Durk, went to City Hall to tell the mayor.
A Lindsay aide, Jay Kriegel, told them to speak to the city's
commissioner of investigations instead. They did, but nothing happened, and so they turned to David Burnham, the
Times police reporter, who then set up a meeting among Serpico, Durk, and Arthur Gelb. Arthur was skeptical when
they met. Serpico was talking about a system of bribes and
payoffs that infested the entire New York Police Department. Everyone knew about cops' getting envelopes at
Christmas, but Arthur thought this was too big. All his life

he had believed there were good cops and bad cops, but while bad cops were rotten, they were shunned by the good cops around them. Serpico, though, presented a different picture: Good cops tolerated and even condoned bad cops, because "good cops" got paid off, too. Arthur had a hard time with this. Besides, Serpico had long hair, an earring, and the unmistakable look of a zealot. Arthur had never seen a policeman like that.

"I knew damn well the *Times* wouldn't print this," Serpico said when Arthur expressed reservations. But the policeman did not understand. Arthur loved the idea of turning the city upside down. Though he could not write the story himself, he could oversee it, and this story had the best parts of *The Front Page* and Lincoln Steffens. Arthur said the *Times* would go with the story if Burnham could document Serpico's allegations. The last big New York police scandal had been in the 1940s, when it was found that Harry Gross, a bookmaker, was paying off cops in Brooklyn. The *Daily News* had run with that one, but it was child's play next to this. Serpico was talking about drugs, corruption, the buying and selling of whole precincts. Arthur told Burnham to go ahead anyway. But what if he found the *Times* itself was paying off cops, Burnham wondered. *Times* delivery trucks blocked traffic when they picked up the papers on West 43d Street, especially on Saturday nights, and routinely violated parking rules. The police always looked the other way, and it was understood in the newsroom that an arrangement was in place. Arthur fretted about that, and then went to a *Times* vice-president. He asked whether the paper was paying off cops. The vice-president said no, and Arthur, much relieved, returned to the newsroom.

Burnham pressed ahead. There are two kinds of investigative reporters—blustery types like Seymour Hersh who pride themselves on their toughness, and intense types like Burnham who seldom raise their voice but always look preoccupied by something important. Burnham worked for months. Serpico, meanwhile, grew increasingly worried. He feared that other cops knew he was a snitch, and would try to hurt him, perhaps even kill him. Some nights he slept on the couch in Arthur's office. A few times he brought over his girlfriend. Arthur was unsure of what he really thought of Frank Serpico, but he loved the drama. Rumors grew about the *Times*'s working on something big. When Lindsay and his people heard them, they reacted as politicians always do, with a preemptive strike.

Word reached the newsroom on a Thursday night that City Hall would announce in a press release the next day that it would investigate police corruption. The gesture was unimaginative. Lindsay should have waited for the *Times* stories to appear. Then he could have furrowed his brow and looked concerned, and said he had been looking into police corruption, but because it was so sensitive he had not wanted to say anything until he was ready to seek indictments. As it was, however, he only incited Arthur. The man who had dreamed of glory on the copyboys' bench called his best reporters together that Thursday night and had them go over Burnham's notes and taped interviews. Then he began organizing a four-part series. How would it open, where would it go, and what could it say without being libelous? Years later Arthur would look back on this as perhaps his finest hour. The newsroom resounded all night with the plink of typewriter keys while Arthur sat in his office and pored over the reporters' copy. In the morning, he sent Marty Tolchin to read the most damaging accusations in the series to Lindsay. The mayor, in turn, summoned the police department's highest officials and had them listen, too. For the most part they denied them.

The series began on page one the next day, and stayed there for three more installments. Whatever the average citizen thought of the *Times*'s charges, Lindsay was upset. He asked Abe and Arthur to meet with him and two assistants. They did, but to no avail. Lindsay was angry and aggrieved, as were the two assistants. Abe and Arthur were firm. They were journalists and had the *Times* on their side, while Lindsay was caught up in the matrix of his own ambition. Cops had been accepting bribes long before he took office as mayor, and even his most ferocious critics could not say it had started with him, but the stories sullied what was left of his promise. Police corruption was sordid, low-life, and scummy. Corruption was inconsistent with Lindsay's vision of himself and the city. The vision had been enchanting, but when the spell faded it was as if it had never existed at all. When Lindsay campaigned in the Florida Democratic presidential primary in 1972, a plane flew back and forth over Miami Beach trailing a banner that read: "Lindsay Spells Tsouris." He went on through the Wisconsin primary, but then gave up the campaign and returned to New York. Four years later he tried to win nomination to the U.S. Senate. He visited political clubhouses and spoke at sparsely attended rallies, but he was like a ghost from the past, and hardly anyone bothered to listen.

CHAPTER EIGHT

ABE, SCOTTY, AND ME

he New York Times has always anguished over the state of its soul and its role in American life, and that is only appropriate. The *Times* is a beacon for journalists, and although its influence has waned in the media age, it still represents the best of print journalism. Newsroom debates over how to keep it that way touch on practical matters: Where are reporters assigned, and what do they write when they get there, and how are their stories then played? The big subjects discussed in public-television seminars or in schools of mass communication seldom arise. I never heard working reporters discuss the limitations of the First Amendment, or whether the Freedom of Information Act should be revised. When one of the big subjects occasionally did surface, however, personal style as much as journalistic principle would determine what a reporter thought about it. Editorial policy and individual temperament were always intertwined.

For years the two most influential, and opposing, temperaments at the *Times* were those of James Reston and Abe Rosenthal. Reporters did not necessarily have to choose between the two, although invariably some did, and their choices reflected their view of journalism. Shortly after Abe became managing editor, for example, the *Times* published a story saying that Mario Biaggi, a Bronx congressman, had not told the truth when he denied having pleaded the Fifth Amendment before a grand jury that was looking into his finances. Biaggi at the time was favored to win the Democratic nomination for mayor, but the story killed his chances. It also upset the reporters in the Washington bureau of the *Times*. As a group they wrote to Abe, pointing out that grand jury proceedings were secret, and that Biaggi had done no more than exercise his constitutional prerogative when he invoked the Fifth Amendment. Therefore, they said, the *Times* had trampled on his rights when it published the story.

The Washington reporters were Reston disciples, and there was no question but that I was a Rosenthal man. I thought the Washington reporters had missed the point. The question was not whether Biaggi had invoked a constitutional right; it was whether he had lied about invoking it. Biaggi had not told the truth, and surely that was a more important matter than the peripheral one the Washington reporters had raised. It seemed to me the Reston school looked at the world as it wanted it to be, and the Rosenthal school looked at the world as it was. Abe had a built-in bullshit detector. He saw journalism not as a set of rules easily followed but as a profession filled with traps for the unwary. Ask him how he ran the paper and he would say, "With my stomach." The *Times* was reborn every day, and he agonized over each conception. Good stories thrilled him and bad stories depressed him, and a lone word used unfairly or inaccurately in a news article would set him off brooding. Sometimes then he would burst forth in wrath like an Old Testament prophet, although almost always the wrath would be directed toward another editor and not toward a reporter. Editors were expendable, but reporters were not. Abe could

sink into gloom if he thought he had hurt a reporter's feelings. He sometimes sent me stiff notes objecting to the tone
of an article I had written or disassociating himself from my
views, but I knew it distressed him when he did. Occasionally he would rebuke a reporter too severely, and then be
stricken by conscience. Six months or a year later, the reporter would find he had a better assignment than the one he
had when he was rebuked.

Abe's reign at the *Times* was personal, idiosyncratic, and
rooted in elementary principles. He said he wanted to keep
the news columns ''straight,'' meaning they should be fair
and objective, but he seldom explained editorial policy
beyond that, and he did not often talk about journalism's
high calling. He was running the most successful and prestigious of all newspapers, but he shunned the public trap-
pings of high priest. Journalism has organizations dedicated
to its own betterment, but he held the *Times* and himself
aloof from belonging. He did not aspire to lead any journalists other than those at the *Times*. He joined no cliques, en-
rolled in no movements, and remained his own man, even
down to his unexpected displays of emotion.

I was in the audience when *42nd Street* opened at the
Winter Garden Theater in 1980. Rumors about the musical
had circulated for months: Gower Champion, its director-
choreographer, was about to be replaced; the ingenue was on
her way out, too; the book was lousy and the dance numbers
weak, and the production an utter disaster. David Merrick,
the show's producer, was, and is, an eccentric man whose
outrageousness was matched by his shrewdness, and he
probably planted the rumors himself. The show's opening
was postponed and rescheduled, and then postponed and rescheduled again. When it finally arrived, *42nd Street* was the
most talked-about show on Broadway. Everyone wondered
whether it would be a hit or a turkey. By intermission, that
was no longer a question. Champion's choreography was

spectacular, and the old plot held up wonderfully well. Pro-phetically, it was about the heartbreak involved in putting on a Broadway musical. When the final curtain fell, there was the beginning of tumultuous applause. Then it stopped. Mer-rick was onstage, holding up his hand for silence. Gower Champion, he said, was dead. Here it was, the night of his triumph, and the director of *42nd Street* had died. The shock in the audience was palpable: a gasp and then a deep hush, and everyone filed quietly out of the theater.

My reaction was different. My God, I thought, what a story. I remembered when the baritone Leonard Warren had collapsed and died on the stage of the Metropolitan Opera years before. The *Herald Tribune* reporter who wrote about his death had won a Pulitzer. I suggested to my date, the ac-tress Barbara Feldon, that we walk over to the *Times*. Years later she told me I was quivering. I wanted to write about Gower Champion, but as a reporter I also had to tempt fate. It was almost ten P.M., and the second edition would close at eleven-thirty. If I took my time getting to the newsroom, someone else might write the story. Rationality is not always the long suit of someone whose life is spent on deadlines. Your thinking goes like this: The more heroic the effort to beat the deadline, the greater the feeling of accomplishment, and thus the deeper the inner peace. It was how you re-deemed yourself as a reporter, and I had not done that since I covered a plane crash at La Guardia and called in the story, in the rain, from a phone booth. I could redeem myself now if things would go just right. Redemption, however, had to be extended as an act of grace, a gift freely offered.

And so it was. In the newsroom I saw Abe and Arthur, both in black tie because they also had been at the opening. They already had given the story to someone else, but then they saw me. It was the act of grace I had sought. Of course I would write the story. Casually I asked Barbara if she would mind going home alone. Gracefully she left the newsroom.

Then I took my tuxedo jacket off and sat at a desk. I was trying to look detached and professional, but I was thinking of the *Herald Tribune* reporter who had won the Pulitzer. Meanwhile, it was getting close to deadline, and Abe had opened a big hole on page one. I would find out now whether I was still any good. I had no notes, and could not remember a word Merrick said, so I checked the Associated Press wire. It had the cause of death and the name of the hospital where Champion had died. That meant I had a lead. It would not sing, but I could cover all the essentials. I wrote about Merrick's onstage announcement and worked in some color: the murmurs, the shock, how people looked when they left the theater. I found out about the blood cancer that caused Champion's death, and put that in, too. I called for his clips from the library, scanned them quickly, and wrote about his life in show business. Then I described *42nd Street* and its choreography. I was going to hit a home run or die trying.

I made the second edition, and pretended not to notice that the young deskman who handled my copy was looking impressed. Then I added some filigree for the third and final edition. When I finished I felt sick, because earlier I had missed not only lunch but dinner. That did not matter. Suffering was essential for redemption, and I had hit the home run I wanted to hit. I knew no one could have beaten me that night. For a while at least, I had been the best in the world at what I was doing. I swaggered out of the newsroom and on a hunch dropped by Sardi's. The restaurant had just closed, but Vincent Sardi, the owner, had allowed some theater people to stay on and talk about Champion, and they had the *Times*'s second edition. Extraordinary, I thought: I was looking at them, while they were reading me. The configuration put me at the center of the universe. In no time at all, I was happily drunk. Forsaking a reputation for stinginess, Vincent Sardi bought the drinks.

When I awakened at home much later, I was possessed by

a single thought: I had to get back to the newsroom. A reporter always wants to see other reporters when he has a good story in the paper. It is his chance to be admired. I wanted to be admired, but I had a more serious mission. For some time I had been feeling sorry for myself, wrestling with old worries and sinking into gloom while I did. The night before, though, I had been uplifted. I wanted to thank Abe for opening the hole on page one, and tell him I thought myself fortunate to work for the *Times*. When I saw him in the newsroom and started to speak, however, emotion, fatigue, and the debilitating effects of a hangover undid me. To my horror, I started to cry. I almost choked when I tried to stop, and then I saw Abe was teary, too. He understood what I had wanted to say. By reputation he was one of the toughest men in American journalism, but he was standing there almost bawling. We quickly drew away from each other, of course. It would not do to be seen that way in the newsroom, and we were never to speak about it, not even when the *Times* nominated me for a Pulitzer.

ABE WAS AN OUTSIDER in an insider's world. He was too independent to be comfortable in a crowd, and he lacked the temperament to be a guru. James Reston functioned differently. In the fifties and sixties he became spiritual leader to a generation of reporters, and even now, I suppose, he still is, emeritus. I saw a documentary about him on public television recently. "Scotty had an entire nation paying attention to his words," Diane Sawyer, the program host, said admiringly. Then Reston read some of those old words from his column. They made it clear he was comfortable in areas usually visited by preachers and poets. Reston thought of journalism as a moral force that enlightened the public and fostered good government. Central to this was the idea that the journalist was franchised to tell people what was good

for them. Central, too, was the idea that if the polity did not
listen, it got itself into trouble. As Reston said in the documentary, "Television has shaken my faith in democracy."
He seemed to think the wrong people were running the
country.

Reston's career had mirrored the changes in the country's
ruling classes, and showed the passage of power. For
decades he was esteemed by newspaper people who had
never been in sight of West 43d Street in Manhattan or the
Times bureau on K Street in Washington. He elevated the
trade, and he was often described, as *Time* did when it put
him on its cover, as the conscience of the press. There was
no doubt he was concerned about the press, and while being
an official "conscience" might have burdened a lesser man,
he carried the title lightly. The reporters who worked for
Reston in the Washington bureau respected and liked him as
a man without pretense, and even the bureau clerks called
him Scotty. If he had enemies in the business, they kept their
mouths shut, and although Turner Catledge, managing editor of the *Times* in the era I am speaking of, would complain
to his New York subordinates that the Washington bureau
ignored too many stories, he knew he could not do much
about it. James Reston, bureau chief and Washington columnist, was too prestigious.

In the summer of 1963, I met him, when I was lent to the
Washington bureau by the national news desk in New York.
I felt honored by the posting, and intimidated as well. I had
never been in Washington, and most of what I knew about it,
or thought I knew about it, had come from Allen Drury's
1959 novel *Advise and Consent.* Whatever that book implied
about politics left no impression, but it did convince me that
Washington was important and glamorous, and so were the
people who worked there, and that I had best make an effort
to fit in. I bought a cotton seersucker suit at Brooks Brothers
to look more presentable. I also tried to memorize the titles

of congressional bills, thinking that all Washington journalists knew them. The seersucker suit turned out to be useful, but in the months I was in the capital I never heard anyone refer to a bill by title, so that part was wasted.

Nonetheless, I fit easily into the bureau, and thought the city a wondrous place. My first morning there, as I walked to the bureau from the hotel where my wife and I were staying, a cab stopped in front of me at a red light. The passenger in the back wore a Panama hat with the brim turned down all around, and he smoked a cigarette in a holder tipped jauntily upward. My God, I thought, it's FDR. In fact, it was Felix Belair, a longtime Washington reporter whom I would meet minutes later in the bureau. Still, Washington was such that you did expect to meet FDR. Shortly after I arrived, Tom Wicker, who was covering President Kennedy, and who would be with him in Dallas only a few months later, generously offered to show me the White House. He took me to the press room, and down a hallway to the Oval Office. John Kennedy was scheduled to be somewhere else. I looked at the rocking chair, presidential seal, and American flag, and was happily overcome. In the midst of my reverie, Wicker urgently yanked me. Kennedy had stepped through the French doors opening from the garden and was now in the room, where Wicker and I, of course, were not supposed to be. For a moment the president and I looked at each other. I was thrilled, and he, I suppose, mildly baffled; then Tom pulled me out of the room and into the hallway, and my encounter with a president was over.

I found it easy to think of Washington as the center of the universe. The city was full of important men who did important things in a civilized way, and whole chapters of American history lay all around me. Unhesitatingly I adopted the attitude *Times* editors in New York deplored. For years they had complained that the Washington bureau under Reston, and before him Arthur Krock, had been run as a separate duchy, oblivious to the rest of the world and the exigencies of a daily newspaper. The editors also thought the bureau missed too many good stories. They were not exactly sure what good stories the bureau missed, but to a man they were convinced there had to be more interesting things going on in Washington than found their way into the bureau's reporting. After no more than a week, however, I was on the side of the bureau. The office was pleasant, and morale was high, and people seemed pleased with what they were doing. The newsroom in New York was grungy, and morale was low, and everyone bitched all the time. The social life was different, too. When I got off work late at night in New York, I went across the street to Gough's bar, and drank with other deskmen, reporters, printers, and inky pressmen in homemade white paper hats. Everyone tried to sit as far away as possible from the men's room. When its door swung open, the smell of urine knocked you off your bar stool. (If there was a ladies' room I never saw it. For that matter, I don't think I ever saw a lady in Gough's.) In Washington, reporters invited you and your wife to their homes for dinner. You arrived at eight and left at eleven, and always met interesting people. You also attended embassy parties. Third world embassies were particularly keen on attracting *Times*men, but invitations from the French and British were most prized.

In almost no time at all, I felt as if I belonged in Washington. I did not meet James Reston right away—he was off somewhere on vacation—but I did meet Arthur Krock, his predecessor as bureau chief. Mr. Krock—even Scotty Reston called him "Mister"—was a monument, and as such was so regarded. He was imposing and commanded pro forma respect, but he harked to a more rococo time, and many thought he was irrelevant, and perhaps just a little embarrassing. Mr. Krock had arrived as a reporter in Washington in 1910, and gone on to hector presidents, win two Pulitzer Prizes (and turn down a third, for an interview with

Harry Truman), and write a Washington column. In 1963, he was still writing the column, densely argued and polemical, and stuffed with long sentences that always threatened to spin out of control and fly off into disparate pieces. His critics at the *Times* wished he would go away, but did not know how to get him to do so. Mr. Krock regarded them with disdain, aware he had walked with giants while even the oldest among them was still wearing knickers.

He rarely visited the bureau, instead filing his column from home, and he had not set foot in the *Times* building in New York in years. He did drop in at the Washington bureau, though, one day when I was there. Reporters greeted him respectfully, but with some apprehension. I thought of Don Giovanni saying hello to the Commendatore. When Mr. Krock saw me, a stranger, he courteously introduced himself and we talked. For some reason, I told him my wife and I had a bad-tempered Manx cat named Wolfgang who terrorized all our visitors. I saw Mr. Krock only once more. He stopped in at the bureau to pick up his mail, and when he passed my desk he said, "How's Wolfgang?" Some time later, when I was back in New York, I wrote and asked if he would recommend me for a Nieman Fellowship at Harvard. I wondered whether he would remember who I was. Shortly afterward, however, I received not just a copy of his glowing recommendation, but the recommendation itself. If I liked it, Mr. Krock said in an accompanying note, I should send it on to Harvard; if I did not like it, he would be happy to write a new one. At the bottom of the note he had written, "Regards to Wolfgang."

My job in the bureau was primarily to act as an intermediary between New York editors and Washington reporters. I also edited copy and, as my self-confidence grew, suggested stories that might be covered. Eventually I learned the bureau practiced its own style of journalism. I was unsure whether it was better or worse than what I had known, but it did take some getting used to. Nothing happened in Washington on Saturdays or Sundays, and so on weekends I was entrusted with running the news desk alone. Most probably New York would bother me for no more than the middle initial of a foreign ambassador, or a short insert on a piece already written. On one particular weekend, however, the Canadians did something important about tariffs. Just what they did I no longer recall, but whatever it was, New York called and demanded a story. Why, yes, I said, and tried to reach Eileen Shanahan, who wrote about economics. Unfortunately, she was not at home. Then I turned to the two reporters stuck with weekend duty in the bureau. One specialized in foreign affairs and the other in domestic politics, and they were men of wide experience—although, as both made absolutely clear, the experience did not include Canadian tariffs. Neither reporter would write the story. I did then what I thought I should do: I called the Canadian embassy and other places, and asked questions, beginning with, What the hell is a tariff? Then I wrote the story. It appeared on page one the next day, and though it carried no byline I was well pleased. Nonetheless, I said nothing about it when I saw my colleagues after the weekend. Reporters were supposed to write about anyone or anything, and then forget all about it. They knew that the day after their stories ran, the newspapers in which they appeared would line the bottom of bird cages. Reporters were supposed to keep things in perspective.

I still had not seen Reston, although certainly I felt his presence. Reporters mentioned him often, always warmly, and frequently with the obeisance that dutiful sons render their fathers. With the exception of a few old-timers, Reston had handpicked everyone in the bureau. He was renowned for spotting young talent and bringing it along; ''Scotty's boys'' were all marked for prominent places at the *Times* or elsewhere in journalism. Most seemed to have come from towns and small cities in the Midwest and South, and then gone on to one of the better colleges or universities. Harvard, I think, predominated. One of the jokes in New York was that Scotty's boys all looked alike, and while that was not quite correct, they did share a style, clearly modeled on Reston's. I did not know three people in New York who smoked pipes, but in the Washington bureau every other male reporter had a meerschaum on his desk or in his breast pocket. Reston, of course, was a pipe smoker. He also wore bow ties and rep ties, shirts with button-down collars, seersucker suits in the summer, and tweed suits with vests in the winter. Your first impression of the bureau was that everyone shopped at J. Press. Reston talked slowly and deliberately, never giving away too much or too little, while appearing to weigh every word, and clearly leaving the impression he could swim in far deeper waters than you. That was also much imitated in the bureau. Scotty's boys were affable, intelligent, and self-confident; they were industrious, productive, and ambitious, and like Reston, serious about their profession. They were also political liberals—not dangerously so, but modestly certain where virtue lay, and eager to assist in its propagation. In time, many would grow critical of Reston—finding him insufficiently hostile to the Vietnam war, or too eager to cooperate with official Washington—but they would do so with regret. He had, after all, been their mentor.

A week or so after the Canadians fiddled with the tariffs, I was back on the desk, expecting a quiet weekend. On Saturday afternoon, however, the AP wire announced that Philip Graham, publisher of *The Washington Post,* was dead, apparently a suicide. I called New York and said the bureau would file a story, and then asked one of the veteran reporters on hand to check it out. He said nothing, but looked uncomfortable, and after a while said he didn't know; it didn't seem the kind of story we should do. Besides, he declared, he did not know whom to call. He could hardly disturb the

Graham family, and no one else would have the information. The cops, I told him, you call the cops, and they will give you what they can. The reporter looked even more uncomfortable, and said he had never called them before. (I discovered later that no one in the bureau had ever called the cops. I doubt anyone even knew the name of the police chief or the location of police headquarters.) I persisted, and the reporter said he would try. Minutes later he came back, looking plaintive. He really could not do the story unless he called Scotty first; Reston and Phil Graham had been good friends, and indeed, Reston was close to the whole family. Donald, Phil's son, had been one of Reston's clerks at the *Times*. At first I thought the reporter simply wanted to make a courtesy call to Reston, who was still away on vacation, to tell him the sad news, but then I realized it was not that at all. The reporter wanted Reston's permission to say in the *Times* that Phil Graham was apparently a suicide. Go ahead and call, I said, but if you are still reluctant to use the word "suicide," I will write it into the story for you.

And it was then I realized I had reservations about James Reston. He represented a kind of journalism I thought unhealthy. It was elevated, sober, and virtuous, but it had a specious core. A journalist could write about great issues, but an uncomfortable fact could undo him. The reporter who thought he needed permission to report on a suicide was being unfaithful to his trade in a way that rummy old sportswriters who accepted free bottles of liquor were not. It was one thing to enjoy petty graft, but another to suppress hard facts. It was the difference between venial and mortal sin, and while both were part of the human condition, the second could lead to perdition. I was learning a new lesson about journalism, even if I did not yet know its full meaning. Faintly, though, a message did come though: Beware the people who moralize about great issues; moralizing is easier than facing hard facts.

I was sitting at the news desk when Reston appeared in

the bureau on Monday. I saw him when he arrived. He passed up the aisle from the back to the front of the bureau, and as reporters became aware of his presence they rose from their desks. They were glad to see him, and he was glad to see them, and there was bonhomie all around—until he got to me. He slowed down a moment and nodded, and I nodded back. Then the man whom even the clerks called Scotty marched silently past me into his office. I wondered whether the reporter who had called him had said this new guy on loan from New York did not understand how things were done; I had told the reporter a suicide was a suicide no matter what James Reston said. I can only speculate about the phone conversation, of course, but I do know that after his return to the bureau, Reston never acknowledged my presence unless he had to, even though I sat just in front of his office, where it was hard to be overlooked. To retaliate, when we did speak, I called him Mr. Reston, not Scotty. To hell with him, I thought, I'll keep my distance, too.

I was indulging in personal pique against one of my elders and betters, but there was more to it than that. Reston publicly pondered the role of the press, and wrote thoughtful essays about its failure to explore great issues. He also mourned America's failure to use the talents of her wisest and best people. But it seemed to me that when he thought of the wisest and best people he thought of people who shared venues with him. Outsiders need not apply; they would never understand the high purpose toward which the insiders worked. Insiders were big-picture men, eyes fixed on large matters, but feet planted firm on the ground. Actually, I was learning how the establishment worked. When Richard Rovere described the establishment, in a famous essay of the late 1950s, he said its titular head was the sometime government official John J. McCloy, and its bank Chase Manhattan, and its house organ *The New York Times*. Rovere was being facetious, but not very, and if the *Times* was house organ, then Reston was principal scribe. He addressed himself to the men who ran things. Other prominent Washington columnists did that as well, but few showed the same empathy as Reston. Indeed, Mr. Krock had been renowned for fighting with presidents, and the great Walter Lippmann had often condemned warm ties between journalists and the people they wrote about as the biggest threat to honest reporting. Lippmann called this "cronyism."

SEVERAL YEARS after my tour in Washington, I was involved in a minor piece of American history: Jacqueline Kennedy's efforts to prevent the publication of *The Death of a President,* William Manchester's book about the assassination of John Kennedy. I had broken the story about Mrs. Kennedy's suing Manchester, his publisher, Harper & Row, and Cowles Communications, which wanted to excerpt the book in *Look* magazine. Other reporters then descended on the story in what media critics now call a feeding frenzy. Rumors lay thick on the ground: Manchester, driven into a nervous breakdown, had fled to a Swiss sanatorium; a *Look* editor had cracked up, too; the book said a Cabinet member once thought Lyndon Johnson had ordered Kennedy's assassination; it said Mrs. Kennedy had sexual problems; it described the Kennedys as boors; it described Lyndon Johnson as a boor; it would finish off Robert Kennedy as a presidential contender; the Kennedy family had offered Harper & Row $3 million not to publish the book; Mrs. Kennedy had offered *Look* $1 million to kill the excerpts. Another rumor said that the family patriarch, Joseph P. Kennedy, was working out some dark design of his own. No one knew what was going on.

The Death of a President was supposed to be the authorized work about the assassination. Jacqueline Kennedy had told Manchester she would cooperate with no other author.

Robert Kennedy, her brother-in-law, had drawn up a memo of understanding about the project, and he and Manchester had signed it. Manchester had worked diligently and finished the book, but now Mrs. Kennedy wanted to take everything back. In a decade that can countenance Oliver Stone and his vaporings, this may not seem all that contentious, but in the sixties it was very big stuff. Day after day I was on page one, tracking the story in its political, social, and literary developments, and happily beating the opposition while I did.

Eventually I began to go dry. The story became harder to do. Sources grew increasingly wary. Kennedy spokesmen, advisers, and confidants had been all over me at first. They were forever phoning to ask how things were going, and what could they do to help. The most persistent caller, Richard Goodwin, who had written speeches for John Kennedy, would wake me in my apartment on West End Avenue. Other Kennedy people would check in during the day. Things went on in this way for a week or so, but then the calls stopped. The Kennedy people had become unhappy with my stories. They also had become unhappy with me. You were either with the Kennedys or against them, and they recognized no middle ground. I had been found wanting when I turned down an interview with Jacqueline Kennedy and Robert Kennedy. A Kennedy aide called to say that Mrs. Kennedy and the senator would like to meet with me privately and explain what was going on; they would not do this for attribution, however, and certainly I could not quote them. No, I said politely and piously, I will speak to them only if they talk on the record. The story was too important to be covered in any other way. In the background, or perhaps on an extension, I heard a muffled "Oh, for Chrissake." It sounded like Bobby Kennedy.

The spokesmen and advisers stopped phoning after that. They also grew lax about returning my calls. They had decided, understandably, to freeze me out. One day I could not reach a single Kennedy person by phone, not even Dick Goodwin. I was scheduled for page one, although as yet I had nothing to write—one or two cloudy ideas and a few stray facts, but not enough for a story. Late that afternoon, however, my phone rang. It was James Reston, whom I had not spoken to or seen since I worked on the desk at the Washington bureau. He wanted to know what was new in the Kennedy–Manchester dispute, and what I would say in the next day's paper. Possessed then by a whim I cannot fully explain even now, I said I was going to write about the increasing friction between Jacqueline Kennedy and Robert Kennedy. A reliable Kennedy source had told me, I said, that the senator thought Jackie was screwing up his career. Uh-huh, Reston said, and thanked me. A short while later, my phone rang again. It was Goodwin, who ingenuously said he had just heard I had been trying to reach him. What could he do to help? Not much, I said. I told him I already had my story: How Bobby Kennedy was annoyed with Jackie. I left out the part about the reliable source, of course. I was pretty sure Goodwin would know I did not have one.

But when I had hung up on Reston and begun to think about it, I realized that Bobby Kennedy probably was annoyed with Jackie. He had his eye on the White House, and she was attracting unwanted attention. Camelot was being tarnished. Already there had been stories about the collapse of the Kennedy myth. Annoyed? Bobby Kennedy had to be pissed. I decided to write about that, and flesh it out with odds, ends, and informed speculation. Indeed, when Goodwin called I had begun to write. He firmly denied the existence of a Kennedy rift—he had to do so as a family spokesman—but that was fine, too. I put the firm denial high up in the story, as any responsible reporter would do. Then I went home and worried about what I would write the next day. The story, I thought, was getting me down. A few days later, I saw Reston's column in the Sunday paper. He had been writing it when he called me. The lead had something about Kennedy blood being thicker than water, and that Bobby would support Jackie, no matter what anyone said. You sly bastard, I thought; you found out what I was going to say in a news story and then you modified it in your column. Reston would never accept free bottles of liquor, but he did comfort famous men.

STRICTLY SPEAKING, THOUGH, Robert Kennedy was not a member of the establishment; none of the Kennedys was. As Irish Catholic Democrats from Boston, they simply did not fit. Joseph Kennedy resented that, although I do not think his sons John or Robert ever cared much. Even when Richard Rovere wrote about the coterie of rich New Yorkers who made up its board of directors, the establishment—or more accurate, the Eastern establishment—was fading. It lost the presidential election in 1960 when it backed Richard Nixon, and four years later, when the Republicans nominated Barry Goldwater for the presidency, it lost control of the Republican Party. Meanwhile, the counterculture was beginning the long march that would end in the transformation of so many institutions. Reston lent himself to the change, even if he did not mean to. Almost ten years after Rovere wrote about the establishment, Reston published *The Artillery of the Press,* based on a series of lectures he had given to the Council on Foreign Relations, itself a bastion of the establishment. In the book he advocated a new freemasonry of public servants, drawn from the "triangle" of universities and foundations, government, and the media. They would, of course, be the best and wisest people around, and they would join in common cause to handle great issues. This was a perfectly terrible idea, although much applauded back then, and *Time* put Reston on its cover. Implicit in the concept of the triangle was the requirement that its members all think alike. If they did not, the freemasonry would fall into factions, and the triangle would no longer exist. There had to be shared purpose, common goals, and mutual understanding. As a practical matter, outsiders would not be welcomed any more than they had been in the old establishment.

The triangle was the new elite, franchising academics, intellectuals, and peripatetic members of the media. The establishment had seldom looked beyond Washington and Wall Street, and Marxists had to be conceded a point when they said it was rooted in money. The new elite, however, would operate from a loftier plateau. Its currency was ideas, not money, and in no time it would spend freely, driving out what it thought was false coinage. Eventually, this would promote what is now called politically correct thinking. By the 1970s, only those on the left and right fringes of American politics still believed in the establishment. In fact, all that really remained was the one family that had always been at its heart, and around whom other members of the establishment had clustered. The Rockefellers still flourished and made themselves felt. Their relationship with the *Times,* though, was changing.

There had always been a feeling in the newsroom that critical stories about the Rockefellers and their interests might not be welcome. Older reporters felt that especially. One of them told me Turner Catledge had once called him into his office and halfheartedly reprimanded him after he had written a story that embarrassed Nelson Rockefeller. Catledge did not care himself; but he had heard from Reston, who had been staying at the Rockefeller estate in Pocantico Hills, New York, when the story appeared. The story was not factually incorrect, but Reston had been annoyed, and he might mention his annoyance to the publisher. The establishment was liberal Republican, internationalist, and pro-business. The *Times* was those things, too. Neither survived the sixties with all the old postures intact, although the affinity for the Rockefellers persisted. In 1968 the *Times* editorial page broke a tradition when it endorsed Nelson Rockefeller for the Republican presidential nomination over Richard Nixon. In previous elections, the *Times* had stayed aloof from the nominating process and supported a candidate only in the general election. Bright reporters noticed. They would have enjoyed annoying Rockefellers, but it hardly seemed worth the trouble. Besides, the Rockefellers were famous for employing retainers to defend their interests. They had been doing it ever since old John D. Rockefeller had hired the public relations man Ivy Lee to burnish the family image. You always had to go through a retainer, so to speak, before you hit a member of the family.

I wrestled benignly with one myself. When David Rockefeller got behind the plan to build Battery Park City in Lower Manhattan, he spoke to Punch Sulzberger. Then Punch spoke to Abe, and Abe spoke to Arthur, who summoned his most experienced reporters. Arthur candidly told us Punch was excited. Battery Park City would rejuvenate Lower Manhattan. The reporters were skeptical; some of them hooted and hollered. Projects to rejuvenate Lower Manhattan sprang up regularly and just as regularly faded. Nonetheless, Arthur said, this one was really big, and gave us our assignments. Mine was a take-out on how the project was being assembled.

I called David Rockefeller, and was put on to one of his aides, who told me to meet him the next day in Rockefeller Center. When I arrived I followed instructions: Take the public elevator to one floor, and then a private elevator to another; he would meet me in the office with glass doors. The doors had no name on them, and the room they opened into was nondescript. A middle-aged man who looked like a retired cop was sitting at a desk. When I introduced myself, he nodded. Then a secretary came out from behind a door I

had not seen, and led me down a corridor. Pictures hung
along the walls. I recognized a Dufy and a Picasso. The corridor led to a room done in Japanese style, sparely furnished,
with sliding panels. The secretary asked if I wanted tea or
coffee, then left me alone. David Rockefeller's man slid
open a panel moments later. He looked like a squash player.
"What can I tell you?" he said briskly. "Where the hell am
I?" I answered. I was in the family's private office, of
course, the inner sanctum for serious business. The squash
player and I talked for almost three hours, and when it was
over I was exhausted. I had thrust and he had parried, and he
knew a lot more about Manhattan real estate than I did. After
three hours, he was not even winded. As a reward, then, he
took me on a tour of family headquarters. Each Rockefeller
had his own file of offices on a separate corridor, the walls
all hung with art. The corridors radiated from a central conference room, which was dominated by a table with chairs
for all the Rockefeller brothers and sisters. I sat down in Nelson Rockefeller's chair and realized how adroitly I was
being handled. An interview at Chase Manhattan would
have been impersonal, but a visit to family headquarters was
like being asked to join the team. Not bad, I thought, and
admired the squash player's perspicacity. Years later I heard
that Ronald Reagan had named him as an ambassador. The
family was represented in the White House then by Michael
Deaver, and so I suppose he and David Rockefeller arranged
the appointment.

Even without trying, the family could make itself felt. I
was interested when it was disclosed that Nelson Rockefeller had given money to important people, supposedly in
interest-free loans. One recipient was Henry Kissinger. The
news stories about this had been straightforward, correctly
so, and never suggested that anyone was being bought.
Subsequently I decided to write about the loans in my
"About New York" column. The best way to do this, I

knew, would be to keep the tone light and breezy, and so I
chose my words carefully and tried to amuse. Then I handed
the column to Arthur Gelb. Ordinarily, I did that on deadline, but this time I chose early afternoon. I did not want to
take advantage of Arthur. He would have no problem with a
news story about Nelson Rockefeller, no matter how damaging, but it would be hard for him to admit that a skeptical
column might not be appropriate. I wanted to give him time
to find a better excuse than that and, if he so chose, to tell me
to write a new column. It worked out exactly that way: Arthur told me we had published too many stories about Rockefeller that week, and one more would be superfluous.
Meanwhile, I should write a new column. When I mentioned
the Rockefeller column again several days later, Arthur said
the timing still wasn't right. A week later, it still wasn't
right. By then we both felt embarrassed. I loved Arthur, but I
did not want to kill the column myself. He was at a loss, too.
When Happy Rockefeller, Nelson's wife, had a miscarriage,
we both finally found an out. ''That family's had so much
trouble—we don't want to seem to be going after them,''
Arthur said seriously. I agreed, and I never mentioned the
column again.

As it happened, I encountered Nelson Rockefeller a year
or so later. At the time I was unattached, and available as an
''extra man.'' Extra men, especially those not noticeably ill-
mannered or alcoholic, were always in demand on the Upper
East Side. An extra man who played his cards right could eat
out three or four times a week if he chose, and while that
would have been dreary, an occasional night out was not
bad, particularly if the food was good and the woman you sat
next to attractive. When I was invited to be the extra man at a
dinner party where the Rockefellers would also be guests, I
accepted; only twelve or fourteen people would be there, and
I would sit next to Clare Boothe Luce. I had never met Mrs.
Luce, but certainly knew who she was: playwright, wit,

glamorous conservative icon, former congresswoman, former ambassador, and widow of Henry Luce. I thought I would hear a bon mot. Unfortunately, though, I did not. Either Mrs. Luce had an off night, or she was disappointed I was not William Buckley.

Toward the end of the dinner, Nelson Rockefeller, slightly boozy, stood up to offer a toast. He wanted to honor another guest, a newspaper publisher from South America, whom he had first met in 1940. Those were the days, Rockefeller said; the world was run very differently. Sensible men in one country could call sensible men in another, and settle important matters between them. There was no need for tribunes, commissions, or intermediaries; lone individuals could do things themselves. "Hear! Hear!" Mrs. Luce said, and held aloft her wineglass. The other guests were rapt. Rockefeller went on to recall his time at the State Department. He had been barely past thirty, but he coordinated Latin American affairs. It was his first excursion into public life, and he had learned he could make himself felt. Once again he said all he had to do was pick up the phone, and a "counterpart" would answer. Rockefeller was getting almost weepy, and when he finally lifted his glass to the newspaper publisher, it seemed he might break out in tears. As for me, I had a creepy feeling. I have never believed in conspiracy theories, but I thought he had just explained how we made such a mess of Vietnam.

CHAPTER NINE

ABOUT MEN AND WOMEN

The first time I was in family court with my daughters I saw a man with a paring knife in his back. The handle was sticking out from beneath his shoulder, and although there did not seem to be much blood, the man had dropped to one knee, with his palms on the floor and an expression on his face that said, Why me? His wife, who had stabbed him, was yelling in Spanish, but then she stopped and, for a moment, or until someone grabbed her, looked just as surprised as he. I do not know what happened to either of them or why, exactly, she stabbed him, but I suppose it was the usual thing—love requited and unrequited and some fooling around on the side, along with alcohol, emotional problems, and fierce fighting over money and children. One way or another, all those dreary circumstances were intruding also on me. I was in family court that day because I was being sued for child support. The inconsistency was that my daughters lived with me and I already was supporting them, while I faithfully paid alimony to their mother. My being sued for child support was absurd, but it is no good now saying I was a victim, or that my ex-wife was just out to get me. Life is more complicated than that, and perhaps the wife was correct when she stuck the knife in her husband's back. My ex-wife worked her way through three lawyers, one of them from a feminist collective, and all of whom sent me bills, and while my ex-wife and I eventually became friends, I still dislike the lawyers.

I tell you this because I cannot separate my views about life from the life I actually have lived, and so I think you should know about me. I have lived through the time that things changed between men and women. People do not form their ideas independently of how they have lived, or where they have been, or whom they are still mad at. Hardly anyone ever admits this, and those who write or speak most firmly about politics or social ills never admit it at all. They pretend detachment and rational analysis, while they are only paying back old scores. They are sore at their parents or at the hand life has dealt them, and they work out their feelings on other issues. They thrive especially in New York. The city was, and is, the blah-blah capital of the world, and while the country pays less attention than it once did, the chattering classes still flourish. In the sixties they began to rewrite the rules that governed the war between men and women.

Civilized society had always recognized a battle of the sexes. Men and women might wound one another, but they knew they had shared needs. Aristophanes understood that when he wrote *Lysistrata.* In the new world I moved into, however, Gloria Steinem could say, "A woman needs a man like a fish needs a bicycle," and help found a national movement. I remember seeing Steinem up close at about that time: at a cocktail party in East Hampton, Long Island, where she glowed and glimmered among fellow writers. Someone told me she was more or less in love with a playwright, and while I do not know whether that was true, I did notice that when he arrived at the party, Steinem became agitated and breathy. The fish-and-bicycle simile fell apart.

Steinem was subject to the same disturbances as the rest of us. She ignored this when she wrote, though, and no good could come from that. Revolutionaries who neglect real-life experience are left with unworkable theory, and Steinem was advocating a more sweeping revolution that anything proposed by Karl Marx. If men and women no longer needed each other, there was no point in practicing restraint. On the ancient battleground where combat took place, there was now carnage in the war between the sexes.

I was, of course, caught up. I began the decade married and ended it alone, and while the intervening years were not all dismal, I hardly would want to repeat them. My wife and I separated in 1972. Her name was Irmie and we had been married twelve years, suffering all the usual problems as well as the ones that leave you altered. Two babies died. Irmie became sick. I began to drink. Perhaps we should have split up before we did, but we stayed together, so we thought, because of our two daughters. Meanwhile, Irmie, who was highly intelligent and very much a part of her time, began to attend consciousness-raising sessions with other West Side women. I met one of them once on the street. She looked at me with a basilisk stare and refused to speak when Irmie introduced us. What, I wondered, had my wife told her about me? What did these women say to each other? Acrimony was resounding in apartments up and down West End Avenue. One night Irmie returned from a meeting boiling over with rage, and in a voice that seemed to resonate out of a deep well said men were no good, and women were better off without them. She meant every word, and although the new feminism did not break up our marriage, it had the paradoxical effect of allowing us both to think of ourselves as victims. The night I finally left, we solemnly told our daughters my departure was all for the best. Colette, our older daughter, cried; Janet, her sister, looked bewildered.

I left with two suitcases and a typewriter, and moved in

with a friend of Willie Morris's, a kind woman who put me
up in the maid's room of her brownstone. On weekends she
went away, and then I would have Colette and Janet over to
stay. I fed them tiger's milk and orange juice, and took them
to Central Park, where I would see other men who held their
children's hands too tightly, and who also had a look on their
faces that said, Why me?

The Central Park fathers all seemed about forty. They
were too old to join the sociosexual revolution and too
young to be able to ignore it. They were caught in generational stasis. There were also the fathers with gold chains
around the neck and silk shirts unbuttoned to the navel. They
sauntered about with their children and young girlfriends as
if they were showing off trophies. The other fathers disliked
them on sight, partly on the grounds of good taste and partly,
of course, out of sheer envy. Most of the Central Park fathers
were men out of place. Their stuff was packed in boxes in
other people's basements, and they were never quite sure
where they lived. Some moved in with new girlfriends,
while others took furnished rentals and wondered what to do
with their laundry. They drank, watched television, and
poked at dead marriages. They worried about money, missed
their children, and muttered about the feminist writers their
ex-wives were now reading. None of those women seemed
to have children. None of them even seemed to be married.
What could they know about families, except that they
didn't want one? The Central Park fathers felt aggrieved and
misused. I was a Central Park father, too.

On the other hand, I had an out. I worked for *The New
York Times*. I could rise above whatever torpor or self-pity I
sank to, and prove to myself I existed. In fact, I could do
even better than that. In *The Kingdom and the Power,* his
book about the *Times,* Gay Talese described me in this way:
"John Corry was a clean-cut, outwardly bland but pleasant
man of average height and build, neat but not fastidious."

Gay also said that while I was seen by my editors as solid, reliable, and not likely to cause any trouble, I had a hidden longing: I wanted fame—''not great fame, just a touch, enough to lend a bit of flicker to his name, a few nods of recognition around New York, enough to justify the secret little outbursts of absurdity and wildness that he knew were within him, awaiting the slightest chance to erupt.'' When I first read that, in 1969, I did not like it very much, but now I think Gay had me just right: I did want fame, at least a touch, and the *Times* was where I could find it. There was something else I could find there: a sense of myself as a man, a confirmation of my own masculinity. The newsroom was a place for male bonding.

That may seem quaint, or perhaps despicable—depending how you look at these things in an age so determined to stamp out sexism. I know only that I took the masculinity of the newsroom for granted, and so did most of my peers. In the nineties, men dance around campfires and beat drums to get in touch with their lost maleness. They look remarkably silly, and it may be they are out around the campfires because they have nowhere else to go. For years I had the newsroom. The feeling there was that journalism was a man's game. There were great women reporters, but we all assumed they were more like us than like other women. Journalism demanded toughness, coolheadedness, and rationality—masculine not feminine virtues. This was simply understood, the same way it was understood you wore a shirt and tie, and did not allow your hair to curl over your collar. There was no precise moment when everything changed, but the first stirrings came early in the sixties, and in no time moved almost everywhere in the newsroom.

In the mid-sixties I was a rim man, or copy editor, on the national news desk, the last all-male desk at the *Times*. The desk was shaped like a splayed horseshoe. The rim men sat along its outer edge; the slotman, who ran it, sat on the inside, in the middle. The slotman at the time was John Stephenson, but everyone called him Steve, and it was at his insistence that the desk remained all male. Women worked on the city and foreign desks only a few feet away, but the national desk harked back to green eyeshades, cigars, and elastic sleeve bands. My colleagues, all older than I, were free to discuss their hemorrhoids, money problems, or prostates. The atmosphere was pleasantly cranky, and humor was conveyed in puns. I do not think I ever heard a dirty joke. Steve would have expressed disapproval. He was a squat man with a rumbling voice and a pouchy face, and he wore very thick glasses. A cartoonist would have drawn him as a benevolent, elderly bullfrog. As had so many old-time deskmen, he had lived much of his life in great books. On slow nights he rewrote our headlines into Latin for amusement.

What I remember most about Steve, though, was his kindness. One night I edited the lead story in the paper, and in nervous haste sent up to the composing room a headline with "Khrushchev" misspelled; I think I left out an *h.* The press run had started before the news editor, Lew Jordan, caught my mistake. He stopped the presses for a replate. When he appeared in the newsroom minutes later, he held up a page proof with my faulty headline. "Who did this?" he asked Steve. "It doesn't matter," Steve answered slowly. Jordan, a tall, dignified man who seldom smiled, let it go. Steve was too good a newspaperman to be argued with, and he carried a certain moral weight. But he was an anachronism, almost the last of his kind, and the *Times* could scarcely wait for him to leave. Betty Friedan had already published *The Feminine Mystique,* and discontent was rising. The national desk got its first woman copy editor the week after Steve retired.

That seemed to me sad. I thought the desk ought to have been preserved under glass, or kept on as a cultural artifact. The rim men had known that one day there would be a woman among them, and none complained when she appeared, but they plunged into mild bereavement. They had lost their singularity in the now integrated newsroom. I left the national desk about the same time as Steve, not because of the arrival of a woman, but because I had decided to do full-time reporting. For several years I had been moving back and forth between the desk and writing, unsure of where I wanted to stay, but proud I could be so mobile. I wanted to compete wherever I could, and while male bonding was one thing, competition was better, especially on a personal level. It was wonderfully stimulating, and always easy to find.

When I had first thought of applying for a Nieman Fellowship at Harvard, I had approached Anthony Lewis. I was new to the national desk then, but I knew that Lewis, a columnist who had won two Pulitzers, had been a Nieman Fellow. When he visited the newsroom I introduced myself. "Mr. Lewis," I said, and began to talk about wanting to go to Harvard. I did not get far; Lewis cut me off in mid-sentence. "But," he said, "you're only a deskman." Then he turned and walked away. It was the word "only" that did it. Lewis, you son of a bitch, I thought to myself; I will become a Nieman Fellow if only to spite you. I did not see him again until months later. It was in the parking lot of the stadium in Cambridge on the day of the Harvard–Yale football game. Lewis was there as a Harvard alumnus, and I was there, of course, as a Nieman Fellow. He looked at me uncertainly, and I passed by him without speaking.

That was childish, but no matter. It seemed to me I had to get even; getting even with other men what was men did. Freud said it had to do with our fathers. Popular psychologists claim that men work well in a corporate structure because they know about being on teams. Women, these psychologists suggest, are not accustomed to joint efforts. There may be something to that, although it ignores the male compulsion to butt heads and measure penises. The chance to compete was surely one reason I had gone into journalism, and chosen the *Times* above all other papers. Getting a good story and then writing it is not ordinarily an exercise in teamwork. It is mano a mano, and the *Times* was the world's best arena. This was a feeling easier to sustain when I first walked into the newsroom. Male reporters went into combat by day—figuratively speaking—and then returned at night to home, hearth, and family. Parameters were circumscribed. Everything was of a piece. Women, children, and work existed in some kind of balance. But the old balance disappeared at approximately the same time as did the old national news desk. The moral compass became uncertain. True north had been displaced. Men my age began picking their way through a changed landscape with all the surefootedness of stranded beach birds. The women's revolution was bewildering and the sexual revolution disconcerting, and the two revolutions had led to an irreconcilable clash. Women wanted new rights, but seemed to be giving up old privileges. Men no longer knew what they owed them. I think men are still trying to figure it all out.

Everything had once been much simpler. Men and women might not have been entirely happy with one another, but some discontent was a given, and responsibilities were defined. My father and uncles complained about their wives, but they handed over their paychecks, and considered themselves partners in lifetime contracts. Their marriages were not always blissful, and constant discord echoed through some, although divorce was unheard of and infidelity rare, perhaps nonexistent. Obviously, I cannot be sure of that last point, but I suspect that no matter how much anyone lusted, consummation seldom took place outside marriage. Sex outside marriage would have violated the lifetime contracts. My Uncle Willie once padded out of the house in bedroom slippers and disappeared for two days, but when he returned his wife forgave him, and it was understood that Willie had just lost track of time. That he might have been in someone else's bed was unthinkable. Marital battles were waged on other issues, and wives gave as good as they got, which meant that warfare was inconclusive. Uncle Jimmy once tried to beat up Aunt Jessie, but she hit him in the head with a lamp and he did not try it again. Indeed, Jimmy took to drink soon after and cowered whenever he saw Jessie. Aunt Mamie buried three husbands, and never doubted after each one died that she would have any trouble finding another. When she died herself, she was married to number four, a man with a stammer who adored her, and to whom she had lied about both her age and the three previous marriages. The women of my childhood were not helpless. They may have been denied access to the workplace, but they had their own prerogatives and they used them. They knew that they knew things their husbands did not, and that this knowledge was a useful weapon. The husbands knew this, too. No matter how they swaggered or preened, they were intimidated by women's superior knowledge.

This was generally recognized, even if seldom expressed. Men did not admit to being afraid of their wives. As a boy, however, I was told that women were smarter than men, and I think there is some truth there. Women have taught me most of the important things I know, and I have always found them somewhat mysterious. Most men of my generation found them mysterious, and in the mystery lay some sense of awe. My father and uncles capsulized this when they said they did not understand women. Sex was one way of exploring the mystery, and sex was approached with apprehension and usually some sense of guilt. Exactly what you were guilty of was unclear, although the feeling of doing something forbidden had its uses. There is something to be said for bridling sexual impulses. I clearly remember the first time I was unfaithful to my wife: in a car in the desert outside Tucson, where I had been covering a murder story

for the *Times*. I did not enjoy myself much, and when I returned to New York I was remorseful. I had betrayed not
only my wife but my sense of what it meant to be husband
and father. As I said, I remember this well, although I am no
longer sure where, or even with whom, I next was unfaithful.
It may have been with the Dutch au pair girl who was mind-
ing my neighbor's children on Fire Island, or perhaps with
the writer who had painted the walls of her Greenwich Village apartment all black, but wherever it was or whomever it
was with, I know it was not very graceful. Sweaty thrashing
and grunting are the stuff of low comedy; when practiced by
a man with a sense of his own naughtiness, they begin to
look like farce. Infidelity, once embarked on, may become
progressively easier; even so, I was not very good at it, and I
do not think many men of my generation were very good at
it, either.

The new world we entered was more permissive than the
one we had grown up in, yet we were still burdened with old
psychological freight. We were tantalized by the sexual revolution, but out of place at the barricades. When we tried to
ascend them, we fell in a heap, often dragging our partners
down with us. We wounded them while wounding ourselves, and pretended there was no problem. I think it made
us cranky. Our sensibilities were too close to the surface,
and when they erupted they came out skewed. Crisis struck
unexpectedly. For a while I wrote a column, ''About New
York,'' in which I was given editorial freedom. I once used
the freedom to write an arrogant piece about middle-aged
men who made fools of themselves with younger women. I
also pontificated smugly about the joys of sex, and how we
all ought to get some. Soon after the first edition was on the
street, my phone rang, and when I answered I heard an icy
voice. I could not tell at first whose it was.

''This is the managing editor,'' the voice said with no pre-
amble.

''Abe?'' I asked.

"What do you think you're doing?" the voice replied.

I stammered something or other, but then Abe cut me off. He said he did not want to speak further. I waited five minutes and then called him at home. "Abe?" I said hesitantly. "I just killed your column," he said, and immediately slammed down the phone. I had never had a story killed before. Besides, a survey of *Times* readers had found that my column was highly popular. The promotion department was even advertising it on the sides of city buses. Now, however, I faced public humiliation. When the final editions appeared, the world would know I had been disgraced.

I was being imaginative, of course. I doubt that even a single reader wrote the *Times* to complain about my absence from the paper. Still, a killed column could not be taken lightly, especially not by me, and in the newsroom the next day I was torn between mortification and anger. Fortunately, then, Arthur stepped in. He pulled me into Abe's office that evening and left me. I found myself looking at Abe, while he looked at me, and then I realized we both were embarrassed. "The hell with it," Abe said, and asked if I'd like a drink. I did, and neither of us said anything about the column. Indeed, we were never to speak of it all. He was too prudish to say what had wounded him, and I was too prudish to ask. In my maundering about sex in the column, he thought I had been writing about him. I suppose I had, but I had not done it intentionally. Abe's marriage was in trouble and he was seeing someone else, and like me, he had found an infinite number of ways to make a fool of himself. Men had always made fools of themselves over women, but the new age of sexual freedom allowed them more chances than before. They tried to explore them with aplomb, although they worried someone would notice. Therefore they pretended nothing was happening, but if something was, it was not what everyone thought. Abe was just being self-conscious. Stories in the *Times* were self-conscious about these things, too. I know because I wrote them; for a while, I had the sex beat.

That happened first in the 1960s, when sex was becoming too visible to ignore. Plays and books were using more explicit language, while hippies wore buttons that said "Go Naked," and the Supreme Court struck down the last state law banning contraceptives. The *Times* had to recognize the revolution and escape its fastidious past. Two decades earlier, the book review had declined to accept ads for Alfred Kinsey's *Sexual Behavior in the Human Male.* Kinsey, a respectable biologist, who once had spent years studying the gall wasp, wrote in dry, dusty paragraphs, but the topic was unacceptable, and the *Times* would not be a party to spreading such filth. The Kinsey Report became a best-seller, although the ensuing fame and opprobrium took a toll on its author. Before his death, in 1956, Dr. Kinsey became severely depressed. Sex was a difficult topic in American life, and the poor man ought to have stayed with the gall wasp.

Nonetheless, Dr. Kinsey did leave a legacy: Americans were freer now than they had been to talk about sex, and even if the level of dialogue was not necessarily higher, there was far more of it than before. Under those circumstances, America's greatest newspaper could not be left at the post. In 1966, Harrison Salisbury assigned me to write about the big study by Dr. William Masters and Virginia Johnson. Kinsey had tried to find out through questionnaires and interviews who was doing what to whom and how often. Masters and Johnson, however, had done field work. For eleven years, at a research clinic in St. Louis, they had watched men and women practice coitus and masturbation; in fact, they had observed, recorded, and analyzed some 15,000 orgasms. Now they were releasing their findings in a book, *Human Sexual Response.* Harrison Salisbury knew a big story when he saw one. He told me to write five columns, or 4,000 words, and said the *Times* would splash them over page one. The *Times,* after all, always covered new developments in science.

I thought myself fortunate. A five-column spread that began on page one was important. Moreover, Masters and Johnson, mindful of the derision heaped on Kinsey, said they would talk only to members of the prestige press and not to tabloid journalists. That put me at the top of the list. I plodded through galley proofs of their book, and then flew to Boston for the interview. Masters was a small, dour gynecologist and Johnson a big, handsome psychologist, and we met in a suite at the Ritz. They sat side by side on a sofa, and Masters did most of the talking. Johnson, meanwhile, smiled warmly. She would gaze first at Masters and then at me and then again at Masters, reminding us both, so to speak, that we were all joined in the interest of science. Masters said vaginal lubrication came from the vagina itself and not from the uterine cervix and Bartholin's glands, that a naturally occurring agent in the vagina could kill or immobilize sperm, that vaginal and clitoral orgasms were biologically the same, that there were no anatomic reasons why elderly people could not function sexually, that the size of a penis had nothing to do with performance, and so on. He also spoke of electrodes, electrocardiographs, electroencephalographs, and cunningly devised miniature cameras.

Everything was high-minded and antiseptic until Virginia Johnson shifted position on the sofa and crossed her legs. I found myself looking up her dress, and when I did I started to giggle. I excused myself then, and said I had to go to the bathroom. When I got there I locked the door and had a small fit of laughter. Kinsey, Masters and Johnson, five columns in the *Times,* and even Krafft-Ebing had just fallen into place. They all offered us men an excuse to look up some woman's dress, while we pretended we were not, but if we were caught, they allowed us to feign lack of interest. Masters and Johnson had written a book about fucking after observing all the fucking up close and firsthand. The important thing, however, was not what they had seen, but that they had seen it. In the bathroom at the Ritz, I knew what I wanted to ask them but couldn't: Was it exciting, how did you feel, and did it make the two of you want to get it on together? Did the people in the laboratory enjoy being looked at, and would the rest of us enjoy being looked at, too? I could not ask questions like that, of course, although clearly they were of more interest than vaginal lubrication. Sexual behavior had to be approached obliquely, through surrogate questions. You had to pretend indifference.

The *Times* in its way was more honest. In the sixties it still had many strictures. The paper approached sex gingerly, and when I turned in my story on Masters and Johnson I initiated a crisis. I had written the piece with great delicacy and tact, but unquestionably it was still about fucking. When he first read it, Theodore Bernstein, the news editor, said it should be cut from 4,000 to 800 words, and that under no circumstances would it run on page one. Salisbury remonstrated with Bernstein, while other editors looked for an intermediate position, or else walked away. Sex was the last great battleground, but whether that led to news fit to print was an unsettled question. Editors struggled with their souls and psyches, and of all the disputes I ever had at the *Times,* this was the strangest and most protracted.

I no longer remember how many times I had to rewrite my story, or what anyone's specific objections were. The story was passed from editor to editor, each of whom wanted some particular item deleted or altered, but few of whom spoke to me. Their subordinates relayed questions. Did the book contain offensive material? God forbid the *Times* should be promoting a dirty book. I added a new sentence to my story: "Dr. Masters and Mrs. Johnson have taken pains to purge the book of anything that might be considered salacious." Were they treating sex as nothing more than a bodily function? I inserted another sentence: "Neither Dr. Masters nor Mrs. Johnson believes, and the book does not suggest, that sex is merely a physical response.'' The story shrank, expanded, and then shrank again. I revised whole sections and handed them in, only to be told they would now be killed. I seethed, became angry, and had the first of several tantrums. The narrow-minded old men who ran the *Times* were opposed to truth, justice, and beauty. Obviously, they had problems with sex. That they might have had legitimate concerns never occurred to me; that they were fighting a losing battle never occurred to me, either. Modernity was on my side, and we were entering the new age of permissiveness.

My story kept being passed around, and editors continued to ask for more changes. At some point, Claude Sitton, the national news editor, told me the *Times* wanted me to do a big take-out on sex. I was to find out ''what's new on the new frontier,'' and update old Alfred Kinsey. Fine, I said, and began making calls around the country to set up appointments. The assignment was a big breakthrough. The Masters and Johnson story, which had not yet appeared in the paper, had been more or less forced on the *Times* because the two researchers were about to publish a book. My new assignment, however, meant the *Times* would now look at sex on its own. That's progress, I thought, and felt mollified, although I was still being asked to make changes in the Masters and Johnson piece. The story was scheduled to appear on a Monday, and as the day drew nearer, my resistance to making changes grew. The Friday before that Monday I became downright sullen. I thought the story finally had been put to bed, but in the morning I was asked to revise it. I did, and was told that was it; there would be no more requests for changes. The next day I went to the newsroom to check the proofs; by now I trusted no one and wanted to be certain there was not even the smallest alteration in anything I had written. There was not, and I felt a guarded relief. Surely, this was now the end of it. But before I left the office, I thought to leave word with the national news desk: If anyone touched my story in any way, or even looked as if he were about to do so, I was to be called at home immediately. I was going to see this through to the end.

The next morning, of course, my phone rang. It was Sunday, and the senior editors were off, but the assistant news editor in charge of the paper had taken one last look at my story and decided he still couldn't stand it. He had dispatched a copyboy to Ted Bernstein's home with the galley proofs, and Ted had taken his one last look and decided he still couldn't stand it, either. He told the national desk to tell me to make more changes. The national desk then called me.

The hell with it, I said, and refused to change a word. Moreover, I was supposed to fly to Kansas City that afternoon to attend a conference on sex education, and I said I would not do that, either. Then I slammed down the phone. A few minutes later, Claude Sitton called, and I let him have it, too. There is no rage like the self-righteous rage of a young reporter who thinks the integrity of his story is being sullied, and I am surprised now I was not fired. Sitton just told me to stay where I was and not do anything rash. He said he would call back later, and after an hour or so he did. He had talked to Ted Bernstein, and they both had talked to Clifton Daniel, the managing editor. Daniel, in turn, had talked to Turner Catledge, the executive editor.

A decision had been reached, and I am telling you now what it was, not because I want to make those editors look foolish, but because you should know how seriously these matters were taken once. It had been decided that my story could remain as it was except for one word. That was "penis." "Vagina" was acceptable, but "penis" had to be replaced by "male sex organ." I told Sitton I could live with that, and flew off to Kansas City.

CHAPTER TEN

A DIFFERENT WORLD

I never had enough money, not nearly, and sometimes I really had none. When I returned to the *Times* from *Harper's,* I was paid $500 a week, and while that was quite good by newsroom standards, it fell far short for me. I had always been more or less broke, but when I became a divorced man with two children I spiraled right down to indigence. The years were full of doctors, lawyers, and tuition bills, and I would skip paying rent, phone, and electricity while I kept up with what seemed more important. I went without haircuts and dentists, say, or dry cleaning, and never owned more than one suit, and when the spavined armchair in my living room finally ruptured, I made do with the wreckage rather than get a replacement. Penury is wearisome and I grew awfully tired, but unquestionably it was easier for me to bear than for most. The fact was I still had the best of things. These were not always things of the spirit, but often of a baser kind. Penurious or not, I was a *Times*man. I was invited to opening nights at the theater, and became accustomed to seats on the aisle or eighth row center. I saw movies at private screenings, and never had to stand in a line to buy tickets. I was sought out and praised and deferred to, and was part of a privileged class. In a society unsure of itself, I had stature. New York is a city of indistinct structure. Everything about it is transient. A few old families may abide, but celebrities come and go, and fame has the permanence of hoarfrost. Respectability is prized and sometimes purchased dearly. The very rich pay for wings on museums or endow dance companies, although money alone will not buy distinction, which is why so many of the rich look unsated. They want to be thought of as serious, but they know they are not thought of that way, and they have an ongoing identity crisis. I was unlikely to suffer from that. Each story I wrote defined me. In a society where so many ache to be heard, a byline was better than money.

Nonetheless, I still had to pay bills. Psychic rewards did not cover alimony and school tuition. I decided to write a book, but had no topic in mind until a friend suggested the rich American Irish. I liked the idea and decided to center the book on a single family, and consequently met Jeanne Murray Vanderbilt. She was beautiful and fascinating and divorced from Alfred Gwynne Vanderbilt, and our meeting was blessed by its timing. My relationship with the woman in Washington was ending. Our three-year affair had been conducted with passionate intensity, but most of it had been at long distance. She had traveled with me once when I was on a story for *Harper's,* and we had been together one whole week, but otherwise there had been only daily telephone calls and furtive weekends. The secrecy at first had been exciting. We tempted fate by appearing in places where people we knew might see us. I did not have the means, or will, to take her away from her husband. She did not have the nerve, or need, to leave him. If our affair became known, though, it could force things. It was not grown-up thinking by either of us, but love affairs are not always conducted by grown-ups, and in any case our thinking was probably irrelevant.

A friend once invited me to spend a few days at her house
in the Hamptons. Coincidentally, my love and her husband
were staying nearby. While walking on a quiet road one evening at sunset I saw them, out strolling with Katharine Graham and some other Washington people. I began to turn
away, but my lover's poodle caught my scent, let out a yip,
and barked deliriously. The poodle ran ahead and threw herself against my legs. I bent down and patted her head, and
she ran around me in a circle. It was clear the dog and I were
old friends. Obviously, I had spent time with her owner.
Meanwhile, the other people kept walking. When they
reached me, I smiled an all-purpose smile, and everyone
more or less smiled back except my love's husband. He
looked at me sadly and turned his head. He was a man full of
woe and embarrassment. I realized then he knew all about
his wife and me but had no idea what to do, and so had
chosen hurt, dignified silence. In fact, he was a decent
man who feared the breakup of his marriage and thought
he had no other option. I felt no pity, however, and wished
only that he were out of the way. He was cheating me out
of a life that was rightfully mine and the woman with whom
I could share it.

Or so I believed, and certainly my passion was real. Unquestionably, too, the passion flowed so freely because the
woman in Washington was unattainable. She was married
and had a social position. The possibility that she might
leave this and settle down with me was minimal. Therefore I
could be as passionate as I chose. I had nothing to risk but
hurt feelings. It is liberating to plunge into an affair that can
never come to fruition. You do not acknowledge to yourself
it is doomed in advance, and you are free to suffer and bleed
and enjoy being semi-demented.

I remember being overcome by desire one morning when
I awoke. I went downstairs, took a cab to the airport, and
flew to Washington. When I got there I took another cab to a

street near my love's house. I did not know whether she was home or not, and when I called I got the answering service. I moped about uncertainly—it was cold and drizzly—but then I saw her coming down the street. We spent the afternoon with our arms around each other on the wet, empty pathways of Theodore Roosevelt Island. Our affair was soulful and satisfying, with an appropriate gleam of madness, although its dissolution was a matter of time. We were carrying on in bits and pieces, with too many vacant spaces between. Mutual devotion is fine, but an accessible partner is better, and the principal worth of a long-distance relationship is that it spares you the burden of real intimacy. My love was a woman of high intelligence, tart humor, and generous spirit, but even the most exciting qualities pall when you call late at night and a husband picks up and answers. What we had was wonderful, but it would never be enough, and in the usual confusion I began a tortuous withdrawal. I suppose it is possible to end a serious affair quickly and cleanly, although I have never known anyone who has, and in my irresolution I was no different. I casually told the woman in Washington I had met Jeanne, but pretended it was of no great importance. I said I wanted only to enlist her for help on my book about the rich American Irish. It may even be I believed that. Men and women have an infinite capacity to delude and lacerate themselves and each other even when well intended. I fumbled around in the usual way, and finally did the sensible thing. I told the woman in Washington it was all over between us. She cried a lot, and I did, too, but I felt a great relief. I was free now to see about Jeanne.

She had been born into a clan, the Murrays and McDonnells, many of whom were rich, and all of whom were Irish and Catholic. Her grandfather Thomas E. Murray, the family patriarch, was a prominent inventor who never doubted the one true faith. His eight children seldom did, either. The principal difference between the generations was that the patriarch had been born poor, while his sons and daughters knew early on they were part of a rising class obliged to be more respectable than Protestants. They either married well or did well themselves, and they passed into a social world that until their arrival had excluded Irish Catholics. I looked them up in the files. The society pages of the *Times* and the old *Herald Tribune* seldom recognized Catholics, and Irish Catholics not at all, but the Hearst papers were not so restrictive. The Murrays and McDonnells had found their first chronicler in the gossip columnist Maury Paul, who was William Randolph Hearst's first "Cholly Knickerbocker." He discovered them in the 1930s in Southampton, Long Island, where they summered on a compound of 160 acres, worshipped in a private chapel, and looked down on the Kennedys of Boston and Hyannis as parvenu and arriviste. Old Thomas E. Murray was gone by then—a bishop, fifteen monsignors, and seventy priests saw him out at a solemn requiem mass—but his legatees included forty-eight grandchildren, most of whom would grow up in great houses, convent schools, and the Southampton compound, and many of whom would make their own feudal marriages. They also would be caught between the exigencies of Irish Catholicism and the demands of a more secular world, and not all of them would survive it.

When I first called and asked to interview Jeanne, she had declined. Soon after, however, I met her on the street with a common friend. She had just read something I had written in the *Times* and liked it. If I called again, she said, we could set up a meeting. I waited several days before I did. I had a sense of closing in on something important, but did not want to look too eager. I was prudent. I was also dead broke, and still living in the maid's room of Willie Morris's friend's brownstone. I was drinking myself into a stupor each night and waking up with a hangover each morning. I was, I suppose, what a psychiatrist would call clinically depressed, or a lay-

person a little bit crazy. The odd thing was that I did not
think of myself as unhappy, and I assumed my life in its essentials was like that of most other people. The newsroom
reinforced my perception. Broken marriages and aberrant
life-styles were not uncommon, and my colleagues included
the mildly daft and a number of walking wounded. One
night I had a drink with a reporter who, when I left him, went
on a three-week bender, then checked into a hospital and did
not turn up in the newsroom again until months later. I am
not sure anyone noticed his absence. The newsroom was a
place for unannounced comings and goings, and personal
trauma was subsumed by daily stories.

Jeanne and I circled each other cautiously early on. She
feinted, I jabbed, and then we both backed off and danced.
The first time I visited her I had been smitten. There was the
obvious attraction of face and figure, and beyond that something keenly felt though dimly understood. She lived in a
penthouse on Park Avenue, and while that was obviously
more alluring than a maid's room in a brownstone, it was the
impress she made it on it that counted. Women build habitats
better than men do, and I look to women to build mine. Most
men do the same, although these days they are afraid to
admit it. As for me, I want to appropriate the places where
women live, and when I have fallen in love, I have fallen in
love not just with a woman but with the world she has built
around her. I mean this almost literally. Jeanne's habitat was
pretty, with style, comfort, and airy lightness. No man could
have created a place like that. A feminine persona was palpable, and I reacted. We no longer speak of a "woman's
touch," though I know one exists, as part of a woman's innate sensibility and not merely as social conditioning.

Jeanne and I continued to meet. My book was our excuse.
We went out to lunch. We sat in Central Park. One day she
walked with me to the *Times,* and I showed her the tin desks,
linoleum floor, and seedy disarray in the newsroom. She re-

sponded as I had hoped, with a deeper interest in me. The newsroom was not a bad place for a courtship. Its functionalism made you get down to essentials. When we left it we went upstairs and drank coffee in the cafeteria. I remember the printers from the composing room who sat at the next table staring. Jeanne talked to me about her family, the people she had known, and her marriage to Alfred Vanderbilt. I listened with the avidity of a reporter and the wonderment of someone who had grown up in a very different environment in Brooklyn. My amorous instincts were mixed up with an interest in social history and the guilty pleasure of social climbing. Names such as Rockefeller, Astor, and Vanderbilt once had a mythical ring. The people who bore them lived in marble halls or on the covers of *Life* magazine, and the social divide was much clearer. The rich may have been silly, shallow, or unpleasantly eccentric, although you were aware of that only when reminded by a scandal in the *Daily News* or *Mirror.* Of course the glamour attached to great names is no more. It faded in the social levelings of the sixties, and disappeared almost entirely when Americans began to surrender their privacy and fall in love with self-exposure. Watch almost any afternoon talk show on television: no one has any secrets, and everyone gets fifteen minutes of fame. The mysterious glamour of the unapproachable rich disappears when so many others demand attention. The solitary figures on the covers of *Life* have given way to the forgettable faces on the covers of *People,* and the supposed high style of a Vanderbilt or an Astor to the conspicuous gluttony of a Donald Trump or an Adnan Khashoggi.

I pressed Jeanne for details about her life, ostensibly because of my book, but really because I was fascinated. She and Alfred had lived in a Georgian mansion called Broadhollow on the North Shore of Long Island. It had ten master bedrooms, an uncounted number of fireplaces, and a dining room that was semicircular at one end and opened onto a garden. The household staff numbered twelve during the week and fifteen on weekends, and that did not include the six gardeners. The Vanderbilts' neighbors, and close friends, were William S. and Babe Paley and John Hay and Betsey Whitney. Bill Paley owned CBS, and Jock Whitney owned, among other things, the old *Herald Tribune.* They all watched new movies together in the Paleys' living room, or played softball on the Whitneys' lawn while butlers stood by with iced drinks on trays. Jeanne and Alfred did not show movies or hold athletic contests, but they did entertain—generals, former kings, current statesmen, and movie stars. Jeanne was describing a world that glittered and shone, but what she talked about most lovingly were particulars—a piece of porcelain, the kindness of Babe Paley, or how the curtains at Broadhollow drifted gently when the French doors were open and a breeze blew in from the garden.

It is unlikely that Jeanne and I would have become lovers if I had not been a reporter. I would have been intimidated by the social divide between us. Journalists are class-conscious people, and much of the so-called liberal bias in the press is really a mild form of class warfare. The solemn cluckings about the 1980s being the "age of greed" have less to do with the economic malpractices of the time than they do with a distrust of people who make big money. (There is a wonderful comic irony, incidentally, when television anchors and commentators with seven-figure salaries and William Morris agents denounce the age of greed.) Old money may be respectable and really old money sanctified, but generally the press does not like the rich. Rich politicians may be treated nicely—Kennedys and Rockefellers, for example, have done well—but only if they appear to have populist instincts. Then the politicians and reporters will even invite one another to their homes for dinner. Jeanne was not seriously rich, but she lived among people who were, and in the beginning they made me nervous. I got over that when I found I made them nervous, too. Money was losing the authority it once had, and many of the rich seemed baffled. All they had left was the ability to buy things. The power to bring about change or grant stature now rested with me and those like me, people who controlled words and images. The rich might go here and go there, and buy this or buy that, and have a pleasant time while they did, but they knew they were distinguished only by their money. I had none, of course, and I certainly regretted that deeply, but I had a great advantage being a *Times*man. In a media-oriented society I had stature; my byline gave me that. Better yet, my identity was confirmed by other members of the media. When I was writing "About New York," I was even the subject of a parody in *The New Yorker*. Nora Ephron wrote it, and it appeared under the headline "About (Almost Surely) New York or Something: A Few Stories and Messages Dropped Off for Mr. John Corry at the *Times*, Although Nobody Can Remember Why." Arthur Gelb worried the parody might upset me and said I should not take it seriously. I said I would not. In fact, I thought it very funny, and enjoyed the recognition.

But recognition was not quite enough. Jeanne's world could still leave me off balance. Society had died years before, but social distinctions made themselves felt. Rituals, practices, and passwords identified who stood where and in what order. At a dinner party, for instance, you had to know the difference between a fish knife and dessert knife without having to look to your neighbor. You could not be perplexed by a finger bowl, either. The first one I ever saw arrived on a separate plate atop a lace doily with a slice of lemon floating on top. I thought it was clear soup. There were also certain words. You said "sofa" not "couch," and "curtains" never "drapes," and knew that lamps were attached to the wall with "sconces" not "brackets." With coaching, I could master elementary matters such as these, but more subtle matters intruded. Jeanne's world was constructed

around old-fashioned notions of propriety and virtue and a
keen sense of competition. It helped that she had been born
Irish Catholic. It was not enough to be as good as someone
else; you had to be better. You neither explained nor complained, and you knew that when you were confronted by the
unexpected, the important thing was to display lovely manners. Ostentation was frowned on and vulgarity despised,
and style valued most when it was achieved without effort.
In other words, Jeanne was a lady.

The *Times* had not equipped me for that, and I did not always know how to respond. I did not always know how to
respond to the sporting life, either. Jeanne could jump
horses, sail boats, and ski mountains. Most mornings she
worked out in a gym on West 57th Street with ballet dancers
and Broadway gypsies. She was happiest when raising a
sweat or extending a muscle, while I seldom did anything
more strenuous than open and shut the door on a taxi. Meanwhile, it seemed to me Jeanne had been everywhere and met
everyone, and I was not always sure I belonged in that company. One night Jeanne heard me half sing and half hum an
obscure song by Cole Porter. She said it sounded familiar,
and so I half sang and half hummed some more. Why, yes,
she said; "Colie" had written that for her eighteenth birthday. In time I learned that Charles de Gaulle approved of the
way she spoke French, Lyndon and Lady Bird Johnson had
invited her to the ranch, and when the Duke of Windsor was
in town without the duchess he asked her out for dinner.

Journalists have access to the famous, too, but they know
they have it only on sufferance. Some handle this well,
mostly by ignoring it, while others become truculent, pushy,
or embarrassed. I had always leaned toward being embarrassed. This personage or that, I would think, is opening up
to me only because I am a *Times* reporter. Right or wrong, it
was not a feeling to carry into a living room for conversation
after dinner. I had to rethink who I was. I also had to rethink

what I thought of male rivals. At first I was sullen, but then I congratulated myself for having beaten heavyweight contenders. After Jeanne separated from Alfred, she started seeing a British Cabinet minister, heir to a baronetcy, and supposedly Prime Minister Anthony Eden's choice as successor. Jeanne was not yet divorced, however, and Eden feared a scandal. He lectured the minister and wrote letters, pleading with him to end a relationship with ''that lady in question.'' The minister eventually resigned, and while nothing came of the relationship with Jeanne, it pleased me to think she once almost had caused a Parliamentary crisis. I wondered how I might have written about it if I had covered it as a reporter.

There were also my daughters. Colette and Janet were two little West Side girls with natural grace but no formal training. Jeanne decided to make them into proper ladies. She insisted they shake hands, stand up when an adult entered the room, and write thank-you notes when they received a special kindness. They looked on her with awe, pride, and some trepidation. Sometimes I did, too.

Our first summer together, we all went to Ireland. Jeanne wanted to introduce us to horses, Georgian houses, and other things Irish. I strained to hear about Nixon's resignation on the television set nearby while we sat in the lounge of the Shelbourne in Dublin and had high tea. In Galway we took lessons from an elderly riding instructor. He and his brother, both bachelors, had immaculate barns, well-groomed horses, and a deep conviction anyone could be taught to ride. When Janet fell off her pony and refused to get back on, they looked embarrassed. I sat atop a huge beast called Dracula and feared I might fall off as well.

The next summer we all went to a very respectable place, Dark Harbor. It was on an island off the coast of Maine, and it did its best to stay secret. The same families had gone there year after year. They took pride in the simplicity of their existence and thought Bar Harbor and Kennebunkport were way too flashy. At the annual dance at the ramshackle Dark Harbor Yacht Club, stray dogs wandered onto the dance floor. The island's doyenne was Mrs. Marshall Field, a very nice woman, and the doyen was Clarence Dillon, whose son Douglas had been secretary of the treasury. Old Mr. Dillon sat next to Mrs. Field the whole time at the dance. The principal pastimes on the island were sailing small boats and gossiping, both done very seriously. I disrupted a big sailing race one day when I stalled the outboard motor on a boat I had borrowed, and did not know how to restart it. I sat dead in the water while the sailboats had to veer around me. The whole island knew about it by evening.

One winter we borrowed a house at a ski resort in upstate New York. I had never skied; neither had my daughters. The three of us slipped and slid on the beginners' hill for several days. On our last morning I announced I was ready for the intermediate slope. Jeanne warned me it was too icy, but I ignored her. I took the lift to the top, started down, and immediately fell. My God, I thought, what am I doing? In blind eagerness to get to the bottom in one piece, I mistakenly went on a crisscrossing trail. Without realizing it, I was on the experts' slope. Somehow I finished the run standing up and uninjured. Jeanne, who was at the foot of the slope, said not a word when she saw me. Indeed, she said nothing at all until we were halfway back to New York City in the car. I lightly asked her then what she thought. She said I was lucky not to have broken my neck, and she would rather not talk about it. Jeanne cared for me, but not in a treacly way, and while she was never much for swearing, she sometimes looked me in the eyes and said, ''Oh, bullshit!''

Jeanne and I often fought. Most battles arose like summer storms that darken the sky and drench the earth, and then pass almost as quickly. A few, though, lasted weeks or even months, periods in which we did see each other or talk, but nursed our grievances until we no longer remembered what had caused them. Then one of us would reach out to the other. No apology would be offered and none would be expected, yet we both would feel greatly relieved. Eventually we would have another battle. It is hard now to remember why we fought, or why we thought we did, but it may even be we enjoyed it. I have snapshots in my head of our past. There I am on Lexington Avenue, calling Jeanne from a pay phone and shouting furiously. She hangs up on me, and I walk another block, call from another pay phone, and start shouting furiously again. This goes on until I run out of change. There we are in a car. Jeanne is driving me from where we were staying in Southampton to the train station. Neither of us is saying a word. Earlier we decided it was all over between us. At the train station, I get out of the car and Jeanne drives away without so much as a glance. I stand there with my suitcase and after a while hear the whistle of the incoming train. Naturally I feel miserable. As the train comes into the station, Jeanne returns in the car. She has both hands on the steering wheel and is looking straight ahead through the windshield. I open the door and get in, and look straight ahead, too. Neither of us says anything until Jeanne asks in a very detached voice what I want to do about dinner.

Yet one ongoing conflict we could never really resolve. It was a by-product of my being a reporter. There are women in New York who are out every night and call one another every morning, and they know things before anyone else does. Aileen Mehle, who for years wrote a gossip column in the *Daily News* under the name Suzy, once told me that all she had to do to get a column was to answer her phone. Jeanne was never on the phone to Suzy. In fact, she had asked her never to mention her in the column. But, Jeanne did know a lot of people, and so she knew a lot of things. "Now if I tell you this," she would say, "you won't write about it, will you?" I would always be annoyed when she said that. I prided myself on being able to separate my private life from what I did for the *Times*. Actually, I should not have been annoyed. People are right to be worried about reporters. They are never entirely off duty, and they want to write about what they hear, and thus many people keep them off the premises. Until she began to see me, Jeanne saw Bill and Babe Paley frequently; then she saw them less. Paley might have had journalists on the payroll at CBS, but he did not want one at his dinner table.

So when Jeanne told me something I would file it away and not use it. Generally I would also file away and not use anything I heard at dinner parties. They were New York's clearinghouses for rumors, gossip, and information. The rumors might be unfounded, the gossip slanderous, and the information shaky, but they were notable for their diversity. Dinner parties in Washington trafficked only in political news. Those between East 59th and East 79th streets in Manhattan threw in the arts, finance, and show business. Seating arrangements at dinner parties measured gradations of status. An important man could not be seated next to an unattractive woman. The wife of the important man could not be seated next to someone whose social skills were minimal. Less prominent guests could not be seated away from the prominent man in the descending order of their prominence, because that would be too obvious. Artists and writers were prized because they could be seated anywhere. A successful hostess had not only to serve good food, but also to recognize distinctions in caste. Meanwhile, few dinner parties ever escaped some discussion of politics or world affairs. A hush would fall over the table when a big topic was introduced, and almost everyone would look interested. Guests who did not look interested would not be considered serious. Almost always, though, I thought the gossip was more informative than the discussions. You heard about things you did not read in the *Times*.

I first heard about a prenuptial agreement between

Jacqueline Kennedy and Aristotle Onassis at a dinner party. The cheerful woman seated next to me said Onassis had given Mrs. Kennedy $3 million on the eve of their marriage, and told her to put it in tax-exempts. Apparently, however, she had not done so, and thus had upset Onassis. Before he died, he was thinking about a divorce and had spoken to the lawyer Roy Cohn. How interesting, I thought, even though I had never heard of a prenuptial agreement, and had to have one explained to me. Nonetheless, I did not mention any of this in the newsroom, not even when I heard later that Onassis had asked Cohn also about wiretaps. He seemed to have believed Mrs. Onassis had a boyfriend. Jeanne thought that was nonsense. She said Jackie would visit a male pal on Lexington Avenue, but only to smoke cigarettes and cry. Jeanne did not even bother to preface this with, "You won't write about it, will you?" After all, I was a serious, tasteful journalist, and this was only gossip.

But as I said, people are right to be wary about reporters. Given the proper stimulus, even the best-intentioned among them will surrender to shameful urges. My stimulus came along in no time. I did not want to work on desks and would do anything to get off one. Periodically, though, the *Times* would make me an editor. Arthur would install me at a desk, promising it would be only a temporary assignment. I would distrust his assurances and begin to plot my escape. When I was made an assistant metropolitan editor, I immediately looked for an excuse to go back to being a reporter. I found one on a Friday afternoon, when an Associated Press story speculated briefly about whether there had been a prenuptial agreement between Aristotle and Jacqueline Onassis. Arthur was intrigued. Perhaps he had never heard of a prenuptial agreement, either. He gave the story to Peter Kihss and told him to track it down. Peter was one of the finest reporters ever to work for the *Times*. When Lee Harvey Oswald was identified as President Kennedy's assassin, Peter had traced his movements in the weeks before the assassination, just by working the phone. The next day two FBI agents showed up in the newsroom and demanded to know his sources.

Nonetheless, Peter was unable to find out about the pre-nuptial agreement. He did not go to dinner parties. I could have simply sat down and written the story myself, but I had a dilemma. Serious journalists did not pass on dinner-party gossip, yet I hated the idea of another reporter's writing about something I knew. Self-interest triumphed over scruples. I told Arthur I was sure I could get the story, but that I would need time to do the reporting. I would have to get off the desk. When Arthur agreed, I was filled with relief—and also mild shame, because I was being less than honest. I stole away from the newsroom and went home to think it over. On Monday I called Roy Cohn. I said I had been told by a reliable source that Onassis had been to see him, and I just wanted to be sure of the date. As casually as I could, I also mentioned the wiretaps. Cohn confirmed everything I had heard. He was the kind of man who wanted only to be sure you spelled his name right.

I stayed away from the newsroom until Friday, when I went in and wrote for the Saturday paper. That was a fig leaf for dignity. On Saturday there were fewer readers than on any other day of the week. At home that night I turned on the eleven-o'clock news. The local stations had all picked up my story and were using it at the top of their programs. I took my phone off the hook then, and left it off the rest of the weekend. On Monday when I showed up in the newsroom, an exasperated assistant news editor told me he had been trying to reach me all Sunday. For one thing, he said, one of Mrs. Onassis's lawyers was warning about a lawsuit. He also said that Christina Onassis had just held a news conference in Athens. I had written that she and her stepmother did not get along, but she firmly had denied it. The assistant news editor said we would carry a story about the news conference, and asked if I wanted to add anything. I said I did. I wrote two unsigned paragraphs that were tacked onto the Athens piece, vaguely hinting at further disclosures. I was sending Mrs. Onassis a message and fervently hoping she would receive it. My original story had not mentioned wire-taps or anything truly messy, and I wanted her to know that I knew more than I already had written about in the *Times*. It worked, or at least I think it did. The *Times* never heard again from the lawyers.

A month or so later I met Mrs. Onassis. The bandleader Peter Duchin and his wife invited me to a party at their house in the country, and Mrs. Onassis was the first person I saw when I arrived. She was wearing a black T-shirt, and I thought she looked too sad and too thin, almost like a child. I remembered the famous photograph that showed her turned around in the backseat of the open car in Dallas, apparently trying to throw herself out over the trunk. I thought about that while she and I sat on a stone fence that day at the Du-chins' and talked about horses. She said not a word about the prenuptial agreement, or William Manchester, or even *The New York Times,* and neither, of course, did I.

WHAT TELEVISION WROUGHT

In late 1948, I saw *The Texaco Star Theater,* with Milton Berle. Our neighbors invited us over on a Tuesday night to watch. My mother, my father, and I sat on folding chairs, stayed exactly one hour and then retreated across the hall to our own apartment, aware something new had entered our life. In fact, something new had entered everyone's life, though to what end or purpose no one knew or could guess, save that it was to be approached solemnly, expectantly, and with an inchoate sense that the world of tomorrow and its rich promise were now here. The year before I saw Milton Berle, television had found its first mass audience: 3.9 million people watched while the Yankees beat the Dodgers in the World Series. However, 3.5 million of them were in bars, and none but the fanciful or spendthrift thought seriously of getting a television set of their own. At the beginning of 1948, only one percent of American homes had the new toy, although the floodgates of desire opened soon after and in five years more than half of all homes in the United States had one television set or more. The media age had arrived, and would transform journalism and politics, but in the innocence of the time, it would be a while before anyone knew.

I had a modest connection with the new medium myself. In the late 1950s, I was a substitute coffee boy on Jack Paar's talk show, NBC's predecessor to Johnny Carson's *Tonight Show.* The regular coffee boy was Bob Shanks, a good friend I had made in the Army. He would become a prominent producer, but for a while in those days he cut up Danish and made coffee for the cast and crew around Paar. Bob was paid twenty-five dollars a night, from which he would buy the Danish; NBC, as I recall, supplied the urn and coffee. If you were parsimonious with the Danish, you kept practically all the money yourself. I was making forty dollars a week as a copyboy at the *Times,* and Bob generously offered to let me pull a few shifts in his place. The first time I did I disgraced myself. Joe Walcott, the former heavyweight champion, was a guest on the show, and I neglected the coffee and Danish while I asked him questions so I could write a story for the *Times.* I did write the story, and the kindly sports editor who accepted it said it would carry my byline. I was thrilled as only a *Times* copyboy could be thrilled, and even though the story ran in only one edition, I knew my career had begun.

So I suppose I owed that to television, although I still thought of it as something peripheral, not to be dismissed entirely, but not to be taken very seriously, either. It seemed such a modest medium, better suited for amusement than for anything really important. It was a source of egalitarian fun. When I was at Harvard in the sixties, I visited Arthur Schlesinger, Sr., at his home to watch *McHale's Navy.* Mrs. Schlesinger served tea. My own favorite program then was *F Troop.* On Saturday nights in the late seventies, my daughters and I watched *The Love Boat* on a portable black-and-white set, with a wire hanger for an antenna, that otherwise stayed on a shelf in a closet. In retrospect, I think my taste

was not bad. Much of what is supposedly junk television—
Gilligan's Island, say—will be around far longer than the
sophisticated comedy or drama that began dominating prime
time in the 1970s. Junk TV never pretends to be more than it
is, and it is often done with real humor. This is the opposite
of almost anything produced by Norman Lear.

Even though I was not watching much television, I did
appear on some television programs. I remember two early
appearances best. In one, I was interviewed about Cuba by
Merv Griffin. In a rapid ascent from coffee boy, Bob Shanks
had become Griffin's producer. I was happy for him, but
nervous about being on the show, and before I left home for
the studio, which was next door to Sardi's, I had a couple of
martinis. Then I stopped off at Sardi's, where I saw the co-
median Henry Morgan, who also would be on the Griffin
show that night. I told him I was nervous. He said he would
buy me a drink. Then I bought one for him. Later the bartender bought one for both of us. At the studio, the woman
who was applying my makeup smiled conspiratorially and
told me Bob had tucked away a bottle of gin and some ice in
case I wanted a drink. Yes, I said, I did. I was the last guest
of the evening, and by the time I appeared I could hardly
remember my name. I've forgotten Merv's first question—I
probably didn't hear it anyway—but apparently I answered
by saying there were millions of cows in Cuba. Vivian
Vance, the very pleasant woman who played Ethel Mertz on
I Love Lucy, was also a guest that night and decided to help
me out. She burst out laughing, as if I had said something
quite funny. That made Merv and the audience burst out
laughing, too. I remember absolutely nothing else, although
Griffin thought I was charming and amusing and the next
day invited me to be on the show again.

The other appearance I especially remember was on the
Today show. Barbara Walters and the actor Burgess Meredith, who was filling in as cohost in place of Hugh Downs,

interviewed me about the Kennedys. Walters did the introduction while Meredith smiled thinly. Then, fixing gimlet
eyes on me, he asked, "Don't you think Mrs. Kennedy has
suffered enough?" He was implying that I had made her suffer—I hadn't—but what was I to say? No, Mrs. Kennedy has
not suffered enough? I was in a no-win territory, and unable
to find a way out. Meredith kept paying tribute to the Kennedys while suggesting I had wronged them. When the interview was over, Barbara Walters pointed backstage and
mouthed the word "Wait." She wanted to tell me Meredith
had been at a dinner party the night before with Jacqueline
Kennedy and told her he would get me. Walters apologized
for Meredith's behavior; it was gracious of her to do so.
When I was a television critic years later, I found it almost
impossible to write anything unflattering about Barbara
Walters.

So much for my firsthand experience. I had learned a
drunk could look presentable on television and a talk-show
host could have his own agenda. Generally, though, I liked
television, and so did almost everyone else. Congressmen
and other scolds complained about its portrayals of sex and
violence, while a chairman of the Federal Communications
Commission called it a "vast wasteland," but nattering like
that was ignored because television knew its place. It had the
good sense to leave serious matters alone and to amuse us.
At his "last press conference" in 1962, when he petulantly
told reporters, "You won't have Nixon to kick around anymore"—after he lost the California gubernatorial election—
Richard Nixon compared print and television journalism. "I
think," he said seriously, "that it's time our great newspapers have at least the same objectivity, the same fullness of
coverage, that television has. And I can only thank God for
television and radio for keeping the newspapers a little more
honest." Things were moving fast, however, and two years
later delegates to the Republican National Convention in

San Francisco wore buttons reading "Stamp Out Huntley–Brinkley." When Dwight Eisenhower spoke to the convention about "sensation-seeking" newsmen who were trying to discredit Barry Goldwater, the delegates roared in anger and shook their fists at the anchormen in their booths above the floor. Eisenhower was surprised; David Brinkley, as he admitted later, was damned scared.

It was the beginning of a permanent schism. The modest new medium was finding its voice. In the two years since Nixon had thanked God for television, the evening news programs had doubled in length to thirty minutes and television had begun to do more than regurgitate headlines. It was seeing itself more expansively and exploring new possibilities. On the eve of the move to thirty minutes, Reuven Frank, who soon would be president of NBC News, and was then executive producer of *The Huntley–Brinkley Report,* sent his staff a thoughtful thirty-two-page memo that ended with the exhortation "Get in there and fight!" Before that, however, it said: "Every news story should, without any sacrifice of probity or responsibility, display the attributes of fiction, of drama. It should have structure and conflict, problem and denouement, rising action and falling action, a beginning, a middle and an end."

In other words, a news story should reach out and grab you; it should hold tight and not let go. Frank, a founding father of news television, was mindful of news as a public trust and committed to what he was doing, but his premise had a flaw. A news story that must display the attributes of fiction and drama risks no longer being a news story. It will be an entertainment or a diversion or, perhaps, a morality tale or homily with a sense of didactic mission. It will not want to inform as much as enlighten, and it will breathe with the breath of a priest and not that of a reporter. In 1963, the same year Frank wrote his memo, the Roper Organization, which had been conducting a similar survey since 1959, once again asked Americans: "Where [do] you usually get most of your news about what's going on in the world today—from the newspapers or radio or television, or talking to people or where?" For the first time, more Americans said they were getting their news from television than from newspapers.

The civil rights revolution was under way, accompanied by memorable televised images: firebombed churches, clouds of tear gas, police dogs attacking marchers. The stories told themselves. In a way, they were easy to cover. It was not necessary to draw moral distinctions between Martin Luther King, Jr., and the Alabama politician Bull Connor. The right side was easy to find. Coincidentally, the new politics was beginning to coalesce: Students for a Democratic Society issued its Port Huron manifesto in 1962; demonstrations at Berkeley would erupt two years later. A tatterdemalion revolution was born while television was feeling its oats. Newspapers were burdened with old strictures about who, what, when, and where, told at the top of the story. Television was onto something new: structure and conflict, problem and denouement, a beginning, a middle, and an end. With its growing sense of self it became a perfect vehicle for the new politics. Good and evil clashed, and any issue could be resolved in two minutes.

Correspondents had to know only which side they were on. It was one thing to choose a side, however, in a hot Mississippi summer, and quite another to choose one when the issues were more complex. The best-known and most celebrated piece of television reporting from Vietnam was Morley Safer's 1965 story about the razing of Cam Ne village by U.S. Marines. It opened with a striking shot: a Marine using a Zippo lighter to ignite a thatched hut. Then we heard Safer: "This is what the war is all about: the old and the very young. The Marines have burned this old couple's cottage because fire [gunfire] was coming from here." Moments

later, a breathless Safer interviewed a Marine while they
both lay prone on the ground. Then Safer was on his feet,
following Marines through the smoky village. It was wonderfully dramatic—structure and conflict, a clear problem
and, of course, the denouement. Safer concluded his report:
"The day's operation burned down 150 houses, wounded
three women, killed one baby, wounded one Marine, and
netted these four prisoners: four old men who could not answer questions put to them in English, four old men who had
no idea what an ID card was. Today's operation is the frus-
tration of Vietnam in miniature. There is little doubt that
American firepower can win a military victory here. But to a
Vietnam peasant whose home means a lifetime of back-
breaking labor, it will take more than presidential promises
to convince him that we are on his side."

Years later, an admiring David Halberstam wrote that
Safer's story "helped legitimatize pessimistic reporting by
all other television correspondents." After it was shown,
"there would be a greater receptivity to darker news about
Vietnam." Halberstam was right: darker news soon
abounded. Safer's piece won any number of journalism
awards and was shown to young correspondents on their
way to Vietnam as an example of work well done. Certainly
it reached out and grabbed you. There was the drumbeat of
history in Safer's portentous opening words: "This is what
the war is all about." A judgment was pronounced. Lyndon
Johnson was so upset when he saw Safer's story that he
wanted an FBI investigation. Johnson, however, barked up
the wrong tree. Safer was no subversive; he was a television
reporter, better-looking than most, but with no more perspective than could be anticipated. The dashing CBS correspondent did not lie, but he had seen only what he wanted to
see, and clever film editing had done the rest. The Zippo
lighter became one of the war's great symbols.

Yet Safer's story had left out a great deal. Cam Ne was

not really a single village inhabited only by the very old and the young; it was a complex of six hamlets separated by rice paddies, and it had been a communist stronghold since the Vietminh fought the French. It hid a network of tunnels and was ringed by a trench, and its thatched huts stood near or on top of concrete bunkers. Fighting had begun there long before the correspondent and his cameraman swooped in by helicopter, and it would go on long after they left. Cam Ne was a nasty place, with booby traps, punji pits, and mine fields. Safer and his CBS editors, however, made it appear that the Marines had entered almost casually and then burned the village down for the hell of it, in the process wounding three women and killing a baby, and then arresting four doddering old men. In fact, the Marines had to withdraw from Cam Ne shortly after Safer took off in a helicopter. The Vietcong were still all around them, even though Safer had said "the Vietcong were long gone."

As reporting, that wasn't much, and while the story made for great television, it was slender on facts. Safer said 150 homes were destroyed; the official Marine report said fifty-one, and since no one ever had reason to accuse the military of underestimating battlefield damage, it may be assumed that Safer miscounted. Safer also said the Marines had entered the village after a "heavy barrage of rocket fire," but according to written accounts there was no rocket fire; and afterward, even the Zippo lighter turned out to be suspect. Some Marines said later that Safer had asked one of them to set fire to a hut so CBS could get a good picture.

Still, Halberstam was correct: Safer had legitimated a more pessimistic kind of reporting. Indeed, he had sanctified and canonized it, and even given his story an afterlife. In 1985, twenty years after the story was first shown, Bob Simon, another CBS correspondent, went to Cam Ne. The *Evening News* spliced together pieces of Safer's and Simon's stories in a kind of before-and-after. Once again we saw the Marine ignite the thatched hut. Then Bob Simon spoke: "Of the many new weapons tried out in Vietnam, the most memorable may have been the Zippo lighter." Then Safer said the villagers would always remember what happened that day; Simon, two decades later, confirmed it: "The villagers will never forget, and they still don't understand."

It was more reasonable, however, to think it was CBS that still did not understand. Simon went on to present the man, whom, he said, "the Marines had been looking for year after year—the district commander of the Vietcong." And where had he been hiding when the Marines attacked? "Right here," the old district commander said through an interpreter. "People kept me in their homes and gave me food. I was in the village the whole time."

Safer, apparently, had missed him. You could forgive him for that, although the rest made you wonder. If the man had been district commander of the Vietcong, then why were the villagers puzzled by the attack? Didn't the Vietcong kill Marines? For that matter, didn't they even kill villagers who refused them shelter? After all, the Vietcong killed hundreds, perhaps thousands, of civilians in Hue during the Tet offensive. Did Bob Simon speak Vietnamese (did Morley Safer?), and if he did not, how did he know what the villagers thought? How did he know they were even the same villagers?

Simon did not know, of course, and Safer had not known that much twenty years earlier, although he had had no difficulty in making a profound judgment: "This is what the war is all about." An irony was that at the same time Simon was reaffirming Safer's old story in Vietnam, CBS News lawyers were refuting it in New York. General William C. Westmoreland was suing for libel. He said a CBS documentary that accused him of having suppressed accurate figures on the size of the enemy had defamed him. The principal point of contention was, Who were the enemy combatants? Westmoreland said he had counted only the Vietcong and North Vietnamese regulars. CBS and its lawyers said he should have counted irregulars as well. By not counting them, they insisted, he had willfully underestimated the size of the foe. But if Westmoreland had counted the irregulars, he would have counted women and old men, civilians like the four ancients Safer had discovered in Cam Ne, who could not speak English and had no idea what an ID card was. CBS News and its lawyers were ignoring Safer's story. It had implied that old men could not be combatants.

There is a tradition in television that allows a correspondent to pontificate however he chooses. Words drift off into the ether without being subject to the scrutiny words receive in print. At the same time, television in its way is more demanding than print. Television is a performance medium, and it is by performance that a correspondent is judged. What a correspondent says is less important than how he says it, and while objective truth is to be desired, the appearance of knowledgeability is desired even more. Simon was in Vietnam because the networks were covering the tenth anniversary of the fall of Saigon, now known as Ho Chi Minh City. The big event was a parade starting at 7:52 a.m., the same time ten years before when the last Marine had been lifted by helicopter from the roof of the United States embassy.

On the *CBS Evening News* that night, Liz Trotta reported on the parade and attendant ceremonies: "The Hanoi government has said several times it wants better relationships with the United States, but one would never guess it from the anti-American rhetoric at today's victory parade. Communist officials lambasted the United States, describing it as bellicose and stubborn."

On the *NBC Nightly News,* however, Garrick Utley reported on the parade and ceremonies thus: "The celebration commemorated the defeat of the United States, but neither in official statements nor in the personal attitudes of the people was there any indication of anti-Americanism. Vietnam now wants better relationships with the United States.''

And so it went, two contradictory reports by two veteran correspondents on Vietnamese feelings toward the United States. One correspondent had to be right and the other wrong, and the one who was wrong was operating in the tradition of that report from Cam Ne. (Apparently, it was Utley; print stories confirmed the anti-American feeling.) Safer helped invent the tradition; twenty years later his colleagues affirmed it, and it is so firmly in place now that it is impossible to imagine television without it. In the Persian Gulf war, anchormen pressed correspondents in Baghdad on questions they could not possibly answer. Tell me, an anchorman would ask, how do Iraqis feel about this latest statement from President Bush? And the correspondent, from a cubicle in a hotel an eight-hour time difference away, in a country whose language he did not understand, would be expected to give an instant reply. The correspondent could not have the slightest idea how Iraqis felt, but would answer just the same. In the grand old sixties tradition, veracity was not important.

TELEVISION, HOWEVER, was only part of journalism at large. Ideas and attitudes began in print, and television picked them up later. The *Times* in the sixties was trying to resist that marriage of news reporting and fiction writer's technique called New Journalism. In the great *Times* tradition, reporters had to be anonymous and objective. New Journalists, though, were neither faceless nor disinterested, nor did they pretend to be. Tom Wolfe was writing in italics, ellipses, and capital letters. Gay Talese was testing interior monologues, re-created scenes, and flashbacks. Page one of the second section of the old *Herald Tribune* was dizzy with New Journalism every night. When the paper folded, its best-known writers decamped to Clay Felker's fledgling *New York* magazine. Now known mostly for restaurant reviews and celebrity appraisals, it was once the advance guard of New Journalism. I remember a piece by Gail Sheehy about a prostitute, "Redpants," a fascinating, beguiling, tough, no-nonsense creature with a lot to tell *New York* readers. Unfortunately, though, she didn't exist. Redpants, as Sheehy and Felker explained lamely later, was a "composite." Sheehy had invented her from bits and pieces, and while any one bit or piece might have been real, their assembly was an act of creation. New Journalism was journalism in name only, and its soul belonged to fiction.

That was true from the start. The writers who first inspired New Journalism did not just borrow from novelists; they were novelists themselves, and they had turned to journalism because it seemed more relevant than fiction. Norman Mailer was one of the first. In "The White Negro," published in Irving Howe's magazine *Dissent,* he wrote about hipsterism and the hip unconscious and what white intellectuals might learn from black criminals. Mailer examined a real crime—the beating to death of a candy store owner—and found in it something uplifting. The two young men who murdered the candy store owner were in a rage, and since unexpressed rage stifles creativity, the violence that dissipates rage could be an act of creation. Norman Podhoretz castigated this idea as "morally gruesome," but hardly anyone paid attention. "The White Negro" became a counterculture document of the sixties. Mailer subsequently began writing nonfiction for *Esquire,* and so did Gore Vidal, James Baldwin, and William Styron. Baldwin was particularly successful. His collection of essays *The Fire Next Time* was on the best-seller list for all of 1963. It more or less argued that blacks hated whites and had every good reason to do so, and it was the first big literary-journalistic work to make white liberals feel terrible.

The *Times* newsroom was not hermetically sealed from all this. The paper might turn its face from heresies, but heresies crept in through the cracks. Old rewrite men, tired copyreaders, and reporters long stuck on their beats might not be moved, but others were, especially those young and ambitious. Naturally I was affected. Ralph Ellison, who wrote *Invisible Man,* arguably the great American novel of mid-century, had the temerity to say in an essay that he was not a black novelist but a novelist who happened to be black, and that he should be judged by his art and not his color. He suggested some black authors were being praised when they couldn't write worth a damn. Indeed, they were—who now would want to read Eldridge Cleaver's *Soul on Ice?*—but Ellison's audacity in saying so was too much for Irving Howe. Howe, who, of course, was white, snorted back in another essay that even if Ellison was black, he just wasn't black enough.

Specious arguments like that are still very much with us, but in the sixties they were brand-new, and the *Times* magazine asked me to write a piece about Ellison. We met in his Upper West Side apartment, a modest old-fashioned railroad flat where he and his wife had lived for years. It was filled with books, papers, and notebooks, and its one conspicuous ornament was a Mies van der Rohe chair. Ellison, who had known bitter poverty as a child in rural Oklahoma, had bought it when *Invisible Man* became a success, and it was, I think, his only indulgence. He was a serious man, who insisted literature should be judged by literary standards, and that novelists, black or white, should compete with Tolstoy and Stendhal and not with political rhetoricians. Certainly that made me suspicious. When I wrote about Ellison, I wondered in print whether he were an Uncle Tom, insensitive to the social and political revolution going on all around him. I am ashamed of that now, but I was part of the media culture, and like so many others who lived and worked in that impudent realm, I just didn't know any better.

But there was always another story. I asked the *Times* to let me visit college campuses to report on drug use by students. The editors said yes, and off I went to Pennsylvania, Colorado, Illinois, and California. The drug users were children of the middle and upper-middle classes, and my story about them was mildly alarming: There were more drug users in the humanities than in the sciences, and more in the English departments than anywhere else; a kilogram of marijuana that cost twenty dollars in Mexico fetched ten times that much in Berkeley; LSD cultists talked knowingly about Zen, Aldous Huxley, and existentialism before they popped off in psychosis. My reporting was the newspaper equivalent of television's coverage of the new politics. Correspondents and anchors clucked disapprovingly at some of the most outré forms, but tried hard to be understanding.

The new breezes blowing through journalism were leaving everyone off balance.

The breezes were so captivating, though, that some people left the *Times* to chase them—including me when I went to *Harper's.* I had read Mailer's marvelous "The Steps of the Pentagon." It had taken my breath away that day on the airplane. Mailer had shown how a writer could get in on the action. I did not notice that he described violence no other reporter saw. I paid no attention to the absence of quotation marks around what were supposed to be quotations. There is a passage about soldiers beating an unidentified young woman—"But there was no face there; all we saw were some raw skin and blood"—and rereading it now I am sure Mailer wrote about something that never happened. Yet the new breezes were wafting everywhere then. When the magazine article was published as a hardcover book, it won the Pulitzer Prize for general nonfiction.

. . .

OLD-FASHIONED OBJECTIVITY had lost its zing. The new sub-
jectivity was more rewarding, and while it was born in print,
it captured television as well: from magazines to great newsrooms to the places where network anchors dwell. What was
important was the moral prism. A news story would be re-
fracted accordingly. In the watershed year 1968, television
helped shape a major party, realign the political system, and
decide a presidential election. The quintessential television
story of the decade was the Democratic National Convention that year in Chicago. It had everything, including an
angry anchorman, Walter Cronkite, who found what he saw
on his monitor intolerable and on the air described Mayor
Richard J. Daley's policemen as "thugs." In 1968, Cronkite
moved from reporting news to making it, and from telling us
about affairs of state to instructing us in how those affairs
should be handled. Other television newsmen had been
slouching toward that for a while, but none had Cronkite's
stature or his niche as household god. He was called America's most trusted newsman, and what he said was so. On the
night of February 27, 1968, he unilaterally said the Vietnam
war was over. The Johnson administration had declared that
the Vietcong attacks during the Tet holiday the month before
had led to a communist defeat. America's most trusted
newsman, however, did not believe it. As he told millions of
viewers, he had been "too often disappointed by the opti-
mism of American leaders." At best, he said, Vietnam
would be a "stalemate." Therefore, he concluded, the only
"rational" thing left to do was "to negotiate, not as victors,
but as an honorable people who lived up to their pledge to
defend democracy, and did the best they could."

As it happened, Cronkite was dead wrong about Tet. As
Hanoi conceded after the war, Tet was a communist defeat.
The South Vietnamese did not rise up in support of the Viet-

cong, and the Vietcong military and political structure was destroyed. Objectively, the war was at a turning point, although it would swivel now in a direction other than the one that might have been expected. Lyndon Johnson watched Cronkite that night and knew his days were numbered. He told his press secretary that they had "lost Walter," and that in losing him he had lost the "center" of public opinion. Johnson was not entirely correct; public opinion is more complicated than that, but he knew that in losing Walter the White House had lost something important. Congress confused the voice of an anchorman with the voice of the people—a mistake it also would make regularly in years to come. More important, Cronkite had issued a hunting license to all his colleagues. If America's most trusted newsman could do it, why couldn't they? A few nights after Cronkite told America to negotiate because the war looked like a stalemate, Frank McGee, the NBC anchor, simply threw in the towel. "The war is being lost," he told his viewers.

Put aside the question now of whether negotiations were in order or whether the war was being lost; there was a larger matter than that. Until the night Cronkite confessed his unhappiness with elected leaders, it had been understood anchormen would hide their opinions. They were supposed to be old-fashioned reporters, presenting facts in an old-fashioned way. Their audience was huge, and their influence substantial; it was unthinkable they would be anything other than objective. Cronkite himself radiated sincerity so unaffectedly he no longer even seemed to be a reporter. Ordinary reporters mixed half-truths, gossip, and speculation in with a few precious facts, and retailed the product as news. Anchormen were supposed to be different. Their covenant with the audience recognized that news was slippery, elusive, and quite often incorrect. What was true one day was not necessarily true the next, and judgments would be made by historians and not journalists. As network executives said, news was a sacred trust and the professionals who dispensed it would observe high standards; they would offer fact not opinion. Network executives still affirm this, although they do it now mostly by rote, and not many people believe them. It would be unfair to blame Walter Cronkite for all that went wrong, but in that one broadcast he changed the rules. Television newsmen were now free to dispense advice and counsel while giving viewers their opinions.

And so they did, and their stories became self-fulfilling prophecies as they looked through their moral prism. Stories in print could be done that way, too, but the difference between print and television was that television was much bigger. Hundreds of thousands might read an article in the *Times.* Cronkite and his colleagues shared their thoughts with millions and millions. Their coverage of the New Hampshire Democratic primary, barely two weeks after Cronkite had declared that the Vietnam war was over, was an example of wish fulfillment. To a man, anchors and correspondents called Senator Eugene McCarthy the primary's "real winner." They were so insistent most people remember the dovish Minnesotan as the actual winner. He was not. He received 42 percent of the vote, while Lyndon Johnson received 48.5 percent, and Johnson had entered the primary so late there had been no time to enter his name on the ballot; voters had to write it in. Meanwhile, the anchors and correspondents interpreted the showing by the "real winner" as the voters' call for peace.

Polls taken after the primary, however, indicated that the majority of people who voted for McCarthy did so not because they liked him or his politics, but because they were displeased with Lyndon Johnson. In the presidential election in November, when Richard Nixon and Hubert Humphrey were the principal candidates, a plurality of the old McCarthy voters in New Hampshire cast their ballots for

George Wallace, a right-wing hawk at the other end of the political spectrum from McCarthy. New Hampshire sentiment never was antiwar; it was anti-defeat. Television, however, shaped viewers' perceptions, and in doing so altered the event. The New Hampshire primary was really marginal, but because the media thought otherwise, history was rearranged. If McCarthy was the real winner, then something had to be done. Four days after the New Hampshire primary, Robert Kennedy said he would enter the presidential race and make Vietnam the issue. Fifteen days later, Lyndon Johnson said he would not run again.

Television was on a roll, a Cyclops running on instinct. It knew what it knew because it knew it, and the Democratic National Convention in Chicago confirmed all its feelings. The anchors and correspondents had only to look at their own pictures: policemen swinging nightsticks, demonstrators running away, a war up and down Michigan Avenue. Cops backed kids up against the Conrad Hilton and drove them through a plate-glass window, then followed them over the shards and into the hotel and pursued them around the lobby. It looked like a revolution, and it was. An old order collapsed, brought down by the marching young and the force of media opinion. In his book about the 1968 campaign, *The Making of the President, 1968,* Theodore White described how the nomination of Hubert Humphrey looked to millions of viewers: "[San Francisco mayor Joseph] Alioto rose on screen to nominate him; back and forth the cameras swung, from Alioto to pudgy, cigar-smoking politicians, to Daley with his undershot, angry jaw, painting visually and without words the nomination of the Warrior of Joy as a puppet of the old machines." When Carl Stokes, the mayor of Cleveland, rose to second Humphrey's nomination, NBC cut to scenes of street violence. In fact, Stokes spoke at ten that night, and the disturbances that week took place in the afternoons and early evenings. All the networks, however—splicing, intercutting, breaking away and then coming back—made it seem everything was happening at once. We saw the streets and then the convention podium. Senator Abraham Ribicoff of Connecticut was there, denouncing "Gestapo tactics." From the convention floor, Mayor Daley shouted and shook his fist and called Ribicoff a son of a bitch. In the anchor booth, Walter Cronkite looked distressed. Then we were back on the streets. It was wonderfully dramatic—electoral politics as a morality play, a compelling production with snow-white heroes, the darkest of villains, and no indeterminate shades between them. Humphrey, Theodore White wrote, "was nominated in a sea of blood."

It had to be that way. The script was written in advance. On the eve of the convention, organizers had predicted that more than a million demonstrators would show up. Reporters early on staked out the best places to watch a riot. Yippies had threatened to dump LSD into the city water supply. Mayor Daley had reports of plots to assassinate prominent Democrats. The Chicago cops were edgy, and they had a sorry record of hitting people with nightsticks in previous demonstrations. The violence sprang from bad judgment on all sides. Television, however, made no concessions. Newspapers had limits imposed by an editorial process, but television had almost no process at all. It was practicing journalism, but everything it did was outsized. One moment led to the next and then that to another, until news moved in one seamless flow, driven by the original assumptions and shown with a lot of swell pictures.

And the pictures were shown again and again, certifiable proof that something awful had gone on in Chicago. But just what did go on, and how did you describe it? When the cops charged demonstrators and swung nightsticks, were they practicing brutality or only overreacting? When Mayor Daley cheered the cops on, was he blundering or miscalculating? Questions such as these might seem insignificant now, but in the heated soul of sixties journalism they could lie like burning embers. J. Anthony Lukas, a *Times* reporter in Chicago, opted for "brutality" and "blundering" when he wrote about what had happened. Abe Rosenthal, not yet managing editor, but for all practical purposes the man then running the *Times,* changed "brutality" to "overreaction" and "blundering" to "miscalculation." On learning this, Harrison Salisbury, who was directing *Times* reporters in Chicago, angrily called New York. It wasn't the first time; he and Abe had fought about the coverage all week. "You're taking the guts out of the story," Salisbury charged once again. No, Abe said; he was taking out the "goddamn editorializing."

Salisbury would have been at home in one of the network vans. Abe would not have lasted. The passions of the decade tugged at him, but he had decided to resist. Yet Salisbury had never met a revolution he didn't like, and he throbbed with excitement in Chicago. His dispute with Rosenthal might have seemed ephemeral, but in its way it would go on for years, transmogrified into other disputes and with adherents on both sides, but always rooted in the passions aroused in the sixties. When Tom Wicker saw the cops hitting demonstrators, he had shouted, "These are our children," and as a columnist on the op-ed page he could do all the editorializing of his choosing. The day after Abe struck "brutality" from Tony Lukas's news story, Wicker wrote a column that began, "After Mayor Daley's brute policemen clubbed down American youngsters in the streets," and went on to describe the demonstrators as "political dissidents, many of them radical, most of them idealistic, demonstrably brave, concerned for their country and their fellow men. . . . These were our children on the streets, and the Chicago police beat them up."

Almost everyone in the respectable media agreed with

Wicker. The tawdry old political order had collapsed, done in by the marching youngsters. Mayor Daley and other party bosses were to be replaced by more virtuous men. The perception of a Democratic Party tearing itself apart became the reality of its aftermath. Eugene McCarthy loftily declined to endorse his party's ticket, and the Humphrey campaign was slow to start. Liberals deserted the candidate, wanting no part of a man already tainted by his association with Lyndon Johnson and now so identified with the cops in Chicago. Humphrey, a decent man, deserved far better than that, but the marching children and the media had created a political reality too great to overcome. Humphrey lost to Nixon by the slender margin of some 500,000 popular votes. Years later, a former aide to Humphrey wrote that shortly before Nixon was inaugurated, "a world-famous network correspondent visited Vice President Humphrey in his White House office and tearfully apologized: 'We defeated you, Hubert' was his confession."

Network executives argued in 1968 that they were only reporting the news that week in Chicago and the rules of journalism determined the coverage. It should be remembered, though, there was another party convention that summer: the Republican in Miami Beach. Six people died then in riots. No one died in Chicago, and despite the appalling pictures, no one appeared to be seriously injured. By the standards of traditional journalism, Miami Beach ought to have been the bigger story. The people in nearby Liberty City were not clubbed—they were shot and killed by men no more just or unjust than the Chicago police. Nonetheless, there were no arguments about whether it was appropriate to use the word "brutality," and no one shouted, "These are our children." The people who died were poor and black, and they captured no one's imagination.

The marching children in Chicago, however, had an appealing agenda: ending the war in Vietnam and transforming our political system. The first goal eluded them. In fact, when they gained media attention and presented the world with the picture of a nation so deeply divided, they encouraged Hanoi not to end the war but to keep fighting. On that second goal, though, the marchers were successful. The Democratic Party began to transform itself even before it left Chicago. It decided to open its ranks, rewrite its rules, and accommodate its most dissident voices. Four years later George McGovern was the presidential nominee, and although he went down to an electoral-college defeat second in size only to Alf Landon's, his nomination meant the radical wing of the Democratic Party now controlled party machinery. It was a triumph for the new politics and the culture that had raised it to power, but as always with revolutionary change there were unintended consequences. The most obvious was that Republicans would gain what for years seemed to be permanent possession of the White House.

Television had much to answer for in that great realignment of power, although at the time it was little remarked on. Perhaps because television had moved so fast—from benign new medium that even Richard Nixon liked to fearsome tiger, in only a few short years. Perhaps the country needed to catch up. Perhaps no one knew how to look at television. What did we see when we watched it? For that matter, who watched it, anyway? Abe was in a snit in the newsroom one day when he saw some reporters clustered around a television set, watching a breaking story. "Newspapermen get their news from newspapers," he said tartly, and dispersed them. In his heart he did not take television seriously; somehow it seemed like a toy, a plaything for the idle or bored. I'm not sure the people who worked in television knew what to make of it, either. They were well known and well paid, and in a society where celebrity had weight they commanded enormous attention. But what did they do, exactly, to deserve it?

I met some of them, of course. You hang around New York and you run into everyone sooner or later. The director Joshua Logan and his wife, Nedda, gave celebrated Christmas parties in their big apartment on East 52nd Street. At one party Walter Cronkite did a brief, decorous hula. The other guests, including me, all laughed and applauded. Shortly afterward I mentioned the party and Cronkite's hula, approvingly, in the *Times*. Then I forgot about it. Cronkite did not. When I ran into him months later, he told me I had breached journalistic ethics by writing about a party to which I had been invited not as a reporter but as a guest. I pointed out that Josh Logan had called to say he found the *Times* story amusing. Cronkite was not mollified. He said I had embarrassed him by saying he did the hula. In the fifties Cronkite had been exchanging gags with a puppet named Charlemane on the CBS *Morning Show*. He also had been the host of *You Are There,* in which he "interviewed" famous characters from history. "We are standing outside the tent of Achilles," he said in one episode. "The place: the plains of Ilium outside the great walled city of Troy. The date: 1184 B.C. And—you are there." A decade or so later, he was telling presidents what to do. This was incongruous at best, although in the media age it was accepted without question. Did Cronkite, an honorable man, ever wake up in the middle of the night and worry? Television had thrust him into the role of oracle, but was he really that, or was he only an entertainer? He might have forgotten Charlemane and Achilles, but the hula was hard to ignore.

Did any people in the business know what the new medium had wrought, and were they uncomfortable with the fruits of their labor? Jeanne and I once had dinner with Bill Paley. "Don't mention *The Beverly Hillbillies* or anything like that," Jeanne warned me beforehand. "Bill can be sensitive, and he'll get upset." That night, the founder, owner, and chairman of CBS said he had not read all my recent stories. I less gracefully said I had not seen all his new programs. Jeanne looked at me suspiciously, and I did not mention television the rest of the night. Neither did Bill Paley. He was charming, amusing, and guarded, never talking of his network. Afterward Jeanne said I had made him nervous, but that was only half true. It wasn't me; it was what I was dragging behind me—*The New York Times* and the rest of the print culture. Print had been conduit and repository for all our most solemn thoughts. Television was new, and Paley wondered whether it was really respectable. Gutenberg changed our consciousness when he invented movable type, and now television was changing it, too. *The Beverly Hillbillies,* I think, truly pained Bill Paley.

Sometimes in the seventies I met television journalists— Mike Wallace, Barbara Walters, John Chancellor, Bernard and Marvin Kalb, and others—at Abe Rosenthal's apartment. They were sophisticated and intelligent, and not shy about expressing their opinions, but they were always deferential to Abe. It was as if he were the pope and they made up the college of cardinals. They did not kiss his ring, but when he spoke they listened. Barbara Walters, who was in the midst of a feud with Harry Reasoner, her coanchor at ABC, complained one night about the stories in the press. She said Reasoner was a mean man, jealous of her $1 million salary, and spiteful toward her because she was a woman. Abe did not take any of this seriously; I do not think he could. He told Walters to buck up as if he were pronouncing a benediction.

There was the triumph of print over television in Abe's attitude. The battle was being lost in the larger arena, although one-on-one was still no contest. Walters and her colleagues were not certain what they were—journalists, entertainers, or personalities—but Abe was editor of the *Times,* and that was all the identification he needed. To that older generation of television correspondents, print had a special cachet. They had grown up with print and come to television later. They feared that print was for serious journalists and television was where reporters wore makeup, and they felt ambivalent about what they did. The feeling was appropriate, and it prevented the correspondents from shrugging off all the old precepts of journalism. The generation of correspondents that has grown up with television does not feel this ambivalence; they are more inclined to take the medium solely on its own terms. The media age would be healthier if they did not.

CHAPTER TWELVE

IDEOLOGY
AND THE CULTURE

ichiko Kakutani was one of Arthur Gelb's pro-
tégées. She was gifted and intense, scarcely in
her mid-twenties, and she occupied the desk
next to mine. Michiko wanted more than anything else to be
a book critic, but in 1982 she labored as a reporter, writing
about literary affairs and literary people and literary and cultural matters. She chain-smoked Camels and was barely five
feet tall, and when she sat at her desk, heaped higher than her
head with books, manuscripts, and other debris, she would
have been hidden except for the smoke from the Camels. On
receiving an assignment she would look distressed and say,
''I can't do this,'' so piteously that others would be alarmed.
On the night before the assignment was due, she would write
at her desk until dawn, agonizing over each word. Then,
hours after she had turned in the story, she would reappear in
the office to await an editor's verdict on what she had written, wearing an expression that said she expected the tumbrel. She was, of course, a first-class talent, incapable of
shoddy work, and beneath the hesitancy, despair, and floun-
dering was a firm single-mindedness. When Arthur asked

her to look into charges *The Village Voice* had raised against the novelist Jerzy Kosinski—that he used ghostwriters and was connected to the CIA—she said, as always, "I can't do this," though this time with more feeling. Michiko was under a burden imposed by her peers, and conscious of its pressure. In the New York literary world, Jerzy Kosinski was not a popular man.

For one thing, he was too raffish, too prominent, and too likely to turn up as a guest on *Late Night with David Letterman*. A Victorian might have called him a bounder, without knowing exactly why. There was something about Kosinski—a touch of the garish, a hint of the lurid. Somehow he didn't quite fit. Earlier that year, Arthur's wife, Barbara, had written a cover piece about him for the *Times*'s Sunday magazine. The piece was not bad, although the cover was silly: Kosinski in polo jodhpurs with no shirt on. The bounderism was confirmed. No serious writer would consent to being photographed like that. And for God's sake, the story was written by Arthur's wife—a clear sign of nepotism if ever there was one. It was worse than nepotism, actually; it was the *Times*'s once again promoting the career of someone who was friendly with *Times* editors. Obviously Kosinski was friendly with *Times* editors. Kosinski knew everyone important; bounders always did. Kosinski even referred to Henry Kissinger as "Henry," and that was probably an indictable offense in itself.

When Arthur asked Michiko to look into the accusations in *The Village Voice,* he was placing the world on her shoulders. If she investigated the charges and found they were true, it might not even be a story. What could she write—that an independent investigation by *The New York Times* had confirmed allegations by a left-wing weekly that a prominent Polish-American novelist was a liar and a fraud? Surely Arthur would not want that. Surely he wanted a story that said the *Voice* was dead wrong. The *Voice,* after all, had been braying at the *Times* for years, charging the paper and its editors with a multiplicity of offenses. The *Times* could not possibly publish a story that said the *Voice* was right about Jerzy Kosinski.

Or so Michiko thought; and so she fell into despair, though her thinking was seriously flawed. Kosinski did indeed know *Times* editors, but the acquaintanceships had done him no good. He had never received a favorable book review in the paper, not even for *The Painted Bird,* his first and most enduring novel. The magazine story by Barbara Gelb, a respected biographer and free-lance writer who had written for the magazine for years, had not been particularly laudatory; it said Kosinski was an interesting man, even though some people thought he was spooky. What seemed to weigh most on Michiko, however, was that the charges about the CIA and ghostwriters had been accepted as accurate, if not in all details, then certainly in broad outline, by everyone she knew. There is consensus in the interstices where literature, politics, and journalism meet. Stray from that herd of independent minds and the loneliness can be fearsome. The verdict on Kosinski had been pronounced long before. One way or another, Michiko thought, she was damned: exonerate Kosinski and face the contempt of peers, or indict him and risk the enmity of Abe and Arthur. On that first part, at least, she was prescient.

At the time, I knew only that Michiko was unhappy—a condition relatively common among young reporters, especially the most gifted. They are only as good as their last story, and they are never wholly pleased with what they have done. But this time Michiko's unhappiness was deeper, an inky gloom more palpable than the smoke from her Camels. Ordinary newsroom unhappiness was marked by sighs, scowls, and cries of injustice. Michiko was immobile. She had spent weeks interviewing editors, writers, and Jerzy Kosinski; she had weighed evidence and sought truth, but found only stasis. She did not know how to write the story; she did not know how not to write it, either. She asked me what to do. I told her to write about what she had found. "I can't," she said dejectedly; the tumbrel was approaching. I asked Michiko whether she believed the story in the *Voice*. "There's something to it," she said slowly and painfully. No question now; the tumbrel was here.

I did not know it then, but the story in the *Voice* already had been picked up and commented on by newspapers and magazines around the world. Some had treated it as a literary squabble and some as a joke and some as a serious matter, but none had dismissed it entirely. The emissions had spread like a fat cloud of swamp gas. Kosinski was well-known in Europe, where he lived part of each year and where his books sold better than they did in the United States. Whatever his eccentricities, it was agreed he had something to say. If he was not a major warrior in the world battle of ideas, he was clearly a certified foot soldier. When Solidarity rose in Poland in 1980, Kosinski championed the nascent labor movement, making speeches, giving interviews, and offering encouragement over the Voice of America. When the United Automobile Workers paid a tribute to Solidarity in Washington the next year, he accepted the tribute on Solidarity's behalf. None of this was much noticed in New York, although it was remarked on in Eastern Europe. In Poland, newspapers emboldened by Solidarity's success carried favorable comments about Kosinski, the first ever to appear there. A literary review even published excerpts from *The Painted Bird,* which had been banned for sixteen years. This was the Warsaw spring, but it ended in December 1981, when the new military government imprisoned Solidarity leaders and imposed martial law. On CBS's *60 Minutes,* a uniformed soldier named Wieslaw Gornicki solemnly described the condition for their release: public admission that Poland must remain allied with the Soviet Union.

Kosinski, meanwhile, spoke more often over the Voice of America. Along with other Polish émigré intellectuals, including the Nobel laureate Czeslaw Milosz, he also petitioned West Germany to deny the new Polish government economic loans. As a foot soldier he had a secure place. As a civil libertarian and former president of American PEN, who had worked to free writers and other intellectuals imprisoned under both rightist and leftist regimes, he had moral stature as well. But the *Voice* story ended all that. The indictment could not be woven of whole cloth. There was something to it; there had to be something to it. The *Times* of London even put its account on page one. Italian, French, and West German publications repeated the accusations against Kosinski, and an imaginative few made up some of their own. (*Les Nouvelles Littéraires* in Paris asked why Kosinski carried a gun, had dozens of false identities, and kept tear-gas bombs in his car.) The story turned up also in daily newspapers in Turkey and Japan and Malaysia. In Poland, meanwhile, where the spring had been replaced by hard winter, the government press quoted European and American articles about the *Village Voice* story as proof of what the government had been saying all along: that Kosinski was an inveterate liar. The foot soldier was wiped out.

I knew none of this when I spoke to Michiko that night in the newsroom. I had not read the story in the *Voice,* which had appeared three months before, but as Michiko talked I had a delicious feeling. I knew I wanted to write about Kosinski and what had happened to him more than I had wanted to write anything in years. It is a fine thing to be a newspaperman and know you are about to be consumed. You find a new sense of self and of purpose. A bluebird awakens your soul. You do not mention this in the newsroom, of course. At most, you say you have a good story and try to keep a straight face. The newsroom code requires a neutral decorum. You know from the start you want to get some son of a bitch, and you are certain you can get him, but you are supposed to look disinterested so no one will think you are biased. I yearned to investigate the Kosinski story because I was sure what I would find—my own metaphorical son of a bitch—although the code did not allow me to say so. Besides, it was Michiko's story. I could not ask that it be given to me. The code also rules out poaching. I had no place to go and no license to write until Michiko delivered us both. A few days after we spoke, she went to see Arthur. ''I can't do it,'' she said softly, meaning anything to do with Jerzy Kosinski. This time Arthur believed her. The next day I asked to be assigned to the story.

I had a starting point from which to work. I had known Kosinski when I was at *Harper's*. Late at night he would turn up at Elaine's, the literary bar on Second Avenue where Willie Morris and I whiled away too many evenings. I liked Kosinski very much. He would nurse a glass of wine and talk, firing words in bursts and ricocheting sentences and whole paragraphs off the walls and floor. Then he would fall silent, and suddenly be out the door, taking his puns, epigrams, and dark humor with him. He was witty, charming, and utterly bereft of malice. He was also extraordinarily eccentric. Once he invited me and my wife to dinner at his apartment on West 57th Street. After dinner he told us he had a secret hiding place. If we left him alone for thirty seconds and then came back, he said, we would not be able to find him. My wife and I stepped into the hallway, walked as far as the elevator, and then returned to the apartment. We looked under the bed and in the closets. We examined the furniture, the windows and doors. Kosinski had vanished. I remember being uncomfortable; for some reason I felt embarrassed. Finally, a cupboard door popped open and he unfolded from a shelf, where he had been lying behind some books. No matter where he lived, he said, he always had a hiding place. I had never met a Holocaust survivor before. It was disturbing to meet someone the same age as you who had faced unspeakable horror while you attended first grade. It was better to think of him as merely eccentric.

Once he had missed a connecting flight to Los Angeles, where he was to stay at the home of Sharon Tate and Roman Polanski, because the airline had misplaced his luggage. That night the Charles Manson gang invaded the household and murdered Tate and four others. The next day, Kosinski called the airline again to complain bitterly about the luggage. There were many stories about Kosinski and his adventures and misadventures. You believed some, dismissed others, and treated a few as sly jokes. There were two running jokes in particular: Kosinski worked for the CIA, and ghostwriters wrote his books.

The questions now were, Where had the jokes come from, and why were they reappearing? I was certain Kosinski had been mugged. On the literary-political battleground, he had been living on borrowed time. The year before, 1981, he had been on the wrong side in the argument over Jack Henry Abbott. An imprisoned murderer, Abbott had corresponded with prominent writers, passionately pressing them to adopt his Marxist-Leninist worldview. Norman Mailer and some of the other prominent writers had detected a rare literary talent in Abbott's letters and campaigned to have him released. Kosinski declined to join the campaign; he called Abbott a "misguided leftist." Mailer and his friends persisted, however, and Abbott won his release, a beneficence he repaid by soon thereafter stabbing a young actor to death outside an all-night East Village restaurant where the actor worked as a waiter. In the aftermath, Kosinski spoke of "criminal chic," and said the writers who supported Abbott had been drawn by his ideas and not his talent. Kosinski was moving toward a perilous place on the battleground, and he reached it a few months later.

It happened when *The Nation* sponsored a four-day organizing conference of something called the American Writers

Congress, attended by some three thousand people at the Roosevelt Hotel in New York. A number of famous authors—Mailer, William Styron, E. L. Doctorow, and Kurt Vonnegut among them—had lent the Congress their names, although fastidiousness kept most from appearing. They knew that a gathering of three thousand people who claimed to be writers would include the obsessive, the compulsive, and the demented, even if the Mobil and Ford foundations, *Playboy,* and the National Endowment for the Arts did not. They had given the Congress financial support; their aid was an expression of the cultural death wish that so often has afflicted American institutions in our century. A story in *The Nation* described the "dominant tone" of the conference as "unabashedly and even exuberantly progressive," but *The New Republic* was more accurate: "The Congress was not concerned with literary or cultural questions at all, but was an entirely political undertaking. The principal characteristic of the participants was a virulent hatred of the country for which the American Writers Congress was named." *The New Republic* also quoted Kosinski; he feared the Congress was being "politically exploited." It was, although on the battlefield it was not prudent to say so. Kosinski had passed the point of no return. The only question then was, Who would pick him off first, *The Village Voice* or *The Nation*?

Knowing all this was one thing, though; demonstrating it was another. Could I actually prove Kosinski wrote his own books? It was not likely. How do you prove that, anyway? Michiko's notes were no help—rumors, denials, and thoughts on literary theory. Obviously I would talk to Kosinski, but what could he really say? I had seen him only a few times since the night he unfolded from the cupboard—an encounter on the street, a single dinner party, a Broadway intermission—and wanted to see him again, although I knew he would smell of the gallows. The story in the *Voice* had taken his identity away.

"How can I prove I am not a member of the CIA? How

can I actually prove I have written a book?'' Jerzy said in his apartment. ''Of course I know myself, but who can I point it out to? If I write something, they will put a headline on it: 'Kosinski still insists he writes his own books.' '' Jerzy looked like hell, and when he talked he quivered. Kiki, his wife, said that when he woke up in the mornings he gagged. The worst part, they both said, was the waiting. *The Washington Post* had reported that *The Village Voice* intended to publish ''further allegations and revelations.'' The *Chicago Sun-Times* had reported the same. There would be no end, Jerzy predicted, to the hounding. His publisher in Hamburg had written him just that week, telling him to stay out of West Germany because ''the press will pay more attention to the articles'' inspired by the *Voice* than it would to his last novel. ''There's a venom, a desire to destroy,'' Jerzy said lugubriously. ''They can make up a charge and use it any way they want to. It's as if I'm out on bail. It's the old fear, the fear of a six-year-old. The villagers are still after the little boy—the painted bird.''

Whether I believed all that then was incidental; it was certain that Jerzy believed it himself. The apartment I had visited years before now felt like a bunker: steel shutters on the terrace door, iron bars on the windows, a sense of Stygian gloom. Jerzy was sure someone had tried to break in; he thought somebody would try again. When he and Kiki were in Switzerland the previous winter, he said, someone had read their mail. Moreover, strangers had made inquiries about them in the village where they stayed. Bizarre, I thought. I was in a puzzle factory. I was indeed, but then again, I was also in the twentieth century.

''Kosinski's life and art have been shaped by two of the most cataclysmic movements in the modern world: Nazi Germany and Stalinist Communism,'' the Jesuit magazine *America* once said in an essay. ''From that dual experience, he has survived with very few verities intact.'' No other nov-

elist of his time had so joined his life and art, and no other
novelist had had his life so confused with his art. Kosinski
seemed uncertain about boundaries, too. Critics said his
works were autobiographical; he said they were novels. De-
clare the works pure fiction, however, and he would say everything in them was true. In murk like that, I thought,
perhaps he really did use ghostwriters. I had read *The
Painted Bird, Steps,* and *Being There;* now, on consecutive
nights, I read Kosinski's five other novels. They had the
same voice, same tone, and same sentence structure. It
seemed clear they all had the same author. But what about
The Painted Bird? In the Kosinski mythology, everything
came back to that. The headline in *The Village Voice*—
"Jerzy Kosinski's Tainted Words"—was a reminder. The
Voice said *The Painted Bird* had been written in Polish and
translated into English. If that was so, then Kosinski was not
the author; he said he had written the book in English. I
called the chairman of the Department of Slavic Languages
at the University of Illinois. He had been born in Poland and
was writing a book on literary translation. "When the Slavic
languages are translated, certain seams always show," he
told me. "They don't show in *The Painted Bird.* The book
was written in English." Now, I knew, I could begin. Where
had those rumors started?

I talked to Polish émigrés whose names I could not easily
pronounce, and whose accents I could not always understand, and whose motives I could not necessarily fathom. I
read translations from Polish newspapers, and old files in
English. What I found was gorgeously clear: a trail that
stretched back seventeen years. Kosinski, who fled Poland
in 1957, first published *The Painted Bird* in 1965. It was
about a boy on the run, who wanders from village to village
in an unspecified part of Europe during World War II. I
learned it had caught the attention of a Polish correspondent
at the United Nations named Wieslaw Gornicki. He seemed

to have been quite popular. Unlike other communists, he was thought of as a liberal, virtually Westernized, a man you could sit down with for a drink. He made small talk, was fond of new movies, and invited other correspondents to his home in Forest Hills for dinner. They gave him a nickname: "Slavic."

Gornicki, of course, was an intelligence officer, the same man who turned up years later in an army uniform on *60 Minutes* and declared the imprisoned Solidarity leaders had to accept Soviet hegemony over Poland. In 1965, though, he specialized in monitoring the activities of émigré Poles. Kosinski, meanwhile, was not just an émigré Pole; he was an anticommunist Pole, and so he had to be discredited. Gornicki filed stories for PAP, the Polish press agency, that said *The Painted Bird* slandered Poles and glorified Germans. The novel did not, but no matter. Gornicki's superiors in Warsaw recognized a good thing when they saw one. Kosinski, they decided, would have his uses. The Communist press in Poland began to build on Slavic's stories: Kosinski had left his homeland under mysterious circumstances; his American wife had influence in the United States Senate; *The Painted Bird* had been published as part of a larger plan. Bits and pieces of disinformation were scattered about and then arranged in a mosaic. Kosinski, the propagandists eventually said, had been a CIA man all along. The agency had published *The Painted Bird* as part of its campaign to help West Germany obtain nuclear weapons. At the end of 1966, the Warsaw correspondent of *The New York Times* reported that *The Painted Bird,* though unpublished in Poland, "was being written about and talked about with near-obsessive insistence."

The deeper I dug, the more I uncovered. The Polish accusations might have been fantastic—Kosinski supposedly was connected not just to the CIA but to a Zionist conspiracy as well—but they hung in the stale communist air until liter-

ary winds dispersed random whiffs. When had I heard the
jokes at Elaine's about Jerzy using ghostwriters? I reckoned
it was 1970. The year before, Gornicki had charged in a Polish magazine that Kosinski had hired ''an authentic English-
man with an Oxford education'' to write his books for him. I
remembered once hearing that Kosinski had plagiarized a
Polish novel when he wrote *Being There;* Michiko even had
the rumor in her notes. Now I discovered the story was the
invention of a communist literary magazine. The campaign
to discredit Kosinski had gone on for years, fitful and un-
even but never dying, carried along by mindless inertia. In
1979 an English professor from Iowa visited Poland for
eleven days as the happy beneficiary of a cultural exchange.
He said later he had been ''deluged'' with stories about
Kosinski: how he had plagiarized other works for *The
Painted Bird* and *Being There;* how his accounts of fleeing
Poland were ''utter fabrications''; how, in short, nothing he
said could be trusted. Inspired, the English professor wrote
an article he playfully titled ''Betrayed by Jerzy Kosinski''
and circulated it among his literary friends and colleagues.

Harper's had taught me about the literary community. It
was fun to hang out there, but a poor place to find worldly
wisdom. As political activists its members were on the left, a
respectable place to be occasionally, but one they reached so
unerringly the journey required no thinking. Here and there
a well-known writer—the novelist Saul Bellow, for example, or the playwright Tom Stoppard—might take a position
contrary to that of his peers, but he would do so as an individual and not as part of a group. When artists and writers
acted collectively to make their views known, the views
were left of center. Little dissent was tolerated and very little
was found, and apostates faced exile or worse. I was ap-
palled by what had happened to Kosinski, but I was fascinated by how it was done. I could write now about
something that had interested me since the night Midge

Decter and I had talked in the Chinese restaurant while we waited for Larry King and Willie Morris: how lies and disinformation may be spread by, and through, an unfortunately politicized culture.

So I wrote and I wrote. My God, did I write: 6,000 words, at least, on my worn, tired portable Olivetti. If the *Times* published 6,000 words about Jerzy Kosinski and his travail, it would be an event, not so much a news story as a statement. I did not think of it that way; hindsight would tell me I should have. I gave the story to Arthur, and he read it and gave it to Abe. "I don't know how you did it," Abe said admiringly, and shook my hand. We were friends, we were colleagues, we shared the same worldview. Abe hated the mindless wounding of Kosinski, and I despised the forces that did the wounding. Now and then the left might be caught in a particularly outrageous lie, but it was seldom penalized or even chided, and so often it had a free ride. I was certain I would now change that. Abe made one or two corrections in the piece, then gave it back to Arthur. Arthur wanted more about Kosinski's celebrity status in the lead, and more about his personal eccentricities in the next few pages. I complied, but only grudgingly. I had never worked as hard on a story before, and I was wedded to it exactly as written. Meanwhile, I had given the *Times* a problem. What the hell was it supposed to do with an article now grown to 6,500 words? It was too long for the daily edition. Somehow it didn't seem like a piece for the Sunday magazine. I suggested it run in the Sunday book review and said I would trim it to fit the space. Abe pondered and then decided it would appear uncut and undiluted in the Sunday Arts and Leisure section. He wrote the headline himself: "17 Years of Attack on a Cultural Target."

When the section was printed, on a Wednesday night, a few editors who saw early copies told me I had done a terrific job. The next day one editor shook my hand. "I don't

know how you did it," he said. I suspected he had picked up
the words from Abe. The *Times* was run in part by osmosis,
and when Abe expressed enthusiasm (or displeasure), the
mood rippled downward and outward. I should have been
surprised that more editors did not congratulate me than did.

After the story appeared on Sunday, a silence crept into
the newsroom. My colleagues were holding their breath.
Why was the *Times* carrying 6,500 words about Jerzy
Kosinski? Other reporters looked at me strangely; something was not quite right. "I saw you were all over the paper
yesterday," a close friend said to me on Monday. I remembered we once had discussed what to say to an actor who
turned in a lousy performance on opening night. You could
not hurt the actor's feelings; you could not lie to him, either.
We decided you should grip his hand and say, "Well, you
did it again," and then move quickly away. My close friend
was now moving quickly away down an aisle in the newsroom. That was not a good sign. The silence was settling in
more deeply. Reporters love gossip, and while they are paid
to deal in facts, they are enchanted by rumor and speculation. When one *Times* reporter asked another "What's
new?" it always signified the same thing: Who was up, who
was down, and what was the newsroom gossip? Reporters
and editors who had known one another a long time could
reduce the question to a single word: "Well?" The variant
was "So?"—asked expectantly, with raised eyebrows. Everyone knew what you meant.

There was a lot of this in the newsroom that week, although no one asked me "What's new?" because what was
new was me, or at least the argument now going on around
me. Opinion was divided. I had been forced to write the
story because Kosinski was a friend of Abe's and Arthur's,
and the *Times* wanted to punish the *Voice*; Abe was using
the *Times* to push his anticommunist views, and I was a willing accomplice. This second opinion was less widely held

than the first, although in its way it was almost the truth. As a foreign correspondent in the late 1950s, Abe had been based for a while in Poland. He had despised its brutal regime, and the regime had despised him; it eventually expelled him for "exposing too deeply the internal situation in Poland." For his coverage, Abe won a Pulitzer.

The *Voice,* meanwhile, appeared with its expected rebuttal: a long story by its editor, which I did not read, and a nasty piece by its most prominent columnist, which I did. The columnist was Alexander Cockburn, son of the late Claud Cockburn, a British leftist whom I visited in the seventies at a crumbling manor in Ireland. He told me his wife was a member of the Anglo-Irish aristocracy and that the manor had been in her family for years. He went on to talk about the Irish Republican Army and the schism in its ranks between the Regulars and the Provisionals. The Regulars believed the IRA should attack only military targets; the Marxist Provisionals thought it permissible to kill civilians. Cockburn defended the Provisionals while we sat in the garden outside his house that day, and I thought him an immoral man. Orwell alludes to Cockburn in *Homage to Catalonia,* the book about the Spanish Civil War that I had read years before in Greenwich Village. Cockburn, who wrote for various publications, also filed stories under a pseudonym for the communist press, smearing the anti-Stalinist left in Spain as tools of Trotsky and Hitler. Orwell dismissed him as a Stalinist flack. Cockburn hated Orwell for having exposed him; that day in Ireland he vilified my hero. I was pleased when I read his son's column in the *Voice* attacking me. It seemed like a laying on of hands—Orwell and the father and now the son and me. I thought I had stepped into history.

After the *Voice* came *The Nation,* predictable and expected, and saying much the same, but with a better grasp of what was important. *The Nation* said I could teach journalism students "how to practice innuendo, sly insinuation and

the use of irrelevant evidence and invidious comparison.''
Then it recognized the real topic: "The material for *The Village Voice*'s article . . . is made to seem a product of the Polish Communist disinformation mill.'' Well, of course; that was my intention. *The Nation,* however, only mentioned this and then dropped it. In all the outraged discussion to come, that part would always be dropped. That a communist disinformation mill might influence an American publication was a subject beyond the pale. The media accepted the idea that Western sources could manipulate communist thinking, but declined to believe it might ever happen the other way around.

Still, I did think I was ahead. Any sensible person would dismiss the *Voice* and *The Nation.* But that week *The New Republic,* an infinitely more respectable organ, also weighed in. It said the *Times* and I owed the *Voice* an apology. Since I admired *The New Republic,* I felt disappointed, although by now there was no time to feel anything for very long. A *Newsweek* reporter called and asked me whether it was true that Michiko had been removed from the Kosinski story for refusing to write what she had been told to write, and that I had been ordered to write it instead. I knew the *Newsweek* reporter, who once had worked at the *Times,* and told him the suggestion was insulting. Then he got angry and I got angry and one of us slammed down the phone. Subsequently, the silence in the newsroom grew thicker. By tradition and custom, and because they are naturally cheap, reporters prefer to pass around Xerox copies of stories rather than go out and buy the whole publications. There were copies of the *Voice, Nation,* and *New Republic* articles all over the newsroom. Nothing is as engrossing as a scandal, and a big one was taking shape.

At the end of the week, Abe and I sought each other out. He said he was disappointed by what he had been hearing. I said it could be worse, and I was proved right. Arthur called me at home on Sunday night. He had just seen an advance copy of *Newsweek.* "You won't like it," he said, meaning the two-page story that graced the new issue. In fact, the magazine was harder on him and Abe than it was on me, and Arthur was being kind. *Newsweek* had broken the big-media code. Big-media organizations might hint at one another's indiscretions or revel in one another's misfortunes, but the code ruled out public brawling. Most of all, big-media organizations did not question the integrity of the people who ran the other big-media organizations. *Newsweek,* however, declared the editors were running the *Times* as a private preserve and not as a responsible paper. "The Kosinski piece provided the most dramatic evidence to date of their willingness to use the power of the *Times* to reward friends and punish enemies," the *Newsweek* article said, and explained that Kosinski was a friend and the *Voice* was an enemy, and I had been told to write what I wrote accordingly. "Corry says he was terribly eager to write the article," *Newsweek* reported dryly. I seemed to be not only a sycophant but a poor liar, too.

The attack was unsettling. The country's greatest newspaper was being told its ethics were bent, its news columns sullied, and its reputation for probity tainted. The substance of my story was covered in only two sentences. *Newsweek* reported it in this way: "The article suggested that a piece that appeared last June in *The Village Voice* questioning whether Kosinski was the sole author of all his books had been indirectly inspired by a smear campaign conducted by the Polish Communist Government. Neither the *Voice* nor the *Times* provided conclusive evidence on the question of authorship." That was it. *Newsweek* would no more comment directly on the story than would *The Nation.* Certain topics were out of bounds. The lofty pronouncement that "neither the *Voice* nor the *Times* provided conclusive evidence on the question of authorship" was media equivocation. The *Voice* had not proved that Kosinski did not write his own books, and the *Times* had not proved that he did. The burden of proof, therefore, was still on Kosinski, who must be considered guilty until he somehow established his innocence. *Newsweek* brushed him aside while it declared war on the *Times*.

Or more specifically, on Abe and Arthur and me. And while I was a lesser target, I clearly was stuck in the trenches. We coordinated defensive tactics that night by phone. I was furious because *Newsweek* had said I was told to write the story and supinely had acquiesced about what it should say. Abe was shaken because the *Times* was his church and reporting his religion and he had been accused of breaking his vows. Arthur was upset because *Newsweek* had said Barbara was involved. Whatever the individual wounds, though, it was best not to show them. The newsroom was a stage, with hundreds of reporters, editors, news assistants, clerks, and secretaries all functioning as theater critics. A scowl would give you away; a grimace would be your undoing. Appearance was what counted.

So I presented myself in the newsroom at the start of the week, although only to show my flag and pretend nothing important had happened. It was hard. The Xerox machines that had strained the week before with the *Voice, The Nation,* and *The New Republic* almost ruptured themselves that morning with *Newsweek.* Everyone had a copy of the article; the usual procedure was followed. When reading an unflattering story about their paper, *Times* people did so surreptitiously. They put the story on their laps or held it under their desks; they camouflaged it inside other papers or took it to the bathroom to peruse. One young reporter read his copy so avidly at a urinal in the men's room that when he looked up and saw me next to him, he was so startled he peed on the floor. It was a very long day. I read my mail, made needless calls, and several times walked the length of the newsroom just to show I could do it. On a hunch I got *The Washington Post.* Why, of course; there it was. The headline on the story was "*New York Times* Articles on Kosinski Questioned." The last is a wonderful media word; it suggests something is wrong without requiring anyone to say what. The *Post* wanted to embarrass the *Times,* and now it could quote *Newsweek.* Ben Bradlee wanted to annoy Abe, and this was too good to pass up.

It was all very personal. Cultural-political warfare always is, especially when the players know one another. The same morning I encountered David Halberstam outside the *Times,* I saw Harrison Salisbury in the newsroom. When he was national editor of the *Times,* I was his deputy and at least we were collegial. That morning, however, he stared right through me. He wanted no part of a man so clearly wrong as I. In fact, my side seemed to have no adherents at all, save Abe and Arthur and Jerzy, and Jerzy had become incidental. The integrity of the *Times* was now at stake. The Sunday editors wanted to print a sampling of letters from readers, but they had a dilemma. Their practice was to print letters both pro and con, and while con was no problem, pro was in short supply. One editor suggested I promote some favorable mail by asking friends to write. I would have, but I had no idea whom to ask.

Nonetheless, there were secret stirrings. Cultural-political warfare always has its own subtext. Henry Kissinger called Abe and congratulated him on the story. He said it was "brave" of the *Times* to run it; he knew the trouble it would cause. Tell him to write a letter, I suggested, although I did not think the former secretary of state would. Then Zbigniew Brzezinski, national security adviser under Jimmy Carter, passed word he approved of the story, too. Terrific, I thought, but I wished he would go public and say so. The most provocative call came from Senator David Patrick Moynihan. Corry was right, he told Abe; Kosinski was not

involved with the CIA. I never had thought Jerzy was, of
course, and while I was pleased to have this confirmed, I
also wished Moyhnihan would write a letter. The liberal
Democrat was co-chairman of the Senate Select Committee
on Intelligence, and like Kissinger and Brzezinski, he knew
about the effectiveness of communist propaganda. But also
like Kissinger and Brzezinski, he knew there was no profit in
talking about it out loud. Respectable public figures did not
antagonize the left unless it was absolutely necessary, and
they tried not to antagonize the media under any circumstances at all. Moynihan, Kissinger, and Brzezinski might
applaud fervently and speak encouragingly, but it was not
bloody likely they would allow themselves to be heard. It
was getting hard to hold up my head in the newsroom.

The atmosphere was dreary. Old friends grinned word-
lessly, not knowing what to say, while reporters and editors I
barely knew shuffled papers on their desks when I passed.
The boldest raised their eyes and looked at me the way you
might look at leftovers from last night's dinner. Once, when
I was a copyboy, I had looked that way at Bill Conklin, a
sportswriter who covered unimportant ball games. Before
that, however, he had covered politics. Conklin had been ex-
iled to sports, or so I was told, because he supported Joseph
McCarthy and had found ways of bending his political stories to reflect the senator's views. I had avoided conversation with Conklin, thinking him soiled, possibly nutty, no
one I wanted to know. Now it was twenty-five years later
and young Harvard graduates felt the same about me. They
should all have this happen to them, I thought sourly, although I knew in my heart that if circumstances were different I might have been on their side. The young Harvard
graduates could think for themselves, but there was no reason for them to do so. Sensible people might take issue, but
sensible people knew enough not to say so. After that *Newsweek* story appeared, Henry Grunwald, the editor in chief of

Time magazine, dispatched a reporter to interview me; *Time* wanted to run its own piece. The reporter was sympathetic and wrote a favorable story, but it was never published. Grunwald had second thoughts. Before becoming a journalist, the reporter had been a CIA man. Grunwald feared that if *Time* published a story upholding the *Times,* other publications would rake up the reporter's past and suggest a *Time–*CIA connection. What the hell, I thought; Grunwald probably was right.

Meanwhile, the *Voice* struck again; so did *The Nation* and *The New Republic.* The Xerox machines once again got jammed. Would no one support me publicly? It turned out someone would, although I was not sure he counted. William Safire, the *Times* political columnist, wrote a piece endorsing my story and criticizing *The Washington Post* and *Newsweek.* In the torrent of words being thrown about, his were the first—and would be the only ones—to discuss what had happened to Kosinski. My story, Safire wrote, showed "what professional savaging an outspokenly anti-Communist writer could expect from the insular crowd that dominates New York's ideological-cultural establishment." He was exactly right. But I knew the insular crowd he had mentioned; it would pay no attention to him. Safire had written speeches for Richard Nixon. That week Mike Wallace and his wife gave a dinner party, with guests from culture and the media invited. They discussed the hot topic: the *Times,* Kosinski, and me. Everybody at the dinner table had something to say. One guest, the dean of the Columbia School of Journalism, declared that Safire and I were "fascists." I am told reliably that none of the other guests objected.

That was the way it was in high media circles: an orthodox faith defended by orthodox custodians who sometimes became vituperative. They did not always mean what they said—the dean, I suppose, had had a few drinks—but their feelings were clear and their souls untroubled and their minds made up in advance. They took positions without being forced to defend them and they lived by faith and not reason. They were not always wrong and they often did the country good service, but they really did think alike. Mike Wallace, David Halberstam, Harrison Salisbury, and the dean of the Columbia School of Journalism might disagree on whether it was better to spend August on Nantucket or in the Hamptons, but they would be unanimous on Mondale over Reagan and Dukakis over Bush and on whether the Supreme Court should uphold affirmative action. The foreign editors of *Newsweek* and *The Washington Post* and the executive producers of the evening news programs might not all want to join the same golf club, but they would all oppose aid to the contras. Somewhere there might have been a film critic who did not think the CIA overthrew Salvador Allende of Chile and somewhere there might have been a book-review editor who favored nuclear power and somewhere there might even have been a documentary filmmaker who liked Margaret Thatcher. On the other hand, I never actually met any.

The crisis wound down as media crises always do, in confusion and with sour feelings. I stopped counting my unfavorable mentions and decided to pull up my socks. I had been around too long and was too good a journalist to think anyone could drive me out of the business, even if a *Washington Post* columnist did write that I was "stupid," as I read before I stopped counting. I was part of a profession that struck and moved on, and I knew the Kosinski affair would turn into a footnote, probably incorrect but seldom consulted, and unimportant to anyone except the participants. I wondered whether it would mention Michiko. We had barely spoken since the night Arthur took her off the story. She began to work at home and call her stories in by phone. The few times I saw her she said very little, and after my story appeared she said nothing at all.

One afternoon she came to the office to listen to messages on her answering machine. I could not help but hear. The messages were from reporters who were working on their own stories about the *Times* and Jerzy Kosinski. They understood Michiko had been removed from her story for refusing to follow orders and that then I was assigned; they wanted the scandalous details. Michiko switched off the answering machine and got up to leave. Wait, I said; you must call back and tell them those things aren't true. "I . . . I can't," Michiko said. You must, I said; if you don't, that terrible stuff will get all around. "John," she said, "I just can't get involved." Michiko looked more stricken than ever, and her eyes welled up with tears. Sadly she left the newsroom. A few weeks later, a grim Arthur told me Michiko had just announced she was quitting to work for *Time* magazine. Consequently, the *Times* was going to promote her from reporter to book critic and also give her a raise. "If she resigns," Arthur said, "everyone will say we forced her to leave. It will confirm all those goddamn stories." Actually, it all worked out for the best. Michiko's book reviews are now some of the best things in the *Times*.

THE LAST TIME AROUND

J n 1982, I remarried, stopped drinking, and became a television critic—three events all interconnected, although perhaps not in obvious ways. My new wife, Sonia Landau, was a Republican. I point out the identification only to note how exotic that made her in the world in which I lived. I had never met a Republican in the newsroom, and I would have been surprised if I had. I suspect that no one I knew at the *Times* other than the art critic Hilton Kramer had voted for Ronald Reagan, and Hilton left soon afterward to edit a magazine. Reagan supporters were poorly represented in the news trade. Few occupied places of prominence, and the ones who did had about them a vague air of disrepute or eccentricity, and were mysteries to their colleagues. When Sonia, who worked in the 1980 presidential campaign, invited me to attend the inaugural ceremonies in Washington, I did so with mixed feelings. I wanted to see what an inauguration was like, but I was uncomfortable with the idea of crowning a former movie actor as president, and reluctant to grace the occasion. The feeling persisted through the first few days of inaugural activities. Washington was full of rich Californians with great smiles who all seemed to have flown in from another planet. By the time Reagan was sworn in, I had had enough of jostling crowds and group gaiety, and I insisted to Sonia that we stay indoors and watch the parade on television. The parade was the usual—marching bands, sheriffs' posses, and dancing palominos until the very end. Then the Mormon Tabernacle Choir pulled up on a huge float in front of Ronald Reagan. The choir sang "The Battle Hymn of the Republic," and a camera zoomed in on the new president's face. I could see his eyes were teary. It occurred to me then that he was more in touch with himself and the rest of the country than were his critics, and that in a pale, thin-blooded time, he was real.

Sonia had been initiated into politics in California, when she and Shirley MacLaine were the state's two Golden Girls for Kennedy. Then she became disenchanted with the Los Angeles Democratic machine and changed party registration. Eventually she found her way to Washington, where she got a job directing radio and television services for Republican congressmen. The Nixon White House admired her work and drafted her for "CREEP"—the Committee to Re-Elect the President—and told her she would share an office with Jeb Magruder. Her first morning there she met E. Howard Hunt, and was touched by a murky foreboding. She resigned from CREEP before noon. Magruder and Hunt, of course, eventually went to jail.

Sonia was not ideological, and she saw politics not in the absolute moral terms in which it was regarded by amateurs, but instead in the laissez-faire manner of professionals. She knew politics was a game best played with a sense of humor. You did not take politicians as seriously as they took themselves, but you did observe certain rules. Deals were made on a handshake, and a politician's word was his bond until he broke it. Sonia once took me to a function where Richard Nixon was the honored guest. She could not bring herself, however, to join the line of people waiting to shake his hand. Her aversion to Nixon had less to do with any high crimes or misdemeanors than it did with his being an untrustworthy man. Sonia told me she could never forget the tears in the eyes of Republican congressmen who had believed his assurances and then discovered he was lying; she could never forgive him for that. I always thought Sonia had politics in perspective.

Meanwhile, the drinking. I had been using alcohol as an anesthetic for years, and realized I had to stop. I had never collapsed into a gutter, or beaten up either of my wives or my children, but I was drilling holes in my brain. One day, sick with a hangover, I could not make sentences say what I wanted them to say in an otherwise routine story. Years of steady drinking have caught up to me, I thought, and it is essential now that I stop. In fact, I did stop, for perhaps two weeks, and then I went back. Soon I was drunk again. One night I was reading the annotated *Alice in Wonderland,* a bottle of Dewar's at my side, and when I finished the book and stood up from my chair I fell facedown on the floor. I had finished the bottle of Dewar's. Two days later I went to McLean Hospital in Belmont, Massachusetts, to talk to an old friend, Shervert Frazier, McLean's psychiatrist in chief. I told him I feared I could not stop drinking. He said he had been waiting to hear me say that for years. He also said I should check into McLean. Absolutely not, I said, overcome with shame at the thought. My Irish Protestant sense of propriety was reeling. I knew people I suspected of being alcoholics, but surely I was not like them.

A few days later, though, I did check into the hospital, leaving behind me in New York a vague story about having to undergo treatment for a bad back. Arthur saw through that in approximately the time it took poor Sonia to tell it, and the next day he and Abe were on the phone to McLean, wishing me luck and telling me to stay as long as I chose. I stayed

five weeks, and I was almost sorry to leave. McLean is a
mental hospital, and although I was in the unit that treated
alcoholics, Dr. Frazier encouraged me to move about and
talk to other patients. I did, and met some very nice people.
Patients in a mental hospital are without pretense or vanity,
and have very little to prove. They have renounced the competitive instinct and can look at the world quite plain. I was
drinking coffee in the hospital cafeteria one day when a
young man in a black T-shirt walked in. "Maniac," it said in
white letters across the front of the shirt. The patients at the
next table applauded.

I became enormously fond of my fellow drunks. Eighteen
of us lived together in an old frame house. We were of all
ages and backgrounds, and instant partners in one another's
travails. The most important rule we observed was: No
lying. A new patient who denied he was an alcoholic was
treated with short shrift. If he was not a drunk, then why was
he in a hospital? Usually the recalcitrant patient would then
come around nicely. Once a week we played patients from
another unit in softball. In the game I recall most fondly, our
opponents were male drug addicts in their teens and early
twenties. Our pitcher was a one-legged man in his fifties,
and one of our outfielders a woman in her sixties. Our short-
stop was a lovely girl of eighteen who had been expelled
from a Catholic boarding school after someone found vodka
bottles in her room. In the first two innings, the drug addicts
scored a dozen runs, while our side panted, stumbled, and
generally looked foolish. In the third inning, however, the
drug addicts allowed their attention to wander. In the fourth,
they began fighting among themselves. We drunks won after
five innings. I have not had a drink since I left McLean and,
most remarkable, have never seriously missed alcohol.

WHEN I RETURNED to the newsroom, my colleagues followed
the rules. No one asked where I had been or what I had been

doing. I told some, of course, but for the most part it was as if I had not been away. The only thing altered was I. I saw no marked change in my interior landscape, but I did become restless. The first story I wrote after returning was about the actress Colleen Dewhurst. She was an old friend and she was opening in a new play, and Arthur, thinking it would be pleasant for me, told me to write about her for the Sunday paper. I did, and while it was a joy to see Colleen again, my restlessness was not assuaged. I had written about the theater and theater people before. Sobriety meant I should do something different. I had covered politics and the police, written "About New York," worked on desks, had a plethora of general-assignment stories, and been a cultural-news reporter. For a while, I had written a Broadway column and reviewed off-Broadway plays. My sense of self was bound up with my being able to move into different worlds. My worth was commensurate with my ability to change roles and perspectives. Journalists are like actors. They slip into parts assigned them, and transform themselves to fit. My pride was the width of my range. I was sure I could work in more diverse areas than anyone else in the newsroom. I once wrote about an unfortunate young violinist whose corpse had been found at Lincoln Center one morning. Then I flew to Connecticut in a small plane and reviewed the musical *Little Johnny Jones* at the Goodspeed Opera House the same evening. I was proud of myself for days.

Eventually I went to see Abe. I do not want to go back on the street as a reporter, I told him, and I have no interest in being an editor; I want to be able to draw together all my experience and do something different, perhaps analysis or commentary. It was a heartfelt plea, although it did wander off at the end. I was saying that I wanted a new job, but I had no idea what new job it was I wanted. There was, however, a thought I had left unexpressed. I knew a middle-aged reporter could wake up one day and find he was being sent out on assignments by an editor younger than his children. This upset nature's balance, and I did not want it to happen to me. One way to escape it would be to develop a specialty that let me move about on my own. I also knew that old reporters with no place to hide could end up on night rewrite or covering suburban news. The dreary possibilities implicit in aging had helped inspire my plea to Abe, who, noncommittally, said he would think about it. The next day Arthur called. Go see Abe, he said; you are now a television critic. Abe told me I would specialize in reviewing news programs and documentaries, and that when I did I would apply ''journalistic standards.'' Neither of us talked about what that meant. Either you understood journalistic standards or you did not, and Abe assumed that I did.

A few words now about newspaper critics: To begin with, they are really reviewers and not critics. Daily journalism does not give a critic enough time to think, and even if it did, his first allegiance still would be to his publication and not to whatever it is he writes about. Intelligent, literate, and thoughtful reviews do indeed appear in newspapers—certainly they appeared in the *Times*—but most newspaper criticism is a guide for consumers: Should they see a play or movie, and does the critic like it or not? Newspaper critics are more likely to be remembered for snappy one-liners— She ran the gamut of emotions from A to B, say, or Such and such a play opened last night; why?—than for thoughtful artistic or philosophical judgments. The pressure of deadlines means critics seldom have time to form them.

As for the influence critics have on what they write about, it varies from slender to none, although the commercial impact may be considerable. Frank Rich, the *Times* theater critic, can make or break a play whose prospects are otherwise marginal, and he can, to some extent, determine which plays will appear. A producer who thinks of bringing a new play to Broadway will think also of Frank: Is this the kind of play that will please him? Frank is the most powerful

critic at the *Times*. Its movie critics may not have great impact on movies made for mass audiences, but they determine
the fate of foreign films or art films, which have limited appeal. Music critics, by contrast, review performances that
will never be heard again. Their most terrible power is their
ability to further, or retard, the careers of young artists.
Dance critics function in much the same way, although their
reviews are read far more avidly in the dance world than
they are by the general public. The *Times* also employs
book, art, architecture, and photography critics and, increasingly, critics who track the excrescences of popular culture—performance art, for example, or heavy metal or
rap—and find in them an artistic significance that surely
would escape the other critics.

As a television critic, I was unlike anybody else. For one
thing, I was invisible. Theater critics sat in aisle seats and
pretended to be unnoticed, while producers, press agents,
and investors tried to read their expressions. As soon as a
play was over and the audience had started to applaud, the
critics all ran up the aisle and out of the theater. They appeared to be facing urgent deadlines, even when they were
merely going home to bed. Critics were celebrities, instantly
recognized but only deferentially approached in concert
halls, art galleries, screening rooms, or theaters. I watched
television at home with our dog, while Sonia was in a room
somewhere else.

I was surprised at how quickly I got into trouble. My first
Sunday piece suggested that television journalism was not
all that it should be. Deep in the piece I said that *60 Minutes*
had not proved its case when it accused the World Council
of Churches of channeling funds to left-wing African guer-
rillas. In a guest column in *Newsweek* a few weeks later,
Don Hewitt, the executive producer of *60 Minutes,* said I reminded him of a ''dog salivating to a bone.'' He said I
should not write about television, because I knew nothing

about it. I had met Hewitt a few times in the past. Perhaps, I thought, he had just been having a bad day when he read my Sunday story. After all, *60 Minutes*—which supposedly accounted for one-fourth of CBS profits—had pioneered in ambush journalism. The program specialized in the hunt, the chase, and the running down of the quarry, and usually left it for dead. It did not seem appropriate that the show's creator should object when someone criticized *60 Minutes*. Nonetheless, shortly after the column in *Newsweek* appeared, Hewitt was at it again, this time in a speech to an organization of newspaper editors. He left out the part about the dog and the bone, but still insisted I knew nothing about television and should not be allowed to write about it. In a way, he was right. I really did not know much about television, although I was learning about the people who worked in it, especially those at CBS. They were easily distressed and inordinately sensitive to criticism.

Although I had been assigned to nonfiction television, I reviewed entertainment programs whenever I could. Hollywood filmmakers poached on the news, but without being subject to the discipline that presenting the news required. *The Day After,* a three-hour movie on ABC about a nuclear holocaust, was a ripe example. ABC invited sympathetic parties to private screenings in the weeks before the movie was shown. The network and the filmmakers insisted the movie was nonpolitical. Still, the nuclear-freeze movement began to promote it and politicians leaped to endorse it. One congressman from Massachusetts announced on the floor of the House that *The Day After* would be "the most powerful television program in history." My younger daughter called from boarding school to say the students would watch it en masse, and then talk about what they had seen. Favorable publicity about the movie was substantial. When I saw it, however, I thought that as a drama it was lame, and as a cautionary tale confused. It introduced the principal characters, and then blew some up, and allowed the rest to die of radiation poisoning. Physicians for Social Responsibility, one of the groups recommending the movie, had said many viewers would react with "feelings of depression and helplessness." It also said that these feelings were "appropriate" and that the best way to cope with them would be to work for a nuclear freeze. ABC and the people who made *The Day After* were being disingenuous when they insisted it was non-political. The movie clearly stated that we had to get rid of nuclear weapons, even if no one else did. Surely, I thought, journalistic standards could be applied here. A journalist was supposed to give both sides of an issue, and so my review included the case for arming and not disarming. One way to deter a holocaust, I wrote, would be to have an arsenal large enough to deter the Soviets from launching their missiles in the first place.

The Day After attracted one of the biggest audiences in television history, and ABC broadcast a panel discussion when it was over. Henry Kissinger, William Buckley, and Carl Sagan, among others, took part. As I listened, I realized they had read my review. It was influencing their discussion. I was pleased to think I could speak with such authority, even if the authority was not mine; it belonged to the *Times,* which had only entrusted it to me for temporary custody. If I had been writing for *The Cincinnati Enquirer,* for instance, Henry Kissinger would have paid no attention. The *Times,* however, was a way station in Scotty Reston's triangle, and so my voice was heard. Indeed, it was amplified all out of proportion.

Shortly afterward I saw another ABC movie, *Something About Amelia,* a sensitive and responsible work, or so the network and filmmakers said, about incest. Most other critics agreed with the filmmakers. They used words like "candor," "maturity," and "reality," and they said the movie eschewed the usual television "pap." Incest, apparently, was not pap. It was the real thing, and the fact that television would deal with it was taken as a sign of the medium's increasing maturity. Actually, this said more about declining morality and the slough we were sinking into than it did about the movie. *Something About Amelia* insisted that the father, played by Ted Danson, should not be blamed for molesting his daughter, Amelia; the poor man could not help it. As a knowledgeable psychiatrist told the stricken mother (Glenn Close), "He probably had an enormous need that he was unable to fill in any other way." The psychiatrist enlarged on this when he comforted Amelia. She had to understand that Dad had made a mistake, but certainly he was no pervert. "What these men yearn for is comfort, warmth, security, intimacy," the psychiatrist explained. Then, after a long pause, he added, "And love."

Neither *Something About Amelia* nor *The Day After* was the thoughtful work it was supposed to be, but both were similar in spirit to so many television programs I would see in the years to come. *Something About Amelia* had a moral vacuity at its core. It said a wicked or immoral act was to be understood and not censured. *The Day After* was full of political mush. Ostensibly the movie examined the most pressing issue of our time, but it presented such a despairing picture it prevented clear thinking about the issue. It seemed to me that television, or at least the part that sought to instruct us on moral issues or matters of national security, had less to do with the world it pretended to mirror than it did with specious visions of what that world ought to be.

Whatever the intermittent problems I might have been having with Don Hewitt and other television people, I was for a while having a greater problem at the *Times*. Abe wanted me to apply journalistic standards to television, and his wishes, even when barely hinted at, were passed on from editor to editor until they solidified into inviolable rules that assumed the force of law. Editors would act on what they thought he thought or might just possibly think when he read the paper. They knew he had installed me as nonfiction television critic and was watching what I would do. Therefore they watched me, too. I would turn in a review to the copy desk; then the news desk would ask to see it. Eventually an assistant managing editor would read it and look worried. I would be told to change a phrase, delete a paragraph, or modify a conclusion. Most of my reviews were of news programs, and I was treading in sensitive areas. The *Times* was a news organization, and it was chary of criticizing other news organizations. Once or twice the vice-chairman of the *Times* board even asked to see what I was writing. I had more editors overseeing me than did anyone else at the paper, and I hated it.

A critic was supposed to criticize, but I seemed to make everyone uncomfortable when I did. One day I turned in a review for the Sunday paper about a two-hour television movie: Aliens who were really lizards had captured earth and turned it into a slave colony. To show serious purpose, the movie also worked in allusions to El Salvador, Nicaragua, and the Holocaust. The first editor who looked at the review asked for minor revisions. I grumbled but made them. Then three more editors read the review and wrote in questions they thought should be answered: What did I mean by this, and how could I justify that, and wasn't something else ambiguous? The review was only about 1,200 words, but they inserted seventy-six questions. The hell with it, I decided, and swept into Abe's office. "I quit," I said. I told Abe the editors were killing me, and I no longer wished to be a television critic. "Do you think they're overreacting because of me?" he asked mildly. "Yes," I answered, and left his office. He must have made a phone call then. By the time I returned to the Sunday department, the seventy-six questions had disappeared, and the review had been sent up to the composing room.

That ended that, although there was one other big interne-
cine battle ahead. I wanted to write about the 1984 election,
and how it was fought out on television. The Reagan–Bush
campaign had summoned Sonia to Washington and put her
in charge of the women's vote. Her first act was to tell conservative Republican women she would welcome them into
the national campaign only if they did not talk about abortion. They agreed, and abortion never became an issue.
Sonia had a practical intelligence that guided her through
political thickets. I would call her in Washington at eleven
every night, and she would tell me how things were going.
When I saw her on weekends I would riffle through her
briefcase and look for memos marked "Confidential." Outwardly the Reagan campaign appeared to be smooth, efficient, and wrinkle-free. From the inside it looked
overheated, disjointed, and anarchistic. Tempers were short,
and jealousies rife, while everyone fought over turf. White
House aides passed on loopy memos full of bad advice.
Maureen Reagan got upset and made people miserable. I had
met her when she visited us in New York. Sonia had known
Maureen for years; her first visit finished me. On her next
visit, when I walked up the street and saw Secret Service
cars parked outside our building, I headed for Central Park.
Maureen was the Republican Party's Electra. She only recently had reconciled with her father, and now she yearned
to be his principal political woman. The principal woman,
though, was Sonia at campaign headquarters. Their friendship could not survive that. First Maureen stopped speaking
to Sonia. Then she planted a spy in Sonia's office, with orders to report to her, Maureen, at the White House. The spy
confessed when Sonia caught her copying names from her
Rolodex.

Intrigue aside, the most important ongoing factor in the
campaign was television. The Republicans made few decisions without reflecting first about how they would play on

the tube, and I knew the Democrats did the same. Sonia's briefcase contained polling data that measured how voters perceived the candidates. Ronald Reagan, for example, was seen as less compassionate than Walter Mondale; Mondale was seen as weaker or less forceful than Reagan. Republican and Democratic advisers would change the television image accordingly. Reagan would be surrounded at a campaign stop by minorities, or by the handicapped. Mondale would take off his jacket, roll up his sleeves, and loosen his tie for a speech. Campaign strategy and television were inseparable. I wanted to write about this and other matters—Gary Hart's candidacy, for instance, was created almost wholly by television—but *Times* tradition said no. Television critics did not write about politics; politics belonged to the Washington bureau and the national desk. The working assumption was that politics was only about issues. The *Times* no longer believes this, but in 1984 it was just beginning to change its mind. I would sneak in a piece about politics, and the national desk would complain. I would back off, then sneak in another piece. Then the national desk or one of the political writers would complain again. There was nothing personal in this; it was only routine *Times* feuding, but it grew so heated that Abe had to intervene. He invited me to lunch, and we chatted about nothing important until we had coffee. Then he asked, "How are you doing?" and I moaned about being stifled. That afternoon Abe wrote a memo to other *Times* editors, saying there were no restrictions on what I could write. The next day I wrote a Sunday story that began:

"Television is not just showing us the Presidential and Vice Presidential debates; television is determining how we score them, too. What plays well is what wins. . . . Old-style political discourse, imperfect as it was, rested on the assumption that candidates were divided by issues, and by issues they would be judged. New-style television discourse operates under different rules. Do the candidates have presence? Are they showing lots of zip? When we hunker down in our living rooms tonight to watch Ronald Reagan and Walter F. Mondale discuss war and peace, the new rules invite us to be theater critics. It is not the issues we are asked to judge; it is the nuances of the presentation.''

And so on. Almost everything I wrote about politics that year is conventional wisdom now, but I was plowing new ground then. I also was learning more about television. I discovered it was an anesthetic. Hours of uninterrupted viewing seemed to deaden the synapses in my brain, and I would feel the same as I had when I had been drinking. The medium demands nothing except our inertness. At the same time, it homogenizes us in the most profound ways. It blurs the distinctions between men and women, and adults and children, by providing them all with the same information. They grow more alike because there no longer are areas of privacy to divide them. Western civilization took five hundred years to develop the modern idea of childhood, but television has erased it in a few decades.

Good sense and modern psychology recognize that children are not merely small adults, and that they should be shielded from certain topics. Television, though, annuls this. Children's television is an oxymoron. A child of five and an adult of forty can see the same images and hear the same words simply by pushing a button. It is a retrograde way of learning. The printed word demands a rudimentary education before it can be understood, and the more sophisticated the idea the printed word expresses, the greater the amount of education required to comprehend it. What a child once learned through reading, therefore, corresponded roughly with his ability to process the information. But in the media age we all get the same messages, and it shows in our behavior. We are beginning to look like pod people. Children and adults now dress alike, talk alike, and play the same games. The concept of childhood is vanishing as fast as the old notions about the differences between men and women.

Meanwhile, the incessant psychobabble of the media age does its best to legitimate aberrant life-styles. There is endless talk about compassion, respect, and tolerance, and almost none about honor, courage, or duty. I once received a letter from a reporter at *The Washington Post* that read, in its entirety: "There are three things in this century that never should have been invented—psychoanalysis, the atom bomb and television." The reporter may have misdated the birth of psychoanalysis, but at least he was facing an issue, possibly in a way not intended. The spirit of ersatz psychoanalysis hangs all over television. Correspondents explain away misbehavior, while talk-show hosts sympathize with the morally maladjusted, and prime-time dramas excuse the deviant. Remember that Amelia's father was only starved for affection.

Perhaps a person's tolerance or distaste for these matters has something to do with his years. I sometimes thought the true dividing line among Americans was not race or gender, but whether they had grown up with television. Although I never met television critics for other papers, I often read what they wrote. It occurred to me they compared what they saw not with other art forms—theater, say, or dance—but only with other programs they had seen on television. These critics and I seldom agreed on questions of style, content, or art. They spoke for a different aesthetics and worldview. I was sure they were all children of television.

I do not mean to be patronizing about the other critics. Some wrote very well and were serious about their profession. But I did not think any of them had ever worked as reporters. They had no real interest in news. Many network executives and almost everyone in public television—I am exempting MacNeil/Lehrer—had none, either. They had to pretend they did, though, because they were in the news trade. I speak now not about workaday correspondents, but about executives who ran things. CBS News, in particular, was home to people intent on proving they were serious.

They did this in tricky ways. There was a television critic at another newspaper whose reviews I enjoyed reading. Our tastes were different, but he was a better writer than I, and was justifiably esteemed. Yet he appeared to be partial to CBS News and to praise its programs with uncommon zeal. A reporter who covered the television industry told me CBS had hired the critic's male lover. The network once even leaked word to me that I would be considered favorably if I applied for an on-air position on its Sunday-morning news show. It did not really want me, of course; it wanted only to stop my reviews in the *Times,* and hiring me was one way to do so.

On the other hand, if a man could not be bought, perhaps he could be bullied. When Sonia was elected chairman of the board of the Corporation for Public Broadcasting, Don Hewitt told a *Times* reporter that *60 Minutes* might do an investigative piece. CPB passes on federal money to public television, and therefore, Hewitt said, Sonia and I might have a "conflict of interest" because I was a television critic. I sent word that Sonia and I would love to appear on television together and would be happy to cooperate, and I never heard anything more about it. But I did wonder if *60 Minutes* made vague threats like that very often; I suspected it did. A program that successful could be whimsical about its power.

In time the complaints from CBS became almost routine. Hewitt would be on the phone the first thing in the morning, wailing to one or more *Times* editors, and then along would come Mike Wallace. CBS executives and producers weighed in whenever they could. I decided I liked Dan Rather, whom I had never met, because he showed a sense of humor. He asked around to learn what I looked like, and found an actor with the same nondescript appearance. Then he escorted the actor to a CBS party and introduced him as John Corry. Apparently, one producer got so upset he was

ready to assault the poor actor; Rather had to step in and explain his prank. The president of CBS News did not find it
amusing, and he chided the anchorman for a "joke in poor
taste." I was not sure what he meant, although I suppose the
poor taste had less to do with Rather's joke than with CBS's
view of me.

I was writing reviews that said CBS did not understand
news and confused it with entertainment; in fact, NBC and
ABC were doing that, too. Corporate takeovers, new man-
agements, and the passing of an older generation of journalists had left marks. News increasingly was being recited or
acted out by on-air Kens and Barbies. Nonetheless, the networks insisted that news programs were their way of showing their commitment to public service. But what is news,
and how do you define it, and who is to determine whether it
is being presented accurately and well? The late eighties
CBS series *West 57th* exemplified the new media age. The
network said the program would redefine news and how it
was presented. When a *Times* secretary called CBS and re-
quested a review tape for me, however, she was told there
were none. I called CBS myself, the only time I had ever
done so. The acting president told me that the president was
on a fishing trip in Oregon and could not be reached, but that
before he left, he had said *West 57th* was getting too much
publicity and no more tapes could be released. I countered
by claiming I would write a story saying CBS News was
fearful of my reviewing the show. The tape was delivered to
the *Times* in an hour.

I found out later that CBS executives had had discussions
about how to keep me from reviewing *West 57th,* and when I
saw the tape I understood why. The program used music and
MTV-style film editing to gloss over its silly reporting. The
tape opened with a story about the home life of Chuck Nor-
ris, the action-movie star, and then went on to an Oregon cult
and kinky sex, with a little gratuitous nudity and violence.

West 57th explored tabloid topics, and even when it turned to non-tabloid topics—famine in Ethiopia, battered women in Dallas—it did so in a tabloid way: fast, flashy, without substance. None of the stories left any residue. They sped by in a kaleidoscope of images. The young correspondents did not report any news; they emoted captions for the images. If *West 57th* had been offered as entertainment, none of this would have mattered; but it was produced by a news organization, and so it mattered a great deal. I wrote a bad-tempered review characterizing the program as a "supermarket tabloid set to music," and concluded: "If CBS is serious about reshaping our definition of news, and it does seem to be serious, it will have to do better. A little more sex, a little more violence just to grab our attention; then it can get on to new cures for psoriasis and the latest in diets. We may be at a turning point in television journalism."

In retrospect, I think I was right. We were at a turning point. The evening news programs are kitschier now than before. Indeed, the producer of *West 57th* has jumped ship at CBS and is now the president of NBC News. After the review appeared, CBS News complained to Punch Sulzberger. Nothing came of it, although I was getting my first inklings of living on borrowed time. I knew I was good at my job—the *Times* would nominate me twice for a Pulitzer as a critic—but in circles where uniformity was prized, I was an irritant to too many people. One day a friendly secretary slipped me a copy of a letter the columnist Anthony Lewis had sent to a senior *Times* editor. Lewis said that I was using television criticism to express my "political opinions," and that he was writing the letter in protest. Lewis was correct. I was expressing my political opinions, although what bothered him most were the kinds of opinions I expressed.

I was a conservative in a media culture dominated by liberals, and sometimes I stuck my thumb in their eyes. It was never hard to do, and the truth was I enjoyed it. I would write about a nature film or a pleasantly trashy mini-series, and then review a documentary about Fidel Castro or the Nicaraguan Sandinistas. Fidel would be shown as a social democrat, and the Sandinistas as agrarian reformers. Apply journalistic standards there, or indeed to almost any PBS program on foreign policy, and you found a revisionist case. Ted Turner's documentaries were even shakier. On the eve of the Soviet Union's final death throes, Turner Broadcasting presented its *Portrait of the Soviet Union,* a seven-hour series that made the old evil empire look like a Leninist theme park. ''Onward into the future—the dream of the Soviet Union,'' the actor Roy Scheider, the series host, said at the beginning. Seven hours later he concluded that the Bolshevik Revolution had launched ''the greatest experiment in social engineering the world has ever seen,'' and that ''the first stage of the revolution is nearing completion.'' All we need, he said dreamily, ''is the will to understand it.'' Ted Turner, who, according to Turner Broadcasting, ''originated'' the series, is a quintessential figure of the new media age.

THERE WAS NO ONE MOMENT when I knew I would leave the *Times,* although it was inevitable that I would. As I write this it is the summer of 1993, and I have been away from the paper five years. Coincidentally, Willie Morris has just published a book in which he recalls the days at *Harper's.* Willie says that I suffered over my writing more than anyone he had ever known, and that I was never pleased by what I wrote. I do not know about the suffering part, but the rest is true. I have written thousands of stories, and it seems to me no more than a dozen turned out right. I remember a piece about George Balanchine, and a column about children at Christmas. On the two hundredth anniversary of the Declaration of Independence, I visited the festivities in Lower

Manhattan, and then returned to the newsroom and on deadline wrote about immigrants. I was thinking about my family
when I wrote it, and I remember that piece, too. I suppose I
am represented best by a handful of stories that were un-
ashamedly sentimental, and by a handful more that were political. I was at my best when I could either cry or get angry,
but my last few years at the *Times* I did less of both. That
was one sure sign I should leave.

My heart had never left the old newsroom, with its tin
desks, old typewriters, and cigarette-scarred linoleum floor.
Arthur had stalked the aisles, and no one had ever heard of
modems and laptop computers. The old "Hell's Kitchen
boys" were still around then. They had grown up in the
neighborhood, and sought jobs at the *Times* because they
could walk to work. Several had become reporters. The last
one remaining in the newsroom, a round-faced alcoholic Ir-
ishman, was my legman one St. Patrick's Day when I covered the parade. He stationed himself on the steps of St.
Patrick's Cathedral, a few feet from the cardinal archbishop
of New York, and waved boozily at all the marchers. It was
disreputable behavior, of course, but everyone laughed
about it when I told them in the newsroom.

I wonder if conduct like that would still be amusing.
When young reporters and copy editors joined the *Times* in
the 1980s, their pictures and biographies were posted in the
newsroom lobby. Older reporters and copy editors would
read the biographies and look vaguely baffled. The new people all seemed to have graduate degrees and know more than
one language. Affluence, a new sophistication, and the passing of an old immigrant generation had bred different journalists. Perhaps they had no need to find the newsroom
romantic. The older reporters were unlikely to admit there
had ever been any romance to begin with, but among themselves they talked about change. There were fewer eccentrics now in the newsroom, while gentility was settling in,

and life somehow seemed less colorful. In dwindling bands older reporters sought one another out. After the no-smoking signs went up in the newsroom, they caucused sometimes in the men's room. In the antiseptic new environment, it was the only place left for a cigarette.

Speculation about who would succeed Abe as executive editor began long before he was to retire. A monument was about to fall, and everyone knew it, except possibly Abe himself. He had chosen no heir apparent, and showed no sign of wanting to leave. If anything, he dug himself more deeply into the *Times*. In the newsroom we heard that Punch Sulzberger had asked him to suggest a successor, but that Abe had declined. Instead, he shifted a few editors around, presumably to give them more experience while the *Times* prepared for an ''orderly transition'' of power. The older reporters wondered how it could ever be orderly. Abe and the *Times* were inseparable, and there was no graceful way to dislodge them. I thought of Willie and *Harper's*; the difference was that Abe's prolonged departure was played out on a public stage. More than a year before he was supposed to leave, *The Washington Post* speculated about his successor in a waspish three-part series that examined his reign at the *Times*. It said Abe had tried to move the *Times* to the ''right'' and bent the rules of nonpartisan journalism. How he had bent them was not made clear, and coming from a paper that few in Washington ever regarded as nonpartisan, the charge was almost comic.

Abe's real sin was that he was an apostate in a media age of conformity. He was the most honorable man I had ever known, fearless in his devotion to principle, but he had become almost an anachronism. His hands-on style of editing was going out of fashion, and the media ethos was changing. I complained to him once that we had underplayed some story or other, and then brazenly said I thought the news columns were turning soft, bulging with too many features. He looked at me angrily, spread open that day's paper, and began stabbing a forefinger at page-one bylines. This reporter, he said, knows how to write a news story, but this reporter does not; this reporter has an interesting mind, while this reporter will never write anything original; and so on, until he had worked his way through the whole first section of the paper. It was an indiscreet outburst, but there was no mistaking its passion, or how it connected Abe to the *Times*. By contrast, I have just read something by the columnist Anna Quindlen in the 1993 Times Company annual report: "About six months ago I looked at page one and saw that every story on it had been written by a woman, except for one story that had been written by an African-American man. And my heart soared. I thought, Anna, the next time you convince yourself things haven't changed, remember this." I do not doubt the sincerity of Quindlen's feeling, but we are looking here at two journalistic cultures. Friends tell me Anna will be the next managing editor of the *Times*.

The newsroom was divided along generational lines that last year or so of Abe's tenure. Older reporters were uneasy about the impending departure; their younger colleagues were sanguine. While the newsroom did not grind to a halt, office gossip all centered on the succession. Pretenders tried not to look self-conscious, but the strain began to show. Over lunch one of them told me he could stand it no longer and wanted to go back overseas. Another, whose hopes were raised early on and then irretrievably dashed, became so embittered he scarcely spoke to anyone in the newsroom. The irony was that the prize they all sought was changing.

The *Times* feels spongier now, and it has lost much of its old zeal for hard news. Its working thesis had always been that it would tell readers what had happened in the world in the last twenty-four hours. Some days the *Times* did this well, and other days poorly, but its purpose was to describe important events as they happened. The events made up the news, and although editors might disagree on which events were important and how they should be covered, it was assumed they would be reported on as comprehensively as possible and with a maximum attention to facts. Different rules now apply. The *Times* sees itself more as an agent for social change and an advocate of good causes. It still has some of the best reporters in the business, and its foreign coverage is unexcelled, but its news columns now have less urgency, and far more editorializing. The paper follows a liberal social and political agenda, when it ought not to be following any agenda at all. The paradox is that it does not necessarily do this consciously. Abe had always recognized that the *Times* would be pulled to the left unless something held it in place. He wanted to anchor the *Times* in the center. The media culture located that center far from where he did—which is how *The Washington Post* could accuse of him bending the rules of journalism. The *Post* also mentioned me: I was part of Abe's rightward move, and had been made a television critic so I could further his infamous scheme. There was some truth in that. Abe liked hearing my dissident voice in the *Times*.

But dissidence does not play well in the long run. Abe knew that, and so did I. We talked on his last day as executive editor, and he said he could no longer "protect" me. It was hard for him to say that. He loved the *Times* and had made it his life, and now he had to stand apart, knowing it was going to change. Max Frankel, who had been in charge of the editorial page, was the new executive editor; a different vision was coming into the newsroom. Max sent me a note on his second day in office, saying that in my review that morning I had indulged in "impermissible editorializing." A few days later Max passed on a letter he had received from the president of a foundation, imploring him to get rid of me as a critic. At the top of the letter Max had written, "How should I respond to this?" He was sending me a warning, and I knew it. It was an honorable gesture on his part, a polite way of telling me to watch out. I felt no resentment. The *Times* was entering a new era, and I was part of an old one, and I knew it was time to get out. The young man who had filled paste pots in the sports department and worked on the side at the racetrack had become a middle-aged man with two grown daughters, a second wife, and the sure sense that if he stayed on in the newsroom he would calcify. The young man thought the good life had to do with the achievement of goals. The middle-aged man knew better. He knew it was not the goals but how you pursued them that mattered. I had run out of goals at the *Times* and was not going to find any more. If I stayed I would stand still professionally, or more likely slip back, dissatisfied with what I was doing while I watched time pass away. I could not let that happen.

Things fell into place. It has been my experience that they usually do. First Sonia was named an assistant secretary of state by the Reagan administration. Around the same time, I was offered a fellowship by the Gannett Center for Media Studies at Columbia. I was still wondering whether I should accept it on the day my younger daughter graduated from college. I had looked forward to the event for years, but on graduation day I was apprehensive. I knew I would meet my ex-wife, Irmie. Since our divorce I had seen her only in court or when we both showed up at a school function for one of our daughters. Always we were careful not to speak. Our anger toward each other was too great, and besides, I was afraid even to go near her. What I was afraid of I do not know, although I thought of her as some kind of monster— which was how she also thought of me. Indeed, she had made that wonderfully explicit. As a therapeutic exercise a few years after we were divorced, she wrote her ''autobiography,'' a copy of which she gratuitously sent me. It was literate and intelligent, and painted a venomous portrait of the unsuitable man she had married. I read just enough to get the gist, then put it aside. A year or so later, I read it straight through. Surely Irmie could not think those things about me.

But she did, and in my mind I gave no quarter, either. I was carrying my resentment like baggage, although I was scarcely aware of its weight. When I thought of Irmie at all, it was only to count myself fortunate I did not have to see her again. Once or twice I thought I glimpsed her on the street, and fled to avoid an encounter. God forbid we should ever meet. Then, however, came graduation. An attractive woman walked up to Sonia. "Mrs. Corry," she said, and extended her hand. "I'm Janet's mother." The attractive woman, of course, was Irmie; I did not recognize her at first. Irmie was a harridan, and this woman seemed so nice. "John," she said, "how are you?" I do not remember what I said to my ex-wife then, but I remember talking to her later. She thanked me for putting the girls through school, and I surprised myself by thinking I would cry. I was feeling relief: a great burden was breaking up and falling in clumps at my feet. I was casting off part of one life, and in the wondrous way these things happen, I knew I was ready now to cast off more. I left the *Times* a few weeks later.

Sonia went to Washington, while I stayed on in New York for the fellowship at Columbia. It would be pleasant to think that Irmie and I simply put the past behind us, but that would have been too much. We had too painful a history behind us. We exchanged a phone call here, another there, and once we met on the street. We walked together and talked about our daughters. We were reassured we could do that. We knew at least something had survived those dead years, and so we became, once again, parents, or perhaps confidants, sharing thoughts about our children in a private parental way. When Irmie was diagnosed with cancer soon after, we talked about that, too. There was a turning point when she had a mastectomy and I visited her in the hospital. She was propped up against pillows and smiling. "John," she said, "you were the only one I wanted to see."

We stayed in touch regularly after that. I would call her, or she would call me, and I discovered things about my ex-wife I never knew. Once, she talked a long while about Edith Wharton and Henry James. She was fascinated by Wharton and distrustful of James, and knowledgeable in her opinions. In my imaginings about Irmie all those years, I had never imagined her reading a book. How well, I wondered, had I known her?

That last year, I know, she wondered about me, too. My daughters told me about it, although they really didn't have to. I understood what was happening full well. My ex-wife and I simply wanted to like each other. The years we had been together could not have been wasted. They had to have had more meaning than that.

I visited the hospital quite often the last time Irmie was there. One visit fell on my birthday. At the hospital, my daughters suggested we celebrate with balloons and a cake, as Irmie and I had celebrated with them when they were children. I thought balloons and a cake would be out of place, but Irmie smiled and said she would like them. That evening we had a party. Our daughters talked and fussed, while Irmie and I looked on benignly. Then she told me how happy she was that we had two children. She sounded thoughtful; it was as if she was forgiving us both for what we had long done to each other. That night, I think, we reclaimed those lost years.

One day soon after, a new nurse came into the room while I was there. Irmie whispered, "How should I introduce you?" I said it did not matter, I thought "ex-husband" would do. Irmie smiled at the nurse and told her my name. "He's my best friend," she added. Irmie had just given me a great gift, and I knew it. A few days later, she died.

INDEX

I N D E X

INDEX